BLACK TIE
& BLUE JEANS

For Barbara —

Happy "grape day" Celebration!

enjoy!

J Kennedy

BLACK TIE & BLUE JEANS

COOKING ON THE LLANO ESTACADO

Jeanne Kennedy

EAKIN PRESS ⬥ Austin, Texas

Published in the United States of America
By Eakin Press
A Division of Sunbelt Media, Inc.
P.O. Drawer 90159 ⌂ Austin, Texas 78709-0159
email: eakinpub@sig.net
🖥 website: www.eakinpress.com 🖥

1   2   3   4   5   6   7   8   9

1-57168-426-3

Library of Congress Cataloging-in-Publication Data

Kennedy, Jeanne
    Black Tie & Blue Jeans: Cooking on the Llano Estacado / Jeanne Kennedy.-- 1st
ed.
        p.   cm.
    Includes index.
    ISBN 1-57168-426-3
    1. Cookery, American--Southwestern style. 2. Cookery--Texas I.Title

TX715.2.S69 K45 2000
541.59764--dc21

                                                                    00-046243

With love, I dedicate this book to our Gourmet Club members:

Jane and Ronnie Brown

Carolyn and Dan Hook

Nancy and Pat McCutchin

Beverly and Jim Merritt

Glenda and Carl Shamburger

and my husband, Don.

CONTENTS

TEXAS, THE LONE STAR STATE

I CALL IT HOME

Texas is referred to as the "Lone Star State" because of the single star shining bright on our Texas flag. Cowboys still ride the plains on horseback, herding their cattle. And, more often than not, cowboy boots, hats, and jeans make up our everyday dress, even if our occupations are far from ranching. Our Texas heritage runs rich in our veins.

Texas is made up of four land regions, the Basin and Range Region, the Great Plains, the North-Central Plains, and the West Gulf Coastal Plain. I live in the Great Plains region, on the Llano Estacado. Much of this area is on a high plateau, and has little rainfall. Due to its dry climate, people did not settle on the Llano Estacado until the late 1800s. Thanks to irrigation and dry-farming methods, it has become one of the state's richest farming regions, and holds history of being one of the richest petroleum and natural-gas fields in the United States.

People from all walks of life make our great state what it is today. In fact, Texans are so well diversified, one may be riding horseback upon our settled frontier as another sits at a computer planning space travel into a new frontier. Texans are easily recognized by their genuine smiles and cheerful greetings!

A LLANO ESTACADO LEGEND

If you ever plan to go to Lukenbach, Texas, most likely you will experience a sense of nostalgia, combined with a zeal of patriotism. Feed a quarter to the jukebox and twirl around the dance hall, laughing and feeling the country spirit Waylon Jennings instilled in each of us through his singing, "Let's go to Lukenbach, Texas, with Waylon, Willie and the boys . . ." And there you'll be, right in the middle of it all! And so it is here on the Llano Estacado, where Waylon Jennings was born and raised in the small, quaint town of Littlefield, Texas. He formed his own band at

the age of twelve and further pursued his love for music when he became a disc jockey at the age of fourteen. In 1955 he met Buddy Holly, who produced Waylon's first record and used him as a bass player with the Crickets. Waylon has accomplished a lot since those early days. He has earned many Grammy and Country Music Awards, becoming one of the music industry's true all-time legends. Even though Waylon doesn't actually live on the Llano Estacado today, he's close to home, for he lives in our hearts. Thank you, Waylon, for what you do best—you touch our lives through your music. You are truly a living legend!

With special thanks to
Llano Estacado Winery

The first to plant commercial hybrid grapes in Whiteface, Texas, the Sandyland Growers have expanded the agricultural horizons on the Llano Estacado. Their first production, labeled "Staked Plains," consisted of 1,300 cases. They now produce 80,000 cases of wine per year, labeled "Llano Estacado," and their operation continues to grow. Their wine has brought recognition to our region of Texas, and it is distributed not only throughout the United States, but internationally in France, Belgium, and Germany. I am very pleased to have had the opportunity to photograph Llano Estacado wine for this cookbook. One will always find a bottle of their Cabernet Sauvignon on our table for Gourmet Club!

For going beyond the call of friendship, I sincerely thank:

Erik Aagaard at Armadillo Camera, photo critic and processing
Melita Atchison at Atchison Jewelry, china and props
Kirk Brock at Brock's Carpet, rawhide reata
Charlie Brownlow at Luskey's/Ryon's, hat and reata
Casey Critchfield, china and silver
Gary Devitt at Commercial Printing, Texas artwork
Waylon Jennings
Curt Kennedy, computer programming
Beth Ann Mann, via Chuck Kershner at FOUR BAR K, gloves
JoAnn Morris, china
Rochelle Parmer, china
Roger Palacios at Gingiss, tuxedo
Randy Sanders, *Lubbock Avalanche Journal*
Joe & Leslie Schedler, saddle and reata
Glenda Shamburger, critiquing my p's and q's
Lynette Watkins, photo critic
Members of our gourmet club, china, crystal, moral support
And Don—eating peanut brittle for dinner wasn't so bad, was it?

PREFACE

Many times I've asked myself why I've had such a burning desire to write this cookbook. Until this moment, I've not been totally able to express the answer to my question. Sitting quietly, allowing myself to listen to my thoughts, I realize that the answer to my question lies in one simple word—memories.

My earliest childhood memory involving food focuses on my mother. In our small country home, we sat at our kitchen table over bowls of red beans accompanied with pickles, onions, and a pan of cornbread. I recall my mother crumbling cornbread into her beans, which was so out of character for her, for she was, and still is, the essence of grace to me. Perhaps that's what impressed that day so deeply in my memory—seeing her kind hands breaking off small pieces of cornbread into her beans! We talked and enjoyed each other, a special time shared between the two of us.

Many memories rest on the bookshelf in my mind, waiting to be opened. Our family would gather around our dining table for our evening meals. Dad always led our family in prayer to offer thanks for the food before us, and for our togetherness. Through our parents' examples, my brother, two sisters and I learned the importance of God, home, family, and friends. I'm forever thankful that our dad taught us to pray, and that our mother taught us to wait upon the Lord. Gatherings at our family table were cherished then, and still are today.

When I married Don and we began raising our family, daily life was a bit more demanding of our time than I remembered from my childhood! Oftentimes, we found ourselves needing to be in several places at once, and we quickly learned to plan our evening meals for around six o'clock. Don would come home from his office shortly after five, grab his cup of coffee, change clothes, and head straight for the middle of our kitchen floor! There, with me busy cooking, we would visit. The children would end up on top of him, scuffling around as I stepped over them, back and forth, from sink to cooktop. As we sat down to eat, we heard tales from the day and plans for tomorrow—oh, how we cherish those memories! One of our great joys is knowing that our sons, Curt and Kelly, will carry on our family tradition.

Through the years, I've been fortunate to have the opportunity to travel with Don as he continued his professional education. He attended lectures and workshops during the day, while I undertook various activities of interest. We always looked forward to our times together in the evenings at nice restaurants, anticipating cuisine from the region. We not only learned to appreciate fine food, but further to appreciate the joy of sharing fine food with each other. This was the beginning of our realization of the importance of quality nourishment for both body and soul.

Such excitement over a meal may perhaps seem unusual, but we all have it . . . think about it. I enjoy the color, the texture, the combination of foods, but most of all, I enjoy people—and, more often than not, my "people" is Don! I know several women who share similar pleasures. Through the years, I have seen them often at different community functions, club meetings, or in our small family restaurant we used to own. After we shared stories of family, food talk began! We had such fun, chatting enthusiastically, dreaming aloud our desire to expand upon our cooking pleasures. For several years we would casually suggest that we should start a gourmet cooking club, so one day I decided to just do it. I made that first phone call, and we did it, and have continued to do it for years now! Six couples meet six times a year, but we share a closeness that is held in our hearts every day. The host couple plans the menu and is responsible for the entrée, drinks, and clean-up. The guest couples prepare their assigned recipes. We now have the opportunity to enjoy an exquisite meal six times a year, with six sets of "chefs" to make it happen!

We have shared many joys and heartaches through these years. We look at old photos and see how we've changed, and we realize how much our cooking has changed as well! This book contains our best recipes, compiled through our fifteen years together, with a few additional contributions from my family and friends. Without them, this cookbook would not exist. So, as you thumb through the pages of this book, you are scanning memories—memories focused around food. The food is delicious, but it's merely a side dish. The company you share it with is truly your entrée.

Best of memories to you!

With love,
Jeanne

Appetizers

From Wraps to Dips

SAUTÉED MUSHROOMS
in Cream Cheese Pastry

8 ounces cream cheese, softened	8 ounces mushrooms, minced
½ cup butter, softened	½ cup sour cream
1¾ cups unbleached flour	2 tablespoons unbleached flour
2 tablespoons butter	1 teaspoon salt
1 medium onion, minced	¼ teaspoon dried thyme
1 garlic clove, minced	1 egg white, lightly beaten

Place cream cheese and ½ cup of butter in mixing bowl. Mix on medium speed until creamy, adding 1¾ cups flour slowly. Mix well. Divide dough in half; shape into two balls. Cover and chill one hour.

Melt 2 tablespoons butter in a large skillet over medium heat. Add onion; sauté until translucent. Add garlic and mushrooms; sauté until tender. Stir in sour cream, 2 tablespoons flour, salt, and thyme; set aside.

Roll one dough portion to ⅛-inch thickness on a lightly floured surface; cut with a 2½-inch cookie cutter. Place on a lightly oiled baking sheet. Repeat procedure with remaining dough.

Spoon one heaping teaspoon of mixture onto one-half of each dough circle. Moisten edges with beaten egg white; fold dough over filling. Press edges with a fork to seal; prick tops and brush with beaten egg white. Bake until golden (approximately 8 minutes) in 450° oven.

Yield: 3 dozen.

For a variation, substitute ¼ pound cooked ground sausage for half the amount of mushrooms called for in the above recipe.

GUACAMOLE

1 ripe avocado, peeled, seeded, and mashed	1 teaspoon cilantro, chopped fine
2 teaspoons lime juice	1 tablespoon tomato, minced
1 teaspoon mayonnaise	Dash of salt
1 tablespoon onion, chopped fine	Dash of garlic powder
1 tablespoon hot salsa	

Combine above ingredients in a small bowl; mix well. Adjust seasonings, for size of avocados varies!

Yield: ¾ cup.

GARLIC SHRIMP

⅛ cup extra-virgin olive oil
1 tablespoon garlic, chopped
1 bay leaf
½ teaspoon ground red pepper

½ pound large shrimp, peeled, deveined, tails attached
1 teaspoon coarse salt
1 tablespoon parsley, chopped

Using a medium-sized skillet or a wok, heat oil over medium-high heat. Place garlic, bay leaf, and red pepper in skillet; cook for one minute. Add shrimp, stirring until just cooked through (approximately 3 minutes). Sprinkle with salt and parsley. Transfer to serving dish.

Serves 4.

HOT ARTICHOKE DIP

1 (4 ounce) jar pimientos, diced
1 (14 ounce) can artichoke hearts, drained and chopped
1½ cups mayonnaise
1 teaspoon salt
2 (14 ounce) cans diced green chilies, drained

4 ounces Monterey Jack cheese, shredded
½ cup Parmesan cheese, grated
1½ cups cooked crabmeat, optional
Additional grated Parmesan cheese
Tortilla chips

In a medium-sized bowl, mix first seven (or eight) ingredients with a spoon. Spread mixture into a shallow 1½-quart baking dish. Sprinkle additional Parmesan cheese on top. Bake at 325° for 30 minutes, or until it bubbles. Serve with tortilla chips.

Yield: 12 appetizer servings.

STUFFED JALAPEÑOS

12 large shrimp, peeled, and deveined
6 jalapeño peppers, halved lengthwise and seeded

6 slices of bacon, cut into halves

Place one shrimp inside one jalapeño half. Wrap one piece of bacon around width-wise and secure with a wooden pick. Bake at 450° for 20–25 minutes, or until bacon is cooked as you prefer. Remove from oven; drain on paper towels. Serve warm.

Yield: 12.

SPINACH BALLS

2 (9 ounce) boxes frozen
   chopped spinach
1 cup dried bread stuffing
1 cup Parmesan cheese, grated

6 eggs, beaten
¾ cup butter, room temperature
Salt and pepper, to taste

Thaw spinach; squeeze to drain well. Place all ingredients in a medium-sized bowl; mix well. Make into small balls (about one inch in diameter) and place on baking sheet; freeze. Remove from baking sheet and place in plastic zip-closure bags. Return to freezer until ready to use. When ready to use, place on lightly oiled baking sheet. Bake at 350° for 18–20 minutes.

Yield: 4½ dozen.

HOT SPINACH DIP

1 (9 ounce) box frozen chopped
   spinach, thawed and squeezed dry
½ cup milk
1 (16 ounce) box pasteurized
   cheese
1 (8 ounce) package cream cheese

¼ cup green onions, chopped
1 (4 ounce) jar pimientos,
   drained
⅛ teaspoon red pepper
Salt or garlic salt, to taste

Place ingredients in crock pot. Cook on medium heat until cheese is melted, stirring to mix well. Serve with tortilla chips or fresh veggies!

Yield: 3½ cups.

BAKED POTATO SKINS

4 baked potatoes, cut into halves
2 cups Cheddar cheese
8 slices bacon, cooked, crumbled

¾ cup sour cream
½ cup green onions, chopped
   fine

Scoop out insides of potato halves. Reserve pulp for another use. Place potato skins in a 13 x 9 x 2-inch baking dish. Equally dividing ingredients, sprinkle the cheese and bacon pieces onto potato skins. Bake at 400° for 8 minutes, or until cheese is melted. Remove from oven. Spoon a dollop of sour cream on top and sprinkle chopped green onions over all. Serve warm.

Yield: 8 appetizers.

PROSCIUTTO WRAPS
with Goat Cheese and Baby Greens

The Wraps:

12 slices prosciutto, sliced
  paper thin
10 ounces soft goat cheese,
  room temperature
3 ounces cream cheese,
  room temperature

2 teaspoons black pepper
¼ cup green onions, chopped
2 tablespoons olive oil

Line six one-cup ramekins with plastic wrap, leaving two inches of overhang. Place two slices prosciutto, crisscrossed, into each ramekin, leaving overhang. In a medium-sized bowl, combine goat cheese, cream cheese, pepper, and green onions; mix until well blended. Dividing into equal amounts, spoon into prepared ramekins. Fold prosciutto over to encase the cheese mixture. Cover with the excess plastic wrap and press gently to compress. Chill thoroughly.

Two hours before serving, invert ramekins to release wraps. Peel off plastic wrap. Heat two tablespoons of olive oil in a large skillet over medium heat. Place the wraps, bottom side down, in the skillet, and cook until cheese is soft when the tops are pressed (approximately 5 minutes). Transfer to a platter and cover loosely. Let stand one hour before serving.

The Salad:

½ pound slender green beans,
  cut into halves
¼ cup white wine vinegar
3 tablespoons shallots, chopped

½ cup extra-virgin olive oil
Salt and pepper, to taste
8 cups mixed baby greens
¼ cup green onions, chopped

Cook beans in a medium-sized pan of boiling, salted water for approximately five minutes, or until just tender. Drain and rinse in cold water; drain again. Allow to dry slightly; cover and chill.

Place vinegar and shallots in a small bowl. Slowly whisk in the oil. Season with salt and pepper.

Combine greens, green onions, and beans in a large bowl. Pour two-thirds of the above olive oil mixture over all; toss to coat. Divide equally onto six chilled salad plates. Top each plate with a wrap, and drizzle the remaining olive oil mixture over each.

Serves 6.

BROILED TENDERLOIN
with Sweet Onion Sandwiches

1 (4 pound) beef tenderloin, trimmed	2 tablespoons granular Greek seasoning
3 garlic cloves, sliced thin	4 tablespoons browning and seasoning sauce
2 tablespoons fresh ground pepper	

Using a sharp knife, make slanted slits in the tenderloin and insert pieces of sliced garlic into the slits. Rub the seasonings over the meat, and secure its shape by tying with white cooking string. Place the tenderloin on a baking sheet lined with foil. Broil on top rack in oven, seven minutes on each of three sides. Remove from rack and set oven temperature to 350°. Wrap the excess foil around the tenderloin and return to oven for an additional 20 minutes (until it measures 135° on a quick-read thermometer). Remove from oven; allow to cool. Cutting across the grain, slice the tenderloin into thin slices. Spread each slice with horseradish dressing. Roll into a small cylinder shape and secure with a wooden pick.

Horseradish Dressing

3 ounces cream cheese	¼ cup mayonnaise
3 tablespoons prepared horseradish	3 tablespoons sour cream

Combine ingredients in a small bowl. Using a spoon, blend to a smooth consistency. Lightly spread on tenderloin slices.

Sweet Onion Sandwiches

24 slices thin sandwich bread	¼ cup mayonnaise
½ pound butter, softened	½ cup parsley, chopped very fine
2 sweet onions, sliced thin	

Trim crusts from bread slices. Cut into halves, making triangles. Spread each half with butter; place onions between two slices, making a small appetizer sandwich. Dip one tip of each sandwich into the mayonnaise, then into the parsley.

Yield: 24 appetizer sandwiches.

This dish is a favorite at parties!

EGG ROLLS

Pork:

1 pound lean pork, freshly ground	2 teaspoons salt
1 egg	3 tablespoons soy sauce
1 teaspoon ginger, minced	1 teaspoon sugar
2 tablespoons sherry	1 tablespoon sesame oil
2 garlic cloves, minced	

In a large bowl, mix the above ingredients; marinate for four hours.

Vegetables:

4 tablespoons oil, for sautéing	2½ cups fresh bean sprouts
3 cups cabbage, shredded	1 teaspoon salt
⅓ cup carrots, shredded	½ teaspoon sugar
½ cup fresh mushrooms, chopped	2 tablespoons soy sauce
½ cup onion, chopped	12 egg roll skins

Using a large skillet or a wok, sauté first four vegetables in oil, adding bean sprouts just before the other vegetables are cooked to soft-crisp. Add salt, sugar, and soy sauce; mix well. Set aside.

Using a large skillet or a wok, stir fry the marinated pork mixture over medium-high heat until cooked thoroughly, making sure that the pork is crumbled fine. Remove from heat; add the vegetable mixture and mix well.

Assembly: Lay out one egg roll skin, shiny side up. Spoon ¼ cup filling diagonally across, and just below center of skin. Fold bottom point of skin over filling. Tuck point under filling, and fold side corners over to form an envelope shape. Roll up to the remaining corner, and moisten point. Press firmly to seal. Repeat with remaining egg roll skins and fillings. Deep fry three at a time at 375°, or until light golden brown. Drain and serve immediately, or hold in 200° oven for up to one hour.

Yield: 12 egg rolls.

WON TONS
with Dipping Sauces

½ pound precooked shrimp,
    chopped fine
½ pound ground lean chicken
1 teaspoon fresh ginger, minced
2 green onions, chopped fine
1 teaspoon Chinese parsley, minced

2 tablespoons light soy sauce
½ teaspoon garlic powder
½ teaspoon salt
1 teaspoon fresh ground pepper
1 package won ton skins
1 egg white

Excluding won ton skins and egg white, mix all ingredients thoroughly in a medium-sized bowl. Place one teaspoon of filling near corner of a won ton skin. Fold corner over the filling, and roll toward center of skin. Take the two diagonal corners, and moisten with egg white. Pinch together behind the rolled part. Repeat procedure for remaining skins and filling. (At this point, these may be refrigerated up to six hours before cooking.) Deep fry at 375° for 2 minutes, or until light golden brown. Drain and serve immediately, or hold in 200° oven for up to one hour.

Serves 12.

Mustard Sauce

½ cup water, room temperature
¼ cup white wine

½ cup powdered mustard
1 teaspoon sesame oil

In a small bowl, gradually add water and wine to mustard, making a smooth paste. Add sesame oil; mix well. Serve as a dip with won tons and other Oriental dishes.

Yield: 12 servings.

Sweet & Sour Sauce

3 tablespoons plum jam
4 tablespoons pineapple juice
3 tablespoons brown sugar

4 tablespoons water
1 teaspoon cornstarch

Mix above ingredients in a small saucepan until smooth and cornstarch is dissolved. Cook over medium heat until slightly thick. Serve as a dip, or with various meat dishes.

Yield: ⅓ cup.

TERIYAKI CHICKEN DRUMMETS
with Dipping Sauces

24 chicken drummets, skinned
⅓ cup sugar
⅓ cup soy sauce
1 garlic clove, pressed

¼ cup pineapple juice
⅓ cup water
1 teaspoon ginger root, grated
1 tablespoon vegetable oil

Combine ingredients in a zip-closure plastic bag. Seal bag, and shake until chicken is coated evenly. Marinate in refrigerator for eight hours, turning bag occasionally. Pour marinade off chicken into a small saucepan. Bring to a boil for one minute; set aside. Place chicken in broiler pan and bake at 350° for 45 minutes, turning and basting occasionally with reserved marinade.

Yield: 24 appetizers.

Pineapple Sauce

8 ounces crushed pineapple,
    with juice
3 cup brown sugar, firmly packed

¼ cup cider vinegar
2 tablespoons ketchup
2 tablespoons cornstarch

Mix ingredients in a small saucepan until cornstarch is dissolved. Cook over medium heat until slightly thickened.

Yield: 1½ cups.

Peanut Sauce

⅓ cup apricot preserves
⅓ cup light cream
⅓ cup creamy peanut butter

2 tablespoons soy sauce
1 tablespoon fresh lemon juice

Combine ingredients in a blender; mix until smooth. Serve at room temperature.

Yield: 1 cup.

CHILES RELLENOS
with Apricot and Roasted Almond Sauces

8 roasted poblano chiles, centers
    slightly slit, seeds removed, stems
    intact (see index for roasting)
2 tablespoons Roasted Garlic Pulp
    (see index)
8 ounces goat cheese, crumbled
4 ounces Monterey Jack cheese,
    grated

1 tablespoon onion, chopped
1 tablespoon cilantro, chopped
1 teaspoon dried basil
1 teaspoon dried marjoram
2 tablespoons roasted almonds,
    crushed
1 teaspoon freshly ground pepper

Excluding chiles, combine all ingredients in a large mixing bowl; mix well. Spoon mixture into prepared chiles, being careful to not overfill. Close the chiles and place in a lightly oiled 13 x 9 x 2-inch baking dish; cover. Bake at 350° for 10 minutes, or until it is thoroughly hot but the cheese is not running out. Divide onto eight warm salad plates that have equally divided Roasted Almond Sauce spread in the middle of each. Top rellenos with Apricot Sauce.

Serves 8.

Apricot Sauce

¼ cup dry white wine
½ shallot, finely diced

5 tablespoons butter,
    room temperature
1 cup apricot preserves, puréed

Using medium heat, place the wine and shallot in a small saucepan; cook to reduce the liquid to 2 tablespoons. Reduce heat to low; whisk in butter, one tablespoon at a time, until well incorporated. Add apricot purée and whisk well. Serve warm.

Yield: 1 cup.

Roasted Almond Sauce

1 cup heavy cream
½ cup sliced almonds, toasted
½ teaspoon salt

1 tablespoon roasted garlic pulp
2 tablespoons chicken stock

Place cream in medium saucepan over medium heat. Cook until reduced to ⅔ cup, stirring frequently. Transfer to blender; add all other ingredients. Blend on high speed until smooth; strain. Serve warm.

Yield: ⅔ cup.

MUSHROOM & GARLIC OYSTERS

½ cup unsalted butter, divided
1 pound mushrooms, sliced thin
1 quart shucked oysters, in
   their liquor
2 cups parsley, minced

¼ cup fresh garlic, minced
1 teaspoon salt
2 teaspoons fresh ground pepper
French bread, sliced

Melt ¼ cup butter in large skillet over medium heat. Add mushrooms and sauté until just tender, stirring frequently. Set aside. Bring oyster liquor to gentle simmer in large saucepan. Add oysters and poach until edges begin to curl. Drain well; set aside. Melt remaining butter in heavy large skillet over medium heat; add parsley, garlic, salt, and pepper. Cook until garlic is tender, stirring frequently. Add mushrooms and oysters; stir to heat thoroughly. Serve with French bread.

Serves 20.

ROASTED GARLIC

1 head of garlic

Olive oil

Cut garlic in half, width-wise. Drizzle with a small amount of olive oil and wrap in foil. Bake at 400° for approximately 30 minutes, or until pulp is softened. Using a butter knife, scoop cloves out and spread on small bites of bread. (To use in other dishes, squeeze to remove pulp.)

CRAB-STUFFED MUSHROOMS

½ cup milk
1 tablespoon butter
½ cup cracker crumbs
1 teaspoon onion, minced
½ teaspoon prepared horseradish
1 teaspoon dry mustard

¼ teaspoon salt
½ teaspoon fresh ground pepper
1 (6.5 ounces) can crabmeat,
   drained
24 large fresh mushroom caps
2 tablespoons butter, melted

Combine milk and one tablespoon butter in a small saucepan. Cook over low heat until butter melts, stirring frequently. Remove from heat; stir in cracker crumbs, onion, horseradish, dry mustard, salt, pepper, and crabmeat. Spoon mixture into mushroom caps. Place in a lightly oiled, 13 x 9 x 2-inch baking dish; brush tops with melted butter. Bake at 350° for 20 minutes.

Yield: 2 dozen.

LIGHT CHILES RELLENOS

4 roasted poblano chiles, centers
    slightly slit, seeds removed, stems
    intact (see index for roasting)
1½ cups water
¾ cup uncooked quinoa
½ cup green bell pepper, chopped
½ cup red bell pepper, chopped
½ cup onion, chopped
2 garlic cloves, minced
½ jalapeño pepper, seeded and minced

2 tablespoons pumpkinseed kernels
½ cup green onions, minced
1 tablespoon cilantro, minced
1 tablespoon soy sauce
1 tablespoon lime juice
1 (14½ ounce) can garlic-seasoned
    tomatoes
1 cup sharp Cheddar cheese, grated

Combine water and quinoa in a medium saucepan; bring to a boil. Cover, reduce heat, and simmer 12 minutes, or until liquid is absorbed. Set aside.

Place a large skillet over medium-high heat coated with vegetable oil spray. Sauté bell pepper, onion, garlic, and jalapeño pepper for 2 minutes. Add pumpkinseed kernels and sauté an additional two minutes. Remove from heat and stir in quinoa, green onions, cilantro, soy sauce, and lime juice. Spoon approximately ⅓ cup mixture into each poblano chile.

Purée tomatoes; pour into a 13 x 9 x 2-inch baking dish. Place filled chiles in dish and sprinkle cheese on top. Cover and bake in a 350° oven for 15 minutes, or until thoroughly heated. Spoon tomato purée over top just before serving.

Serves 4.

These make an impressive appetizer or a nice lunch entrée!

BASIL-TOMATO TART

1 prepared pie crust
1½ cups Mozzarella cheese, grated
6 roma tomatoes, peeled, seeded,
    and chopped
½ cup fresh basil leaves pepper

3 garlic cloves, chopped fine
½ cup mayonnaise
¼ teaspoon salt
¼ teaspoon fresh ground pepper

Prebake pie crust at 375° for 10 minutes. Remove from oven and sprinkle with ½ cup mozzarella cheese, followed with the chopped tomatoes, basil, and garlic. In a mixing bowl, combine the remaining cheese, mayonnaise, salt, and pepper; evenly spoon over tomato mixture. Bake at 375° for 30 minutes, or until top is bubbly and golden. Allow to stand 5 minutes; slice and serve warm.

Serves 8.

PAULA'S SHRIMP WITH AN ATTITUDE
Dressed in Beer Batter and Coconut

Seasoning Mix:

1 tablespoon ground red pepper	1 teaspoon dried thyme leaves
2 teaspoons salt	1 teaspoon dried oregano leaves
1 teaspoon black pepper	1½ teaspoons paprika
1½ teaspoons garlic powder	½ teaspoon onion powder

Combine seasonings in a small bowl; set aside.

The Flour Mixture:
In a small bowl, combine ¾ **cup flour** with **2 teaspoons of the seasoning mix;** set aside.

The Batter:

The Batter:	The Grand Finale:
1½ cups flour	2 pounds large shrimp
2 eggs, slightly beaten	(peeled, with tails on)
1 cup beer	2½ cups grated coconut
1 tablespoon baking powder	Canola oil for deep frying

In a medium bowl, combine four teaspoons of seasoning mix with flour, eggs, beer, and baking powder; thoroughly mix.

Dressing the Shrimp: Sprinkle both sides of shrimp with remaining seasoning mix. Holding by the tail, dredge each shrimp in the flour mixture, shaking off excess. Dip in batter (except tail), allowing excess to drip off. Coat generously with grated coconut; place on baking sheet.

Cooking: Heat oil to 350°. Gently drop shrimp, one at a time, into the hot oil; deep fry until golden brown. Drain on paper towels. Serve with Spicy Orange Sauce for dipping!

Serves 12.

Spicy Orange Sauce

1¾ cup orange marmalade	3 tablespoons Creole mustard
2 tablespoons prepared horseradish	

Combine all ingredients in a small bowl; mix well.

Yield: 2 cups.

PINEAPPLE & WATER CHESTNUTS
Wrapped in Bacon

15 slices bacon
1 cup ketchup
1 cup sugar
2 tablespoons teriyaki sauce

1 (15 ounce) can pineapple
chunks, juice reserved
1 (8 ounce) can sliced water
chestnuts

Cut bacon strips into thirds. In a small bowl, combine ketchup, sugar, four tablespoons of the reserved pineapple juice, and teriyaki sauce; set aside. Place one water chestnut and one pineapple chunk in middle of one piece of bacon. Fold bacon over top and secure with a wooden pick. Repeat procedure. Place on a baking pan lined with parchment paper. Bake at 450° for 25 minutes, or until bacon is cooked as you prefer. Drain. Dip each piece into ketchup mixture; place on baking pan. Return to oven and cook an additional 8 minutes.

Yield: 45 appetizers.

PARMESAN & ALMOND CHEESE SPREAD

⅓ cup sliced almonds
⅓ cup butter
⅓ cup parsley, minced
⅓ cup heavy cream
1 teaspoon salt

⅔ cup freshly grated Parmesan
cheese
½ teaspoon ground white pepper
24 lightly buttered toast strips

In a medium skillet, sauté almonds in butter until light golden. Excluding toast strips, add all other ingredients; mix well. Spread on toast strips. Heat before serving.

Yield: 24 appetizers.

CREAMY CHEESE BALL

1 pound cream cheese, softened
2½ cups Cheddar cheese, grated
1½ cups green onions, chopped fine
1½ tablespoons Worcestershire sauce

2 tablespoons pimientos, diced
1½ tablespoons hot sauce
1 cup nuts, chopped fine
Assortment of crackers

In a large bowl, combine all ingredients except nuts and crackers. Mix well, then half and chill. Before serving, shape into two balls, and roll in nuts. Serve with an assortment of crackers.

Yield: 2 cheese balls.

ROASTED SWEET PEPPERS
with Cheese and Herbs

3 red bell peppers, roasted, peeled,
    and seeded
3 yellow bell peppers, roasted,
    peeled, and seeded

Pinch of salt
½ pound smoked mozzarella cheese
24 whole fresh basil leaves,
    chopped

Be sure to roast the peppers until they are soft, or they will be difficult to roll! (See following recipe for roasting chiles and peppers.)

Cut roasted peppers into lengthwise strips, 1½ inches wide. Place on work surface; sprinkle with salt.

Cut the mozzarella into thin slices, slightly more narrow than the peppers. Place ½ teaspoon of the basil leaves along the length of each strip. Place a piece of mozzarella at the end of each strip. Roll the pepper over the cheese, continuing to roll the length of the pepper. Secure with a wooden pick; repeat for remaining strips. The flavors will develop as the peppers sit, so they may be rolled in advance and refrigerated. Return to room temperature before serving.

Yield: 24 appetizers.

ROASTING CHILES AND PEPPERS

Place peppers on top of foil in the top rack of oven. Broil until skins are blistered, frequently turning (watch closely!). When completely blistered, remove from oven. Place in a plastic bag, sealing to allow the heat from peppers to create steam (this helps the skins to loosen from the meat). Once cool, remove from bag. The skins are now ready to be peeled away from the meat of the peppers. Proceed to prepare as recipe calls for.

BLUE CHEESE & HAM SPIRALS

2 cups unbleached flour
½ teaspoon salt
1 cup unsalted butter, cut into
    ½-inch cubes
1 egg mixed with 1 tablespoon milk

⅔ pound blue cheese, crumbled
2 tablespoons dry sherry
½ pound shaved ham
2 egg whites, slightly beaten
    (for glaze)

Pastry: Combine flour and salt in large bowl. Cut in butter until coarse meal forms. Stir in egg-and-milk mixture. Knead dough until smooth ball forms. Flatten into a rectangle. Cover and refrigerate until firm.

Roll out dough on lightly floured surface to 16 x 8-inch rectangle. Fold into thirds, as for a business letter. Give dough a quarter turn, so that it opens like a book. Repeat rolling and folding two more times.

Cheese Mixture: Using electric mixer, beat cheese until light; stir in sherry.

Assembly: Cut dough in half. On lightly floured surface, roll each piece into a 12 x 10-inch rectangle. Spread half of cheese mixture evenly, leaving ½-inch border. Cover cheese with half of ham. Starting at one long side, roll up dough, jellyroll fashion. Repeat with remaining dough, cheese, and ham. Place rolls on baking sheet and freeze until almost firm. Cut into ½-inch slices; place on lightly oiled baking sheets and brush with glaze. Bake at 400° for 15 minutes, or until light golden brown.

Serves 12.

CRAB CANAPÉS

1 pound crabmeat, precooked
1 cup celery, chopped fine
⅓ cup soft breadcrumbs
⅛ teaspoon dry mustard
¼ cup light mayonnaise
¼ cup plain yogurt

1 tablespoon chopped pimiento
1 teaspoon lemon juice
¾ teaspoon Worcestershire sauce
1 (18-inch) French bread baguette,
   cut into ¼-inch slices

Reserving bread slices, combine crabmeat with remaining ingredients in a medium bowl; stir well. Spoon two teaspoonfuls crab mixture onto each slice of bread.

Yield: 6 dozen appetizers.

DON'S SHRIMP COCKTAIL

1 quart of Bloody Mary mix
½ cup cilantro, chopped fine
½ cup green onions, chopped fine
1 pound medium precooked shrimp

2 avocados, cut into small,
   bite-sized chunks
6 lemon or lime wedges

Excluding the lemon wedges, combine the above ingredients in a large pitcher; mix well. Thoroughly chill. Equally divide into six chilled parfait glasses. Garnish with a lemon wedge on rim of glass.

Serves 6.

You'll need a tall iced tea spoon for this one!

CHICKEN BITES
Wrapped in Bacon

3 chicken breasts, skinned
¼ cup soy sauce
2 tablespoons dry sherry
1 tablespoon sugar
1 tablespoon white vinegar
¼ teaspoon ginger, grated

½ cup lemon juice
½ cup Worcestershire sauce
¼ cup prepared mustard
1 tablespoon fresh ground pepper
2 garlic cloves, minced
8 slices bacon, cut into
   one-third strips

Cut chicken breasts into bite-sized pieces. Excluding bacon, combine all ingredients in a zip-closure plastic bag and marinate chicken for four hours; remove. Wrap chicken with bacon strips and secure with a wooden pick. Place on a baking sheet lined with parchment paper. Bake 25 minutes at 400°, or until as cooked as you prefer.

Yield: 24 appetizers.

CRABMEAT NACHOS

2 scallions, sliced thin
1 garlic clove, minced
½ cup butter, room temperature
2 large tomatoes, chopped fine,
   divided
1 serrano chile, minced

1 tablespoon cilantro, chopped
1¾ cups cooked crabmeat
½ pound Monterey Jack cheese,
   grated
1 avocado, chopped
Sliced jalapeño chiles (canned)
Nacho chips

Using medium skillet, sauté scallions and garlic in one tablespoon butter until soft (not allowing the butter to brown). Stir in one half of the tomatoes. Add chile and cilantro; reduce heat to low. One tablespoon at a time, whisk in the rest of the softened butter until creamy, not allowing the butter to simmer at any time. Gently stir in crabmeat.

Assembly: On a nacho plate that is suitable for oven use: Place crabmeat mixture on each chip and top with cheese. Place under broiler until cheese is melted. Garnish with diced avocado, jalapeño slices, and reserved chopped tomatoes.

Yield: About 24 nachos.

MEDITERRANEAN TOASTS

Olive Salad:

2 tablespoons extra-virgin olive oil

¼ cup onion, chopped

¼ teaspoon ground fennel seed

⅓ cup fennel bulb, cored & diced

1 garlic clove, minced

1½ cups black olives, pitted and
   chopped fine

½ teaspoon lemon juice

1 tablespoon Italian parsley, minced

1 tablespoon capers, chopped fine

1 teaspoon fresh ground black
   pepper

Place oil, onion, ground fennel, fennel bulb, and garlic in a medium-sized skillet; sauté over medium heat until just tender. Remove from heat; add remaining ingredients. Let marinate for at least one hour.

The Toasts:

1 clove of garlic, pressed

¼ cup extra-virgin olive oil

16 small triangles of bread

Parsley sprigs, for garnish

Mix together garlic and olive oil; brush onto bread triangles. Place on a baking sheet and broil until lightly golden. Place ½ teaspoon olive mixture on each of the toast points. Place a sprig of parsley on top, for garnish.

Yield: 16 toasts.

Variation for olive salad: *Omit fennel; use diced, seeded tomatoes; sun-dried tomatoes; or roasted sweet peppers instead. Include a mixture of chopped fresh herbs if you choose!*

This olive salad is now a popular item as a spread served on warm muffulata sandwiches! Another variation for olive salad is the Black Olive Tapenade, served with Pork Tenderloin (see index). Olive salad is also delicious served on pizza and pasta dishes.

STUFFED CHERRY TOMATOES

12 cherry tomatoes   **½ cup herb-seasoned cream cheese**

Core tomatoes; set upside down to drain. Spoon cream cheese (room temperature) into a pastry piping bag. Using a large, star-shaped tip, pipe cream cheese into the cored tomatoes. Garnish with a sprig of parsley if you choose! Thoroughly chill before serving.

Yield: 12 appetizers.

Variation: *Steam snow peas until just tender; cool. Open center side and remove seeds. Pipe cream cheese into center. Place in refrigerator and serve cold.*

SPICY SPINACH DIP

**1 (10 ounce) package frozen
    chopped spinach**
2 jalapeños, seeded and chopped fine
¾ cup green onions, chopped fine
**2 cups chopped tomatoes, seeded
    and drained**

8 ounces cream cheese, softened
**2 cups Monterey Jack cheese,
    grated**
⅓ cup light cream
¼ teaspoon garlic salt

Thaw spinach and squeeze dry. Mix together the remaining ingredients and pour into a lightly buttered baking dish. Bake at 350° for approximately 20 minutes, or until bubbly. Serve warm.

SWEET POTATO QUESADILLAS

1 large sweet potato, baked
**12 mini-tortillas (see index
    for recipe)**

¾ cup Monterey Jack cheese, grated
**½ cup roasted poblano strips (see
    index for roasting)**

Scoop pulp from inside of sweet potato. Using a fork, mash to a smooth consistency. Place approximately 2 teaspoons pulp in center of tortilla; top with a small amount of cheese. Place on a baking sheet, and broil just until cheese starts to melt. Remove from oven and place poblano strips on top. Serve warm.

Allow yourself to be creative with these. I enjoy making different varieties to serve children at the lake . . . or should I say, they enjoy making different varieties to serve to me?! Their favorite is refried beans topped with melted Cheddar cheese. One of my favorites is barbecue sauce topped with smoked chicken, caramelized onions, and melted Monterey Jack cheese.

QUESADILLAS
with Brie, Mango, and Chiles

1 medium onion, sliced thin
1 red bell pepper, chopped
2 tablespoons butter, divided
1 roasted poblano chile, seeded and
    chopped (see index for roasting)

2 tablespoons cilantro, chopped
1 mango, peeled, pitted, chopped
4 (8-inch) flour tortillas
8 ounces Brie cheese, trimmed, cut
    into ¼-inch strips

Using a medium-sized skillet, sauté onions and bell pepper in half of butter over medium heat. Remove from heat and add the poblano, cilantro, and mango; set aside. Slightly butter one side of tortillas with the remaining butter; set aside.

Assembly: Over medium heat, place one tortilla at a time (buttered side down) on a large skillet or griddle. Place one-fourth of cheese strips on half of flour tortilla. Top with one-fourth of chile-mango mixture. Season with salt and pepper. Fold empty half of flour tortilla over to enclose filling. Grill for about 45 seconds on each side, or until cheese begins to melt. Cut each quesadilla into three pieces. Arrange on platter and serve.

Yield: 12 appetizer servings.

BACON-WRAPPED OYSTERS
For Dan

1 pint large fresh oysters
⅛ teaspoon paprika
½ teaspoon salt

¼ teaspoon fresh ground pepper
2 tablespoons parsley, chopped fine
8 slices bacon, cut into thirds

Drain oysters; place in a small bowl and mix with the seasonings. Lay one oyster across one piece of bacon. Roll bacon around oyster; fasten with a wooden pick. Place on a baking sheet lined with parchment paper. Bake at 450° for 20 minutes, or until bacon is crisp.

Yield: 24 appetizer servings.

DILLED BRUSSELS SPROUTS

1½ pounds Brussels sprouts
2 teaspoons salt
1 teaspoon fresh ground pepper
1 cup prepared Italian salad dressing

2 tablespoons green onions, chopped
1 teaspoon dill weed

In a large saucepan, pour enough water over sprouts to just cover them; add salt and bring to a boil until just tender. Drain and cool. Place Brussels Sprouts and remaining ingredients into a large zip-closure plastic bag. Mix well; refrigerate overnight to marinate. Serve with crackers.

Serves 12.

CLAM CRISP

2 tablespoons onions, chopped fine
1 tablespoon butter
1½ tablespoons unbleached flour
½ teaspoon garlic powder

¼ teaspoon Worcestershire sauce
1 (7½ ounce) can minced clams
1 loaf sandwich bread, sliced thin

Using a small skillet, sauté onions in butter over medium heat. Remove from heat. Add flour, garlic powder, and Worcestershire sauce; blend well. Stir in clams (using liquid) and cook over low heat, stirring constantly until thickened; set aside. Remove crusts from slices of bread. Using a rolling pin, flatten each piece of bread and place one teaspoon clam mixture on each piece. Roll up; cut in half. Baste each piece with a small amount of melted butter and place on a baking sheet. Bake at 425° for 8 minutes, turning once.

Serves 12.

BACON BALLS

1 pound bacon, cooked and crumbled fine
8 ounces cream cheese
1 teaspoon Worcestershire sauce
½ teaspoon ground white pepper

¼ cup evaporated milk
2 teaspoons onion, chopped fine
1 cup fine rye bread crumbs
1 cup parsley, chopped fine

Excluding parsley, combine all ingredients in a medium-sized bowl; mix well. Roll into bite-sized balls, then roll in parsley to coat. Chill until ready to serve.

Serves 12.

MINI CRESCENTS
with Bacon and Sour Cream

1 (8 ounce) can crescent rolls
½ cup sour cream

½ teaspoon onion salt
6 slices bacon, cooked and
   crumbled fine

Remove dough from can. Unroll and separate into two large pieces. Lay each piece on cutting surface and cut in half lengthwise, making four separate pieces. Spread each piece with a mixture of sour cream and onion salt, sprinkling on crumbled bacon last. Cut each of the four pieces into five triangle shapes, using a corner to make first triangular shape. Roll each piece, starting with the flat edge and rolling to the point. Place on a lightly oiled baking sheet. Bake at 375° for 15 minutes, or until rich golden brown.

Yield: 20 appetizers.

PASTA SATCHELS
with Italian Sausage

1 pound bulk Italian sausage,
   ground fine
2 tablespoons Madeira wine
4 tablespoons tomato paste

½ cup black olives, pitted and
   chopped fine
35 won ton skins

Place sausage, wine, tomato paste, and olives in a large bowl; mix well. Set aside. Trim corners off won ton skins, rounding off corners as much as possible.

Assembly: Place a teaspoonful of filling in middle of a wrapper. Bring up the edges and squeeze just above filling to seal, leaving top of skin open (spread top out slightly). Repeat procedure for remaining filling and won ton skins. Slightly press pasta satchels onto a steamer plate (or basket) that is lightly oiled, so that the bottoms will flatten and satchels will stand on their own. Keep separated to prevent from sticking together. Cover with a damp cloth to prevent skins from drying out.

Cooking: Place steamer plate or basket in prepared steamer; cover. Steam for 15 minutes. Place steamed satchels in a lightly oiled 13 x 9 x 2-inch covered dish and hold in 200° oven until all satchels have been steamed. Serve warm.

Yield: 35 appetizers.

BAKED SWEET POTATO WEDGES
with Spicy Hummus Spread

2 medium sweet potatoes
1 teaspoon ground white pepper
1 teaspoon salt

½ teaspoon paprika
½ teaspoon garlic powder
2 tablespoons oil

Cut each potato in half lengthwise. Cut each half into three or four lengthwise wedges. Place in a medium-sized bowl; mix well with other ingredients. Place on a baking sheet. Bake at 425° for 25 minutes, or until soft. Serve warm with hummus on the side for dipping.

Yield: 12–16 Appetizers.

Spicy Hummus Spread

1 (15 ounce) can garbanzo
   beans, liquid reserved
2 garlic cloves, cut into halves
½ teaspoon ground coriander
3 tablespoons lemon juice

3 tablespoons sesame seeds,
   lightly toasted
½ teaspoon ground cumin
½ teaspoon ground red pepper

Mix above ingredients in a food processor (or blender), adding enough of the reserved liquid to make a very smooth consistency (about ⅓ cup). Serve hummus as a dip, as with the above recipe, or for a spread on pita sandwiches with fresh veggies!

Yield: 1½ cups.

SALMON BALL

1 cup salmon, precooked
½ pound cream cheese, softened
½ cup green onions, chopped fine

¼ teaspoon salt
3 tablespoons lemon juice
1 cup pecans, chopped fine

Mix all ingredients together in a medium-sized bowl, using only ¼ cup of pecans. Shape into a ball and refrigerate for 8 hours. When ready to serve, roll the ball in the remaining pecans. Serve with an assortment of crackers.

Yield: 1 salmon ball.

COCKTAIL MEATBALLS
in Cranberry Sauce

2 pounds ground beef	½ teaspoon salt
1 cup corn flakes	1 teaspoon fresh ground pepper
⅓ cup dried parsley flakes	1 teaspoon garlic powder
2 eggs	½ cup ketchup
2 tablespoons dried minced onions	2 tablespoons soy sauce

Using a large bowl, combine all the above ingredients; mix well. Form into walnut-sized balls and place on a baking sheet. Bake at 350° for 20 minutes, or until meatballs are browned. Drain well.

Place meatballs in a 13 x 9 x 2-inch baking dish; pour Cranberry Sauce (recipe follows) over all. Return to oven and bake, uncovered, for an additional 20 minutes. Serve in a chafing dish.

Yield: 12 servings.

Cranberry Sauce

1 (16 ounce) can jellied cranberry sauce	1 tablespoon lemon juice
	2 tablespoons brown sugar

Combine above ingredients in a medium saucepan. Cook over medium heat, stirring occasionally, until mixture is of a smooth consistency.

This recipe may be made in advance and frozen. Place in refrigerator to thaw the night before ready to use. Place in 350° oven to reheat. This is another one of those favored party dishes!

BABY BACK RIBS

3 racks baby back pork ribs	1 tablespoon sherry
2 green onions, chopped fine	2 tablespoons sesame oil
4 garlic cloves, chopped fine	1 cup soy sauce
2 teaspoons ginger root, grated	1 cup club soda

Mix ingredients in a large, heavy plastic bag; seal. Marinate in the refrigerator for at least eight hours, turning occasionally to baste equally.

Remove ribs from refrigerator; allow to reach room temperature. Take ribs from plastic bag and place them in the large baking pan; cover with heavy-duty foil. Bake in 350° oven for one hour.

Prepare on outdoor gas grill by placing a large piece of heavy-duty foil over grill rack, but keep the rack sides free from foil. Make small knife slits in the foil; very lightly oil. Preheat grill to 350°.

Place ribs on prepared grill for 30–45 minutes, turning often. Begin basting both sides of the ribs about the last ten minutes of grilling, being careful not to burn.

Remove from grill, and place ribs into a clean heavy plastic bag; allow to rest for 15 minutes. Remove from bag and separate ribs by slicing between them with a knife.

Serves 6.

Peachy-Plum Basting Sauce

½ cup peach jelly	½ cup chili sauce
½ cup plum jelly	¾ cup cider vinegar
½ cup brown sugar	

Mix above ingredients in a small saucepan. Bring to a boil over medium heat and gently boil for 3 minutes. Remove from heat and allow to reach room temperature.

Yield: 3 cups.

Blackberry Basting Sauce

2 cups blackberries	½ cup honey
½ cup brown sugar, packed	⅓ cup ginger, minced
½ cup ketchup	3 teaspoons hot sauce

Place ingredients in blender or food processor; purée. Pour into a medium-sized saucepan and cook over medium heat 10 minutes.

Yield: 3 cups.

TERIYAKI BEEF KABOBS

1 cup teriyaki sauce	4 tablespoons honey
¼ cup light soy sauce	2 garlic cloves, minced
½ cup water	1 tablespoon ginger, grated
¾ cup pineapple juice	½ teaspoon fresh ground pepper
½ cup brown sugar	2 tablespoons oil

Combine above ingredients in a large zip-closure plastic bag. Allow to stand until the sugar dissolves. Use as a marinade for beef or chicken.

1½ pounds sirloin steak, 1 inch thick	15 wooden skewers, cocktail size
1 (14 ounce) can pineapple chunks, drained	

Trim fat from sirloin steaks; discard. Cut meat into one-inch cubes and place in plastic bag with the marinade mixture. Tightly seal the bag and place in a bowl. Refrigerate eight hours. (Soak skewers in water to prevent burning.)

One hour before ready to serve, remove meat from refrigerator; drain in a colander. Using one skewer at a time, build kabobs, alternating meat and pineapple three times (starting with meat and ending with a pineapple chunk). Place side by side on a baking rack that is placed on a foil-lined baking sheet. Bake at 450° for approximately 8 minutes per side.

Yield: 15.

Option: *After baking, allow the kabobs to cool. Stack in a large baking dish, and cover. Refrigerate until ready to use. Reheat in 350° oven, covered, being careful to not overheat.*

TASTY TAMALES
Wrapped in Bacon

6 fresh tamales, each cut into thirds	6 slices bacon, each cut into thirds

Wrap one piece of bacon around one tamale piece; secure with a wooden pick. Repeat procedure for remaining bacon and tamales. Place on a parchment-lined baking sheet. Bake at 450° for 20 minutes, or until bacon is cooked as you prefer; drain. Serve warm.

Yield: 18.

CHICKEN TOSTADAS

4 cups cooked chicken, shredded

2 cups salsa

12 tostada shells

16 ounces cream cheese, softened

3 cups Monterey Jack cheese, grated

6 cups iceberg lettuce, shredded

4 tomatoes, chopped

4 green onions, chopped fine

Combine chicken and salsa in a medium-sized bowl; toss well. Spread tostada shells with cream cheese and top with the chicken mixture. Sprinkle the grated Monterey Jack cheese on top and place on a baking sheet. Broil in oven just until cheese melts; remove and top with lettuce, tomatoes, and green onions. Serve with additional salsa, pickled jalapeño slices, or guacamole—if you choose!

Yield: 12.

CASIE'S DEVILED EGGS

6 hard-boiled eggs

2 tablespoons mayonnaise

1 teaspoon vinegar

⅛ teaspoon each, salt and pepper

½ teaspoon dry mustard

Paprika, for garnish

Peel and halve eggs. Scoop the cooked yolks into a small bowl; set aside the whites. Mash the yolks with a fork; add all remaining ingredients (except paprika), mixing thoroughly. Adjust seasonings according to size of eggs and personal taste. Equally fill the egg whites, and garnish with a sprinkle of paprika.

Yield 12 eggs.

Variation: *Omit: 1 tablespoon of the mayonnaise, the vinegar, and dry mustard. Add: 1 tablespoon sweet pickle relish, 1½ tablespoons relish juice, and 1 teaspoon prepared mustard.*

FINGER SANDWICHES

1 cup cream cheese, softened

½ cup mayonnaise

⅓ cup chopped pecans

1 cup black olives, chopped fine

1 tablespoon olive juice

1 loaf bread, sliced thin

Place the first five ingredients together in a small bowl; mix well to blend. Refrigerate for twelve hours. Spread on bread, making a sandwich. Using an electric knife, trim crusts and cut diagonally.

Yield: 24.

STUFFED MUSHROOMS

24 fresh mushrooms
½ onion, chopped fine
1 stalk of celery, chopped fine
1 garlic clove, chopped fine

¼ cup butter
1 tablespoon Worcestershire sauce
1 cup breadcrumbs
Salt and pepper, to taste

Remove stems from mushrooms; chop fine. Place stems, onion, celery, and garlic in medium saucepan; sauté in butter over medium heat. Remove from heat; add Worcestershire sauce and breadcrumbs, making sure the crumbs are absorbed by the butter (if it's too dry, add more butter). Season to taste. Allow to cool; stuff mushroom caps with the mixture. Place in an appropriate-sized baking dish. Bake at 350° for approximately 20–30 minutes, depending on size of mushroom caps. Serve warm.

Yield: 24 Appetizers.

ROASTED NUTS

Lightly mist oil onto amount of nuts you choose to roast; sprinkle with some salt (optional). Spread on a baking sheet. Bake at 350° for approximately 8 minutes, stirring once. (Watch closely, for cooking time increases or decreases according to size of nut you are roasting.)

TOASTED MUSHROOM SANDWICHES

8 ounces mushrooms, chopped fine
2 tablespoons butter, melted
3 ounces cream cheese, softened
1 (10¾ ounce) can cream of
  mushroom soup
2 teaspoons Worcestershire sauce

2 teaspoons horseradish
¼ teaspoon garlic powder
½ cup slivered almonds, toasted
32 slices sandwich bread, sliced
  thin
¼ cup melted butter

Using a medium-sized skillet, sauté mushrooms in two tablespoons of butter; drain and set aside. Combine the cream cheese and mushroom soup in work bowl of electric stand mixer; beat until smooth. Add the sautéed mushrooms, Worcestershire sauce, horseradish, garlic powder, and almonds. Stir until well blended; set aside. Trim the crusts from bread slices. Roll each slice with a rolling pin to flatten. Place one tablespoon mushroom mixture in the center of each bread slice. Fold corners of bread to overlap in the center and secure with a wooden pick. Place on a baking sheet and slightly baste with melted butter. Bake at 450° for 5 minutes, or until light golden brown.

Yield: 32 appetizers.

BEAU MONDE DIP
with Fresh Veggies

⅔ cup mayonnaise
⅔ cup sour cream
3 tablespoons green onions, chopped

3 teaspoons dried parsley
1 teaspoon dried dill weed
1 teaspoon Beau Monde seasoning

Place all ingredients in a small bowl; mix well. Refrigerate until ready to use. Serve with an array of cold fresh veggies!

FRESH FRUIT
with Sour Cream Sauce

1 cup sour cream

½ cup light brown sugar

Place sour cream and brown sugar in small bowl. Mix until sugar is dissolved. Refrigerate until ready to use. Serve with an array of cold fresh fruits!

I like this especially well with apples!

CARAMEL FONDUE

6 tablespoons butter
1 (14 ounce) package caramels

2 tablespoons milk
4 tablespoons rum

Place ingredients in top of double boiler. Cook over medium heat until melted. Transfer to a fondue dish; keep warm for dipping apple slices and other fresh fruits.

BREADED BACON

1 pound sliced bacon
3 eggs
1½ teaspoons red pepper

1½ teaspoons dry mustard
3½ teaspoons cider vinegar
4 cups salted crackers, crushed

Slice bacon in half, crosswise. Whisk to blend eggs, red pepper, dry mustard, and vinegar in a medium bowl. Dip each bacon slice into egg mixture, and then press in cracker crumbs to coat both sides. Place on baking sheet and bake at 350° for 20 minutes, or until desired doneness is reached.

Yield: 2 dozen.

PARTY PIZZAS

1 pound lean ground beef
1 pound ground hot sausage
1 pound pasteurized cheese
½ teaspoon garlic salt

1 teaspoon Worcestershire sauce
1 tablespoon dried oregano
48 pieces sliced rye bread,
small (2 x 2 inches)

Place ground beef and sausage into a large skillet. Cook over medium-high heat until browned. Remove from skillet with a slotted spoon; drain on paper towels. Return to skillet; add remaining ingredients, except bread. Cook until cheese is melted. Remove from heat. Spoon a small amount on top of each piece of rye bread. Bake at 400° for 10 minutes, or freeze until ready to use.

Yield: 48.

FAST & EASY SAUSAGE BALLS

1 pound ground sausage
1½ cups Cheddar cheese, grated

2 cups biscuit mix

Place ingredients in a large bowl; mix by hand. Roll into one-inch balls; place on a baking sheet. Bake at 375° for 10–15 minutes. Drain on paper towels. Serve fresh, or freeze.

Yield: 4 dozen.

CINNAMON PECANS

1 egg white
½ cup sugar
2 teaspoons ground cinnamon

¼ teaspoon salt
3 cups pecan halves

Place egg white in work bowl of electric mixer. Beat on medium speed, adding sugar a little at a time, until just foamy. Using a rubber spatula, stir in cinnamon and salt. Stir in pecans; mix well to coat. Place individual pieces onto a parchment-lined baking sheet. Bake at 300° for 30 minutes. Remove from oven; cool.

Yield: 3 cups.

PARTY MIX

½ cup butter	2 cups corn cereal squares
1 teaspoon seasoned salt	2 cups rice cereal squares
1 teaspoon garlic salt	2 cups wheat cereal squares
1 tablespoon Worcestershire sauce	2 cups miniature pretzels
⅛ teaspoon red pepper	2 cups mixed nuts, divided

Place butter, seasoned salt, garlic salt, Worcestershire, and red pepper in a two-cup glass measuring cup. Microwave on high for 30 seconds, or until butter is melted. Combine cereals and pretzels in a large bowl; mix well. Place in two 13 x 9 x 2-inch baking pans; add 1 cup nuts per pan. Drizzle half of butter mixture over each portion; mix well. Bake at 250° for one hour, stirring every 15 minutes. Remove from oven; cool. Place in zip-closure bags to retain freshness.

Yield: 10 cups.

SNACKING CRACKERS

½ cup vegetable oil	1 teaspoon red pepper
1 (1 ounce) package ranch dressing mix (dried)	1 teaspoon seasoning salt
1 teaspoon garlic powder	1 teaspoon Worcestershire sauce
1 teaspoon dried dill weed	1½ cups oyster crackers

Mix all ingredients except crackers in a large zip-closure bag. Add oyster crackers; mix well.

Yield: 1½ cups.

CHEESE STICKS
with Roasted Garlic

1 cup unbleached flour
¼ teaspoon salt
Dash or red pepper
½ cup butter, cold

1 tablespoon roasted garlic plup
1 tablespoon water
1 cup chedder cheese
¼ teasopoon each, dried basil
  and oregano (optional)

Combine flour, salt, and red pepper in a large mixing bowl. Using a pastry blender, cut in butter until mixture resembles coarse meal. Add remaining ingredients. Mix, by hand until thoroughly blended. Should the mixture seem a bit dry, add a few drops of water until a soft dough forms.

On a lightly floured surface, roll dough approximately 12 x 8 inches in size. cut, width-wise, into one-half inch strips. Place on baking sheet (or you may choose to curl or plait strips for amore attractive presentation.) Bake in 425° oven for approximately 15 minutes.

Yield: 2 dozen.

BLACK BEAN RELISH

1½ cups canned black beans
  drained and rinsed
1 cup canned whole kernel corn,
  drained
1 cup red bell pepper, minced fine
1 cup purple onion, minced fine

¼ cup green onions, minced fine
2 tablespoons fresh cilantro,
  minced fine
3 teaspoons sugar
1 tablespoon fresh lime juice

Combine all ingredients; mix well. Cover and refrigerate four hours before serving.
Makes 4½ cups.

SALADS

FROM POACHED PEARS
TO BLACK-EYED PEAS

POACHED PEAR SALAD
with Red Wine Vinaigrette

3 Bosc pears

3 cups dry red wine

1½ cups orange juice, strained

1 cup sugar

½ teaspoon ground cinnamon

2 tablespoons crystallized
 ginger, chopped

8 cups mixed salad greens, torn

Red Wine Vinaigrette (recipe follows)

½ cup feta or blue cheese,
 crumbled

18 walnut halves, toasted

Preparation of pears: Cut pears into halves; peel, core, and remove stems. Combine the wine, orange juice, sugar, cinnamon, and ginger in a large skillet; bring to a boil. Reduce heat; place pears, cut side down, into the liquid and simmer 15 minutes. Gently turn over and simmer another 15 minutes, or until tender. Using a slotted spoon, remove pears from pan; drain (reserve liquid). Place in a 13 x 9 x 2-inch baking dish; cover and chill thoroughly. Bring reserved liquid to a boil over medium heat until it thickens (like thin syrup). Set aside to cool. (This is the "poaching syrup" used in the Red Wine Vinaigrette.)

Serves 6.

Red Wine Vinaigrette

¾ cup extra-virgin olive oil

½ cup red wine vinegar

⅓ cup poaching syrup, thickened
 (see preparation of pears, above)

½ teaspoon oregano, chopped fine

½ teaspoon salt

¼ teaspoon white pepper

1 teaspoon fresh thyme

2 tablespoons green onions,
 chopped fine

Thoroughly whisk the above ingredients together in a small mixing bowl.

Yield: 1¼ cups.

Presentation: Equally mound the mixed salad greens onto six chilled salad plates. Drizzle vinaigrette over the greens, and garnish with crumbled cheese and toasted walnut halves. Leaving the stems intact, slice the poached pears into ¼-quarter inch slices, lengthwise. Place on the side of each salad mound, stem side down, with the slices fanned out.

ROMAINE & ARUGULA SALAD
Dressed in Orange and Avocado

4 cups romaine lettuce, torn bite-sized	¼ teaspoon salt
4 cups arugula, torn bite-sized	2 teaspoon fresh ground pepper
½ cup extra-virgin olive oil	3 oranges, peeled and sectioned
½ cup red wine vinegar	1 purple onion, peeled and sliced thin
¼ cup orange juice	2 avocados, peeled and sliced thin
2 teaspoons honey	6 tablespoons parsley, chopped

Mix the romaine and arugula in a medium-sized bowl; set aside. In a small bowl, combine the olive oil, vinegar, orange juice, honey, salt, and pepper for the dressing; whisk well.

Presentation: Equally divide the salad mixture onto six chilled salad plates. Arrange oranges, onions, and avocados on top. Drizzle a small amount of dressing mixture on top; garnish with parsley.

Serves 6.

CRISPY APPLE SLAW
with Blue Cheese

4 cups Chinese cabbage, sliced thin	2 tablespoons cider vinegar
4 cups red cabbage, sliced thin	½ teaspoon coriander
2 red apples, cored and cut into ¼-inch wedges	1 teaspoon dried celery leaves
3 tablespoons lemon juice	½ teaspoon salt
2 tablespoons sugar	½ teaspoon fresh ground pepper
2 tablespoons water	2 tablespoons extra-virgin olive oil
2 tablespoons red wine vinegar	½ cup blue cheese, crumbled

Using a large bowl, combine the two cabbages, apples, and lemon juice; mix well. With the exception of the cheese, combine all other ingredients and whisk well; pour over the cabbage mixture and gently mix. Place equally divided portions onto six chilled salad plates; garnish with blue cheese.

Serves 6.

TANGY FRUIT SALAD

8 cups red leaf lettuce, torn bite-sized
1 papaya, peeled, seeded and sliced
    ¼-inch thick
1 pink grapefruit, peeled
    and sectioned
8 strawberries, quartered
1 avocado, peeled and sliced
    ¼-inch thick

⅓ cup white wine vinegar
¼ cup orange juice
1 tablespoon shallots,
    chopped fine
½ teaspoon dry mustard
½ teaspoon salt
¼ teaspoon white pepper
¼ cup safflower oil

Equally divide the lettuce onto six chilled salad plates; arrange papaya, grapefruit, strawberries, and avocado slices on top. Combine the remaining ingredients in a small bowl for the dressing; whisk thoroughly. Drizzle the dressing over each salad.

Serves 6.

GRAPEFRUIT SALAD

4 cups green leaf lettuce,
    torn bite-sized
4 cups red leaf lettuce,
    torn bite-sized
1 avocado, peeled and sliced
    ¼ inch thick
1 cup grapefruit sections
8 black olives, pitted and sliced

⅓ cup red wine vinegar
⅓ cup sugar
½ teaspoon salt
½ teaspoon celery seed
½ teaspoon dry mustard
¼ cup vegetable oil
1 red onion, sliced thin

Combine lettuces, avocado, grapefruit, and black olives in a large bowl. With the exception of the onion slices, combine the remaining ingredients in a small bowl; whisk thoroughly. Just before serving salad, add dressing to the lettuce mixture; toss gently. Equally divide the salad onto six chilled salad plates; garnish with red onion slices.

Serves 6.

COLD PASTA SALAD
with Smoked Salmon

½ pound smoked salmon, skinned and boned

8 ounces cooked pasta shells, cooled

2 tablespoons sun-dried tomatoes, minced

2 tablespoons black olives, minced

4 tablespoons red onion, minced

2 tablespoons parsley, chopped fine

¼ cup garlic vinegar

½ cup extra-virgin olive oil

½ cup Parmesan cheese, grated fine

2 teaspoons pine nuts, toasted

Break salmon into bite-sized pieces; refrigerate until ready to use. Excluding the salmon, cheese, and nuts, mix the remaining ingredients together in a large bowl. Cover and refrigerate for two hours. Just before serving, add the salmon, cheese, and nuts; mix thoroughly. Equally divide onto six chilled salad plates.

Serves 6.

ARTICHOKE SALAD
with Mushrooms and Snow Peas

1 (14 ounce) can artichoke hearts, drained

2 cups mushrooms, sliced thin

1½ cups snowpeas, trimmed and blanched

¼ cup red wine vinegar

¼ cup canola oil

2 teaspoons Dijon mustard

1 teaspoon garlic, minced

1 teaspoon dried dill weed

½ teaspoon salt

1 cup heavy cream, chilled

12 large green lettuce leaves

½ cup sliced almonds, lightly toasted

Cut artichokes into halves; combine with the mushrooms and snow peas. Refrigerate until cold. Using a small bowl, combine vinegar, oil, mustard, garlic, dill weed, and salt; whisk the cream in slowly until well incorporated. Pour the vinegar mixture over the vegetables and toss well. Equally divide onto six chilled salad plates lined with lettuce leaves; garnish tops with toasted almonds.

Serves 6.

ENDIVE SALAD
with Champagne Vinaigrette

3 cups Belgium endive

3 cups watercress

1 cup raddiccio

1 green apple

1 red apple

1 Bosc pear, peeled

4 tablespoons lemon juice

Champagne Vinaigrette
   (recipe follows)

¾ cup blue cheese

Pinch endive, watercress, and raddiccio into bite-sized pieces in a large bowl; toss gently. Cut apples and pear into halves; core. Cut into small, bite-sized chunks and lightly coat with lemon juice. Pour a generous amount of vinaigrette dressing over the salad mixture; toss to coat. Arrange salad onto six chilled salad plates; top with apples and pears. Garnish tops with blue cheese.

Serves 6.

Champagne Vinaigrette

½ cup extra-virgin olive oil

¼ cup almond oil

¼ cup champagne vinegar*

3 tablespoons apple cider vinegar

3 tablespoons apple juice

1 tablespoon red onion, diced fine

1 tablespoon Italian parsley,
   chopped fine

⅛ teaspoon each, salt and
   white pepper

Combine the above ingredients in a small bowl; whisk to blend. Refrigerate for 6 hours. Mix well before serving.

Yield: ¾ cup.

To substitute for champagne vinegar, combine ½ cup white wine vinegar, ½ cup Sauvignon Blanc, and one whole clove in a small saucepan. Boil over medium heat for five minutes; cool. Remove clove.

RED CABBAGE SALAD
with Apples and Walnuts

1 red onion, quartered and sliced thin	2 tablespoons balsamic vinegar
2 tablespoons extra-virgin olive oil	1 apple, cored and cut bite-sized
1 garlic clove, chopped fine	2 tablespoons parsley, chopped
1 head red cabbage, cored and shredded	½ teaspoon marjoram, chopped fine
	18 walnut halves, toasted
½ teaspoon salt	3 ounces feta cheese, crumbled
½ teaspoon fresh ground pepper	

Using a large skillet or wok, cook onion in oil until barely translucent. Add garlic, and continue to cook for one minute. Add the cabbage and continue to cook until just wilted. Add the salt, pepper, vinegar, apples, herbs, and walnuts; mix thoroughly. Divide warm salad equally onto six salad plates, and garnish with cheese.

Serves 6.

ROMAINE & TOMATO SALAD

2 tablespoons lemon juice	½ teaspoon fresh ground pepper
1 tablespoon basil, chopped	¼ cup extra-virgin olive oil
1 tablespoon Italian parsley, chopped fine	8 cups romaine lettuce, torn bite-sized
2 tablespoons green onions, chopped fine	6 tomatoes, chopped
½ teaspoon garlic, minced	¼ pound provolone cheese, grated
1 teaspoon salt	½ cup black olives, sliced

Using a small bowl, combine lemon juice, herbs, onions, garlic, salt, pepper, and oil; whisk well.

Equally divide the romaine lettuce onto six chilled salad plates; top each with chopped tomatoes. Drizzle the oil mixture over each, and garnish with cheese and olives.

Serves 6.

BERRY MELON SALAD
with Poppyseed Dressing

1 cantaloupe, halved, peeled, and
    seeded
6 kiwi, peeled, quartered, and
    quarters halved

3 cups strawberries, sliced
6 sprigs of mint, for garnish
Poppyseed Dressing (recipe follows)

Slice each cantaloupe half into thirds and place each on a chilled salad plate. Top with equally divided strawberries and kiwi. Drizzle with Poppyseed Dressing and garnish with mint sprigs.

Serves 6.

Poppyseed Dressing

¾ cup orange juice
½ cup grapefruit juice
2 tablespoons lemon juice

2 tablespoons honey
1 tablespoon cornstarch
1 teaspoon poppyseeds

Combine juices and honey in a small saucepan. Using a small amount of the juice, dissolve the cornstarch; add to the juice mixture. Cook over medium heat until thick and bubbly. Remove from heat; stir in poppyseeds. Chill thoroughly.

ROMAINE & STRAWBERRY SALAD

7 cups Romaine lettuce,
    torn bite-sized
1 cup watercress, stemmed
12 strawberries, stemmed and
    quartered
½ red onion, sliced thin and
    separated

¼ cup wine vinegar
2 tablespoons lemon juice
1 tablespoon sugar
⅛ teaspoon salt
⅛ teaspoon fresh ground black
    pepper
¼ cup extra-virgin olive oil

Using a large salad bowl, combine the first four ingredients. Whisk the remaining ingredients in a small bowl until smooth. Equally divide the salad mixture onto six chilled salad plates, and drizzle the oil and vinegar mixture on top.

Serves 6.

HABITUAL SPINACH SALAD
with Balsamic Vinaigrette

8 cups spinach, torn bite-sized
6 mushrooms, sliced thin
6 slices bacon, cooked and crumbled
½ red onion, sliced thin and separated

3 boiled eggs, chopped fine
Fresh ground pepper
Balsamic Vinaigrette (recipe follows)
4 ounces feta cheese, crumbled

Arrange spinach in even portions on six chilled salad plates. Top each portion with mushrooms, bacon, onion, eggs, and pepper. Drizzle vinaigrette over each; sprinkle cheese on top.

Serves 6.

Balsamic Vinaigrette

¼ cup balsamic vinegar
½ cup red wine vinegar
4 tablespoons honey
1 tablespoon Dijon mustard
½ teaspoon each salt, and
    fresh ground pepper

3 teaspoons lemon juice
¼ cup extra-virgin olive oil
1 garlic clove, pressed
1 green onion, sliced thin
2 tablespoons parsley,
    chopped fine

Excluding the green onions and parsley, combine the above ingredients in a food processor and process until smooth. Add the onions and parsley; mix well.

Yield: 1 cup.

WILD GREENS
with Pears and Blue Cheese

8 cups mixed baby greens
3 ripe pears, peeled, cored, halved
1 cup toasted walnut pieces

½ cup blue cheese
Balsamic Vinaigrette Dressing
    (previous recipe)

Equally divide mixed greens onto six chilled salad plates. Drizzle desired amount of vinaigrette dressing over each salad, and place one pear half in center. Sprinkle with toasted walnut pieces, and place approximately one table-spoonful of blue cheese in center of each pear half.

Serves 6.

DRIED CRANBERRY & SPINACH SALAD
with Raspberry Vinaigrette

8 cups spinach, torn bite-sized
3 tablespoons sunflower seeds,
   toasted
½ cup dried cranberries

½ cup walnuts, toasted and broken
3 green onions, sliced thin
Raspberry Vinaigrette
   (recipe follows)

Divide spinach onto six chilled salad plates; sprinkle with remaining ingredients. Drizzle Raspberry Vinaigrette over top.

Serves 6.

Raspberry Vinaigrette

1 (10 ounce) package frozen
   raspberries, thawed
¼ cup sugar
2 teaspoons cornstarch
¼ cup red wine vinegar
¼ cup cranberry juice

¼ cup raspberry juice
¼ teaspoon celery seed
¼ teaspoon ground cinnamon
Dash of ground cloves
¼ teaspoon fresh ground pepper

Using a blender or food processor, blend raspberries until smooth; strain to remove seeds. In a medium saucepan, stir together the sugar and cornstarch; stir in strained raspberries and the remaining ingredients. Cook over medium heat until slightly thick; chill.

TOMATO & ARTICHOKE SALAD

3 (6 ounce) jars marinated
   artichoke hearts
¾ cup red wine vinegar
½ cup extra-virgin olive oil
¼ teaspoon salt
¼ teaspoon white pepper

6 medium tomatoes, cut into
   wedges
¼ cup green onions, chopped fine
1 tablespoon basil, chopped
6 large green leaf lettuce leaves

Reserving marinade, drain artichoke hearts and cut into halves. Using a large bowl, combine the reserved marinade, vinegar, oil, salt, and pepper; mix well. Add the artichoke hearts, tomatoes, green onions, and basil; toss gently. Cover and chill for two hours. Equally divide onto six chilled salad plates lined with lettuce leaves.

Serves 6.

FRESH BROCCOLI & CAULIFLOWER SALAD

1 bunch broccoli (florets only)
1 medium cauliflower (florets only)
1 cup cider vinegar
3 garlic cloves, minced
1 tablespoon sugar
1 tablespoon salt
1 tablespoon dill weed
2 teaspoons fresh ground pepper
1 cup salad oil

6 stalks fresh asparagus, cut on
   diagonal
1 cup celery, sliced thin
1 cup mushrooms, sliced thin
12 green lettuce leaves
4 radishes, sliced thin (or cherry
   tomatoes)
3 tablespoons parsley,
   chopped fine

Place broccoli and cauliflower, separately, in zip-closure bags. Combine vinegar, garlic, sugar, salt, dill weed, pepper, and oil. Equally divide mixture between the two bags. Place in the refrigerator and allow to marinate for 24 hours.

Using a small sauce pan, bring 1 cup water and asparagus to a boil over medium heat; cook for four minutes. Drain into a colander and refresh under cold water to retard further cooking. Drain and refrigerate.

Just before serving, add broccoli and cauliflower mixtures together in a large bowl. Add the asparagus, celery, and mushrooms; toss to coat evenly. Arrange on lettuce-lined salad plates; garnish with radishes (or cherry tomatoes) and chopped parsley.

Serves 6.

GREEN SALAD
with Apples and Orange Vinaigrette

4 cups each romaine and Boston
   lettuce, torn bite-sized
1 Golden Delicious apple, cored,
   halved, and sliced thin
1 Red Delicious apple, cored,
   halved, and sliced thin

1 large orange,
   peeled and sectioned
4 tablespoons olive oil
¼ cup red wine vinegar
1 teaspoon Dijon mustard
½ teaspoon, each salt and pepper

Equally divide lettuce onto six chilled salad plates. Arrange apples and orange sections on top of lettuce, and drizzle with mixture of oil, vinegar, mustard, salt, and pepper.

Serves 6.

GARDEN SALAD
with Creamy Lemon Dressing

7 cups romaine lettuce,
    torn bite-sized
Creamy Lemon Dressing
    (recipe follows)

1 cucumber, peeled and sliced thin
1 carrot, grated fine
1 purple onion, quartered
    and sliced thin

Divide lettuce equally onto six chilled salad plates and drizzle with lemon dressing. Top each portion with cucumber slices, grated carrot, and pieces of purple onion.

Serves 6.

Creamy Lemon Dressing

1 pint sour cream
⅓ cup Parmesan cheese, grated fine
¼ cup lemon juice, fresh squeezed
4 teaspoons water

¼ cup salad oil
½ teaspoon salt
1 teaspoon fresh ground pepper

Place ingredients in a medium-sized bowl; whisk well to blend.

WALDORF SALAD

2 cups apples (green & red), cubed
¼ cup pineapple juice
1 cup celery, sliced
1½ cups seedless grapes, halved
½ cup miniature marshmallows
½ cup evaporated milk, cold

1 teaspoon sugar
½ teaspoon vanilla
3 tablespoons mayonnaise
2 tablespoons creamy
    peanut butter
½ cup pecans, broken

Place apples in large bowl and pour pineapple juice over all; mix well and drain. Add celery, grapes, and marshmallows; mix well, and set aside. Pour milk into small bowl. Using a handheld mixer, beat milk until frothy. Add sugar and vanilla; mix well. Add mayonnaise and peanut butter; beat until smooth. Pour over apple mixture; mix well using a rubber spatula. Stir in pecans just before serving.

Serves 6.

ARUGULA SALAD
with Honey-Glazed Shrimp

24 large shrimp, peeled and deveined
1 cup red onion, chopped, divided
1 garlic clove, pressed
⅔ cup Italian Vinaigrette, divided
    (recipe follows)
¼ cup chili sauce
¼ cup prepared horseradish
1 tablespoon hot sauce
1 tablespoon Worcestershire sauce
½ cup butter
1¼ cups tomato, chopped

¼ cup molasses
¼ cup brown sugar
1¼ cups balsamic vinegar
2 Granny Smith apples,
    sliced thin
2 cups jicama, julienned
2 teaspoons lemon juice
8 cups arugula lettuce, cleaned
    and dried
1 red bell pepper, julienned

Using a large zip-closure bag, marinate shrimp overnight in mixture as follows ½ cup red onion, garlic, ¼ cup Italian Vinaigrette dressing, chili sauce, horseradish, hot sauce, and Worcestershire. Keep refrigerated until ready to grill shrimp.

Using a medium-sized skillet, sauté remaining onion in butter until translucent; add tomatos, molasses, brown sugar, and vinegar. Cook over medium heat until thick and soft; strain.

Grill shrimp on outdoor grill over medium-high heat. Baste with the above sauce until done.

Toss apples and jicama with lemon juice; set aside. Mix arugula with the remaining vinaigrette dressing and divide equally onto six chilled salad plates. Equally top each with apples, jicama, and red bell pepper. Arrange four shrimp around each bed of greens.

Serves 6.

Italian Vinaigrette

¼ cup salad oil
⅓ cup white wine vinegar
1 teaspoon sugar
2 teaspoons oregano, minced
½ teaspoon paprika

1 teaspoon Dijon mustard
¼ teaspoon celery seed
1 garlic clove, pressed
2 tablespoons Parmesan, grated

Place all ingredients in a small bowl and whisk until smooth.

CAESAR SALAD
with Sourdough Croutons

½ cup lemon juice, fresh squeezed	Salt and pepper, to taste
2 tablespoons Worcestershire sauce	8 cups romaine lettuce, torn
4 garlic cloves, chopped	1 red onion, sliced thin
½ teaspoon hot sauce	Sourdough Croutons (recipe follows)
¼ cup olive oil	1 cup Parmesan cheese, grated

Place first four ingredients in a food processor or blender. With machine running, gradually add oil. Season with salt and pepper.

Combine lettuce, onion, and croutons in large bowl. Toss with enough dressing to season to preferred taste. Sprinkle with cheese and serve on individual serving plates.

Serves 6.

Sourdough Croutons

1 small loaf sourdough bread	¼ cup Parmesan cheese, grated
2 tablespoons olive oil	½ teaspoon garlic powder

Cut bread into ¾-inch cubes. Place in a large bowl and drizzle olive oil over all; toss to distribute. Add Parmesan cheese and garlic powder; toss to coat evenly. Spread cubes onto a baking sheet and bake for approximately 15 minutes at 350°, turning occasionally.

MARINATED TOMATO SALAD

3 tablespoons onion, chopped fine	1½ teaspoons dry basil
¾ cup stuffed sliced olives	½ teaspoon dry thyme
5 large tomatoes, peeled and sliced	2 garlic cloves, pressed
⅓ cup oil	6 green lettuce leaves
½ cup wine vinegar	12 purple onion rings, separated
1 teaspoon each, salt and pepper	½ cup sliced olives

Using a large dish, sprinkle chopped onions and olives over tomatoes. Whisk oil, vinegar, salt, pepper, basil, thyme, and garlic together; pour over tomato mixture. Cover and chill four to six hours.

Arrange lettuce leaves onto six chilled, individual serving plates. Top with tomatoes and garnish with purple onion and olive slices.

Serves 6.

MANDARIN ORANGE TOSSED SALAD
with Caramelized Almonds

3 cups Boston lettuce

3 cups green leaf lettuce

2 cups red leaf lettuce

Vinaigrette Dressing (recipe follows)

2 stalks celery, sliced thin

1 can Mandarin orange sections, drained

4 green onions, sliced thin

Caramelized Almonds (recipe follows)

Combine lettuces in large bowl. Just before serving, add the vinaigrette to the lettuce mixture; toss gently to blend. Equally divide onto six chilled salad plates. Sprinkle with celery, oranges, green onions, and caramelized almonds.

Serves 6.

Vinaigrette Dressing

¼ cup vegetable oil

2 tablespoons sugar

1 tablespoon white vinegar

½ teaspoon salt

¼ teaspoon fresh ground pepper

8 drops hot sauce

Combine all ingredients in a small bowl; whisk to blend. Refrigerate until ready to use.

Caramelized Almonds

½ cup slivered almonds

4 tablespoons sugar

Combine ingredients in a small, heavy saucepan. Cook over medium heat, stirring constantly, until golden. Pour onto parchment paper; cool. Break into small pieces.

This is one of my family's favorite salads—thank you, Jane, for sharing!

FRESH FRUIT SALAD

Arrange assorted fruits such as strawberries, blueberries, blackberries, melon balls, fresh pineapple chunks, grapefruit and orange sections, seedless grapes, kiwi, and sliced bananas on a leaf of red-tip lettuce. Top with Fresh Fruit Dressing, and serve immediately.

Fresh Fruit Dressing

1 tablespoon poppyseeds (or celery seeds)	½ cup applesauce
⅓ cup sugar	¼ cup honey
¼ teaspoon dry mustard	3 tablespoons lemon juice
½ teaspoon paprika	1 tablespoon vinegar
½ teaspoon salt	½ teaspoon lemon zest
	⅓ cup salad oil

Combine all ingredients in a food processor or blender. Mix well and chill. Serve over fresh fruit.

MEXICAN SALAD

3 medium oranges, peeled and diced	2 tablespoons fresh lime juice
3 medium tomatoes, seeded and diced	½ teaspoon each, salt and pepper
2 avocados, peeled, pitted, and diced	3 tablespoons cilantro, minced
½ cup frozen corn kernels, thawed	8 cups red leaf lettuce, torn bite-sized
¼ cup red onion, minced	
3 tablespoons olive oil	

Combine oranges, tomatoes, avocados, corn, and onion in medium-sized bowl; set aside. Using a small bowl, gradually whisk oil into lime juice; season with salt and pepper. Add to the salad mixture, along with the cilantro, and mix well. Mound red leaf lettuce onto six chilled salad plates, and place salad mixture on top.

Serves 6.

CANTALOUPE & BLUEBERRY SALAD

8 ounces vanilla yogurt
1 tablespoon lemon juice
1 teaspoon poppyseeds
1 teaspoon orange zest

1 large cantaloupe, halved
  and seeded
18 leaves Boston lettuce
1½ cups fresh blueberries
6 sprigs fresh mint

Combine yogurt, lemon juice, poppyseeds, and orange zest in a small bowl; mix well and refrigerate.

Slice cantaloupe lengthwise into 24 slices. Arrange 4 slices on each of six lettuce-lined salad plates; top each with ¼ cup blueberries. Spoon a small amount of yogurt mixture over each. Garnish with a sprig of fresh mint.

Serves 6.

MEXICAN SALAD
with Avocado Dressing

8 cups iceberg lettuce, shredded
3 tomatoes, cut into wedges
½ cup black olives, sliced
1 small purple onion, sliced and
  separated

Avocado Dressing (recipe follows)
2 tablespoons cilantro, chopped

Divide lettuce onto six chilled salad plates. Arrange tomatoes, olives, and separated onion rings on top. Drizzle each with dressing; garnish with cilantro.

Serves 6.

Avocado Dressing

1 avocado, peeled and mashed
½ cup sour cream
1½ tablespoons lime juice
½ teaspoon ground cumin

½ teaspoon salt
¼ teaspoon ground red pepper
2 garlic cloves, minced fine
2 tablespoons vegetable oil

Combine all ingredients in a blender and blend until smooth. Chill thoroughly.

CHICKEN SALAD
Stuffed in Tomatoes

5 (boneless, skinless) breasts of chicken	1 teaspoon salt
2 tablespoons dried basil	1 teaspoon fresh ground pepper
4 tablespoons minced onions	1 cup mayonnaise
2 stalks celery, chopped	6 medium tomatoes

Sprinkle chicken breast with dried basil. Place in a baking dish and bake for 35 minutes at 350°, or until cooked thoroughly. Allow to cool; cut into ½-inch cubes. Place in a medium-sized bowl; add onions, celery, salt, pepper, and mayonnaise. Adjust seasonings. Refrigerate.

Core tomatoes, making a large enough opening to remove pulp. Using a paring knife, flute the outside edges for an attractive presentation (should you have a "fluting" knife, just use it and don't core beforehand). Turn upside down on paper towels to drain. Refrigerate until ready to use.

Remove tomatoes and chicken salad from refrigerator. Spoon chicken salad into tomatoes. Serve cold.

Serves 6.

Optional ingredients: *Cashews, bamboo shoots, pimientos, red or green bell pepper, English peas, or chopped cherry tomatoes!*

Suggested presentation: *Serve tomato on a leaf of green leaf lettuce and garnish with a sprig of parsley. On the side: a slice of cantaloupe, watermelon, and small cluster of grapes.*

CHICKEN SALAD SUPREME

2½ cups cooked chicken breasts, diced	1 teaspoon salt
1 cup celery, chopped fine	1 cup mayonnaise
1 cup green grapes, cut into halves	½ cup heavy cream, whipped
½ cup slivered almonds, toasted	

Mix ingredients together, folding in whipped cream last; refrigerate. (Best made one day before ready to serve.)

Mom made this last Christmas, just to have on hand—she does things like that!

TUNA SALAD

1 (6½ ounce) can tuna, drained
¼ cup apple, chopped
2 teaspoons sweet pickle relish
¼ cup purple onions, chopped
1 tablespoon celery flakes
½ teaspoon dill weed

½ teaspoon lemon juice
¼ teaspoon salt
¼ teaspoon pepper
1 teaspoon Dijon mustard
⅓ cup mayonnaise
1 hard-boiled egg, chopped fine

Reserving eggs, combine all ingredients in a small bowl. Mix well to blend. Gently fold in eggs. Cover and refrigerate until cold.

Serves 4.

SHRIMP & AVOCADO SALAD

1 tablespoon lemon juice
2 teaspoons Dijon mustard
¼ cup vegetable oil
2 tablespoons Parmesan cheese, grated
½ teaspoon each, salt and pepper

8 cups mixed salad greens, torn
1 cup Monterey Jack cheese, grated
1 avocado, peeled and cut into ⅛-inch slices
1 pound precooked medium shrimp
6 pieces sliced lemons, for garnish

Using a small bowl, combine lemon juice, mustard, oil, parmesan, salt, and pepper; whisk thoroughly. Mix with salad greens and equally divide onto six chilled salad plates. Sprinkle tops with grated Monterey Jack cheese. Place avocado slices on top, followed by the shrimp. Garnish with a thin slice of lemon.

Serves 6.

HOT GERMAN POTATO SALAD

6 russet potatoes, cooked in jackets
6 slices bacon
¾ cup onions, chopped
2 tablespoons unbleached flour
1 tablespoon sugar

½ teaspoon celery seeds
¼ teaspoon fresh ground black pepper
¾ cup water
⅓ cup vinegar

Slice potatoes thin; set aside. Fry bacon in large skillet over medium-high heat until crisp; remove and crumble. Place onions in bacon grease; sauté until tender. Blend in flour, sugar, celery seeds, and pepper. Stir to make a smooth roux. Slowly add water and vinegar, being careful to avoid lumping. Mix well until slightly thickened; add crumbled bacon and mix well. Add potatoes and gently stir to coat. Remove from heat; cover and allow to stand until ready to serve.

Serves 8.

POTATO SALAD

6 large russet potatoes,
   peeled and sliced
1 medium onion, chopped
4 dill pickles, chopped
3 tablespoons prepared mustard

4 tablespoons vinegar
1 cup mayonnaise
½ teaspoon salt
½ teaspoon freshly ground pepper

Place potatoes in a large saucepan and cover with water. Bring to boil over medium-high heat; reduce heat to medium low and simmer until soft (approximately 30 minutes). Using the pan lid, drain water off potatoes. Add remaining ingredients; mix thoroughly by hand, using a fork. Adjust seasonings to preferred taste.

Serves 12.

This recipe is good with barbecue, and it's what my family expects when I make potato salad! However, for another version of potato salad, try New Potato Salad, using new potatoes, of course—and don't peel them! Add salt, pepper, dill weed, chopped onion, and mayonnaise. Just season to taste; it'll be good!

CRAB LOUIS SALAD

½ cup mayonnaise
½ cup chili sauce
2 tablespoons green bell pepper,
   chopped
2 tablespoons sweet pickle, chopped
2 tablespoons onion, chopped
2 tablespoons lemon juice

1½ cups lump crabmeat
Prepared salad greens
2 tomatoes, quartered
2 green bell peppers, sliced
2 hard-boiled eggs, sliced
Pimiento strips

Using a medium-sized bowl, combine mayonnaise, chili sauce, chopped bell pepper, pickle, onion, and lemon juice; mix well. Add crabmeat and toss lightly; chill thoroughly. When ready to serve, equally divide prepared salad greens onto four chilled salad plates. Spoon crab mixture on top, and garnish with the quartered tomatoes, sliced bell peppers, egg slices, and pimiento strips.

Serves 4.

Crab Louis Salad always makes me think of a very fun skiing vacation we shared with a group of friends in Taos, New Mexico. We dined at Andy's favorite restaurant, and he ordered a Crab Louis Salad before his entrée. It was so huge, and he managed to eat it all! Good friends, happy times, cherished memories!

GRANDMOTHER'S PINK SALAD

1 (16 ounce) can cherry
   pie filling
1 (8 ounce) can crushed
   pineapple, drained
1 (11 ounce) can mandarin
   oranges, drained

1 (14 ounce) can sweetened
   condensed milk
¾ cup miniature marshmallows
½ cup chopped pecans
9 ounces prepared whipped
   topping

Using a large bowl, combine first six ingredients and blend together by hand, using a rubber spatula. Fold in whipped topping, and gently mix until well blended. Chill thoroughly before serving.

FRESH CRANBERRY SALAD
Rochelle's Way

4 cups fresh cranberries, crushed
2 cups sugar
1 cup grapes, halved
1 (15½ ounce) can crushed
   pineapple, drained

2½ cups marshmallows
1 cup pecans, chopped
½ pint heavy cream
¼ cup sugar

Combine cranberries and sugar in a large bowl. Cover and refrigerate overnight. Two hours before serving, add grapes, pineapple, marshmallows, and pecans; mix well, and set aside.

Pour the heavy cream into a medium-sized bowl. Using an electric mixer, began beating on slow speed. Incorporate sugar in small amounts and continue to beat until stiff. Gently fold into cranberry mixture. Return to refrigerator until ready to serve.

FAT-FREE SALAD TREAT
For Don

1 (16¼ ounce) can crushed
   pineapple, drained
16 ounces fat-free
   cottage cheese

1 (6 ounce) package sweetened
   lime gelatin
12 ounces fat-free whipped
   cream topping

Combine the pineapple, cottage cheese, and lime gelatin in a large bowl; mix well. Stir in the whipped topping and blend thoroughly. Cover and refrigerate.

Serves 6.

GREEN BEAN & MANGO SALAD

2 (16 ounce) cans cut green beans,
   drained
1 onion, chopped
4 ribs celery, chopped
½ cup fresh mushrooms, sliced
3 tablespoons pimiento, chopped
¼ cup water chestnuts, sliced

1 mango, peeled and chopped
½ cup salad oil
½ cup red wine vinegar
¼ cup ketchup
½ cup sugar
2 tablespoons Worcestershire sauce

Combine first seven ingredients; set aside. Combine the oil, vinegar, ketchup, sugar, and Worcestershire in a small saucepan. Heat until sugar dissolves. Allow to cool; stir into the vegetable mixture. Refrigerate until thoroughly chilled.

Serves 8.

TABBOULEH

¾ cup cracked wheat
1 bunch parsley, snipped
1 bunch green onions, chopped
1 medium tomato, chopped

1 tablespoon olive oil
Juice of 1 lemon
½ teaspoon salt

Soak cracked wheat in water for approximately two hours, then squeeze dry. Place all ingredients in a medium-sized bowl and mix thoroughly; chill.

BLACK-EYED PEA SALAD

2 cups carrots, chopped
1 medium onion, chopped
1 medium bell pepper, chopped
3 (15 ounce) cans jalapeño
    black-eyed peas, drained

1 (2 ounce) jar pimientos, chopped
    and drained
¾ cup sugar
⅔ cup salad oil
¾ cup cider vinegar

Mix all ingredients together in a large bowl; marinate in refrigerator overnight.

LEMON-MUSTARD VINAIGRETTE

¼ cup salad oil
3 tablespoons fresh lemon juice
1 teaspoon sugar
1 teaspoon salt

1 teaspoon fresh ground pepper
2 teaspoons Dijon mustard
1 garlic clove, pressed
1 teaspoon Worcestershire sauce

Combine all ingredients in a small bowl; whisk well to blend.

SPINACH SALAD DRESSING

¼ cup cider vinegar
¼ cup vegetable oil
2 teaspoons Dijon mustard
2 teaspoons brown sugar

4 slices bacon, cooked
    and crumbled
2 tablespoons sliced green onions

Combine first four ingredients in a small bowl; whisk well to blend. Add bacon and green onions.

GREEN SALAD DRESSING

1 cup cottage cheese
¼ cup skim milk
4 tablespoons chili sauce
2 teaspoons prepared mustard
1 teaspoon paprika

½ teaspoon salt
½ teaspoon fresh ground pepper
2 tablespoons sweet pickle relish
4 teaspoons parsley, minced
3 teaspoons green onions, minced

Combine first seven ingredients in blender; blend until smooth. Add sweet pickle relish, parsley, and green onions; stir well. Cover and refrigerate.

ORANGE-RASPBERRY DRESSING

½ cup orange marmalade
¼ cup raspberry vinegar
1 jalapeño pepper, seeded and minced

1 tablespoon cilantro, minced
Dash of salt
3 tablespoons olive oil

Whisk together all ingredients until well blended.

DRIED TOMATO VINAIGRETTE

7 ounces oil-packed dried tomatoes
1 cup fresh basil leaves,
    loosely packed
2 tablespoons shallots, chopped
1 garlic clove, pressed

¼ teaspoon salt
¼ teaspoon fresh ground pepper
¼ cup red wine vinegar
¼ cup olive oil

Combine all ingredients in a blender; blend until smooth.

CREAMY HERB DRESSING

½ cup mayonnaise
⅓ cup sour cream
2 tablespoons parsley, chopped
2 tablespoons chives, chopped
2 tablespoons tarragon, chopped

1 tablespoon lemon juice
1 tablespoon white wine vinegar
2 teaspoons Dijon mustard
¼ teaspoon salt
¼ teaspoon fresh ground pepper

Combine ingredients; mix well. Cover and chill for at least four hours.

ORANGE VINAIGRETTE

¼ cup orange juice
3 tablespoons balsamic vinegar
2 tablespoons water
½ teaspoon Dijon mustard

1 teaspoon honey
1 garlic clove, minced
½ teaspoon fresh ground pepper
¼ cup oil

Combine ingredients in a small bowl. Stir well, using a whisk.

BALSAMIC VINAIGRETTE
Glenda's Recipe

2 tablespoons balsamic vinegar
2 tablespoons water
2 tablespoons honey
1 tablespoon olive oil

1 tablespoon lemon juice
¼ teaspoon dried tarragon
⅛ teaspoon salt
⅛ teaspoon fresh ground pepper

Combine above ingredients in a small bowl. Stir well, using a whisk.

RASPBERRY VINAIGRETTE

¼ cup seedless raspberry jam

¼ cup raspberry white wine vinegar

2 tablespoons honey

1 tablespoon olive oil

Using a small bowl, combine all ingredients; mix until well blended. This is good over spinach salad, topped with melon balls and sliced strawberries!

Yield: ½ cup.

OIL & VINEGAR DRESSING

¼ cup sugar

¼ cup hot water

½ teaspoon each, salt and pepper

½ teaspoon paprika

½ teaspoon ground mustard

½ cup vinegar

1 tablespoon balsamic vinegar

1 tablespoon lemon juice

1 garlic clove, pressed

3 tablespoons vegetable oil

Combine sugar and hot water in a two-cup container; allow to dissolve. Add remaining ingredients and whisk well to blend.

Yield: 1 cup.

ROASTED RED PEPPER DRESSING

2 roasted red bell peppers
   (see index for roasting)

2 garlic cloves, chopped

¼ cup balsamic vinegar

¼ cup fresh basil, thyme, or
   oregano

¾ cup olive oil

Combine first four ingredients in food processor, and process until smooth. Slowly add olive oil, and process until blended.

Yield: 1 cup.

ROASTED GARLIC DRESSING

¼ cup roasted garlic pulp
1 tablespoon roasted poblano,
   minced fine
¼ cup red wine vinegar
1 teaspoon balsamic vinegar

1 tablespoon water
3 tablespoons olive oil
¼ teaspoon sugar
1½ teaspoon roasted almonds,
   crumbled fine

Whisk the above ingredients together in a small bowl, adding almonds last.

Yield: 1 cup.

FRENCH DRESSING

½ cup brown sugar
½ cup cider vinegar
½ cup ketchup
½ cup vegetable oil
1 garlic clove, pressed

1 tablespoon chopped chives
¼ teaspoon celery salt
½ teaspoon hot sauce (or to taste)
Salt and pepper to taste

Combine ingredients; mix well. Store in refrigerator.

CREAMY BUTTERMILK DRESSING

½ cup mayonnaise
½ cup sour cream
1½ cups buttermilk
1 teaspoon dried basil
1 tablespoon parsley, minced
3 tablespoons fresh lemon juice

½ teaspoon fresh ground pepper
1 garlic clove, pressed
1 green onion, chopped fine
2 tablespoons Parmesan
   cheese, grated

Combine all ingredients in a small bowl; mix well to blend. Cover and store in refrigerator.

Soups

From African Peanut to New England Clam

CREAM OF AUTUMN MUSHROOMS
with Roasted Pecan Nuts and Whiskey

1 onion, chopped
4 tablespoons butter
2 garlic cloves, chopped
1 pound mushrooms, sliced
4 cups chicken broth, divided
2 cups light cream, divided

¼ cup unbleached flour
1 teaspoon salt
½ teaspoon ground white pepper
2 tablespoons whiskey
3 tablespoons pecans, chopped fine
Juice of ½ lemon

Using a large saucepan, sauté onion in butter until barely translucent; add garlic and mushrooms. Continue to sauté until mushrooms are soft and tender. Add 1 cup chicken broth; transfer ingredients to a food processor (optional; you may prefer it as-is!). Pulse just a few times to barely chop ingredients; return to saucepan and add the remaining three cups chicken broth.

In a small bowl, add enough cream to the flour to make a smooth paste; stir into mushroom mixture slowly. Add the remaining cream, salt, and pepper. Cook over medium heat until mixture begins to thicken; add whiskey and pecan nuts. Just before serving, add lemon juice.

Serves 6.

CREAM OF TOMATO SOUP

1 (14.5 ounce) can chicken broth
2 (14.5 ounce) cans chopped
   tomatoes
1 carrot, chopped
2 stalks celery, chopped
1 onion, chopped

1 garlic clove, chopped
1 cup milk or light cream
2 tablespoons unbleached flour
½ teaspoon paprika
½ teaspoon each, salt and white
   pepper

Combine broth, tomatoes, carrot, celery, onion, and garlic in a large saucepan. Heat to boiling point; reduce heat and simmer for 20 minutes. Strain, reserving broth and discarding vegetables. Return broth to the large saucepan.

Using a small bowl, add enough milk to the flour to make a smooth paste. Slowly stir into the tomato mixture, along with the remaining milk. Add paprika, salt, and pepper. Cook over medium-low heat until slightly thickened, being careful not to boil.

Serves 6.

HOT & SOUR SOUP

2 (14.5 ounce) cans chicken broth
4 large mushrooms, sliced thin
¼ pound lean pork, cut
   matchstick style
½ pound chicken breast, cut
   matchstick style
½ cup bamboo shoots, cut
   matchstick style
¼ pound tofu, drained and cut into
   ½-inch cubes
2 tablespoons white wine vinegar

1 tablespoon dry sherry
1 tablespoon soy sauce
2 tablespoons cornstarch
¼ cup water
1 teaspoon ground white pepper
1 teaspoon sesame oil
1 egg, lightly beaten
2 green onions, cut diagonally
   into 1-inch pieces
Salt, to taste

Using a two-quart saucepan, heat chicken broth to boiling. Add mushrooms, pork, chicken, and bamboo shoots. Reduce heat and simmer for 10 minutes. Add tofu, wine vinegar, sherry, and soy sauce; heat uncovered for one minute. Using a small bowl, blend cornstarch and water. Add to soup, and cook until slightly thickened. Remove from heat; add pepper and sesame oil. Stirring continuously, slowly pour egg into soup. Sprinkle with onions, and salt to taste.

Serves 6.

EGG DROP SOUP

1 large bunch watercress, OR
   2 cups spinach, coarsely sliced
4 cups chicken broth

2 teaspoons each, sherry
   and soy sauce
2 eggs
Salt, to taste

If using watercress: Wash watercress and discard stems; break long sprigs in half. Using a two-quart saucepan, heat chicken broth, sherry, and soy sauce to boiling. Add watercress or spinach; simmer uncovered for 2 minutes. Beat eggs lightly. Remove saucepan from heat; add eggs slowly to soup, stirring constantly as they form long threads. Season with salt to preferred taste. Immediately serve in small individual cups.

Serves 6.

CREAM OF ASPARAGUS SOUP

1 cup onion, chopped
1 garlic clove, minced
1 tablespoon butter
2 pounds fresh asparagus
4 cups chicken broth

½ cup sour cream
3 tablespoons unbleached flour
1 teaspoon salt
1 teaspoon ground white pepper
Juice of half a lemon

Using a small skillet, sauté onion and garlic in butter until soft and translucent. Set aside.

Using top five inches of asparagus, cut into thirds. Place in a medium-sized saucepan, along with chicken broth; cook until just tender. Remove from heat. Using a slotted spoon, remove some of the asparagus tips, reserving to use as a garnish. Pour the asparagus and broth mixture into a food processor or blender; add onion and garlic mixture. Process or blend on high speed until smooth. Add sour cream and flour; mix to blend. Return mixture to saucepan; add salt and pepper. Heat until slightly thickened. Add lemon juice; top with reserved tips. Serve hot or cold.

Serves 6.

This is one of our favorite soups. When Ashley first saw it, she was a bit skeptical due to its color. It's now number one on her request list! Thanks, Carolyn!

COLD POTATO & CUCUMBER SOUP

3 medium potatoes, sliced
1 quart water
6 medium cucumbers, peeled,
  seeded, and sliced thin
1 onion, chopped

3 tablespoons butter
4 chicken bouillon cubes
2 cups milk
Fresh chives, chopped

Combine potatoes and water in a large saucepan. Cover and cook over medium heat for 20 minutes or until tender; set aside. Do not drain.

Using a large skillet, sauté cucumbers and onions in butter until tender; add to potatoes. Stir in bouillon cubes and milk. Cook over medium heat for 10 minutes, stirring occasionally; cool. Spoon one-third of mixture into food processor and process until smooth. Repeat two times. Cover and chill thoroughly. Lightly garnish with fresh chives just before serving.

Serves 8.

PRIME RIB SOUP

1½ pounds leftover prime rib
1 onion, chopped
4 tablespoons butter
1 garlic clove, minced
½ cup mushrooms, chopped
½ cup dry white wine
4 cups beef stock
2 cups light cream
2 cups whole milk

3 tablespoons browning and
    seasoning sauce
⅛ teaspoon Liquid Smoke
1 tablespoon dried parsley
2 teaspoons salt
1 teaspoon fresh ground pepper
¼ cup unbleached flour
½ cup water
Juice of half a lemon

Cut prime rib into bite-sized pieces; set aside. In a large saucepan, sauté onion in butter until barely translucent. Add garlic and mushrooms; continue to cook until mushrooms are soft and tender. Add wine; cook over medium heat until evaporated. Add meat, beef stock, cream, milk, browning and seasoning sauce, Liquid Smoke, parsley, salt, and pepper. Continue to cook over medium heat; do not boil.

Combine flour and water, making a smooth paste. Slowly strain into soup mixture, stirring constantly. Continue to cook until slightly thick; add lemon juice, and adjust seasonings to preferred taste.

Serves 8.

POTATO SOUP

2 large russet potatoes
1 cup water
2 cups chicken broth
1 small onion, chopped
2 garlic cloves, minced
2 tablespoons cornstarch
2 cups skimmed milk

2 teaspoons salt
1 teaspoon ground white pepper
1 teaspoon dried parsley flakes
1 teaspoon dried celery flakes
2 tablespoons brandy
4 slices bacon, cooked
    and crumbled
Juice of half a lemon

Peel and cut potatoes in small bite-sized chunks. Place in a large saucepan, cover with water and chicken broth. Cook over medium heat until just barely tender.

In the meantime, sauté onion and garlic in small skillet until barely translucent. Add to cooked potato mixture. Combine cornstarch and enough water to make a smooth paste. Slowly stir into potatoes, along with milk, salt, pepper, parsley, and celery flakes. Add brandy; continue to cook until mixture is slightly thickened. Add bacon pieces and lemon juice.

Serves 4.

BEEF STEW
Jeanne's Version

3 pounds lean stew meat
4 tablespoons browning and
  seasoning sauce
2 tablespoons canola oil
2 quarts water
1 large onion, cut into ⅛-inch
  wedges
1 garlic clove, minced
4 medium potatoes, cut into
  1-inch cubes

4 carrots, sliced ⅛-inch thick
3 teaspoons dried celery flakes
3 teaspoons dried parsley flakes
2 teaspoons salt
2 teaspoons ground white pepper
2 teaspoons paprika
3 cans (14.5 ounce) diced tomatoes
1 can (14.5 ounce) diced herb
  tomatoes
1 can (14.5 ounce) cut green beans
1 cup frozen whole kernel corn

Baste stew meat with browning and seasoning sauce. Heat oil in eight-quart soup pot over medium heat; add meat and sauté until thoroughly browned. Add 2 quarts water and bring to a boil. Reduce heat and simmer for approximately 2 hours. (I use my pressure cooker. If you prefer to use this method, refer to your cooker instructions.) Remove from heat; allow to cool. Remove meat with a slotted spoon, and strain liquid through a fine sieve to remove any meat residue. Return meat and liquid to clean soup pot. Add onion, garlic, potatoes, carrots, celery and parsley flakes, salt, pepper, paprika, and tomatoes. Bring to a boil; reduce heat and simmer gently for approximately one hour, or until potatoes are just cooked. Add green beans and corn. Cook an additional 10 minutes, and adjust seasonings to your preferred taste.

Serves 12.

BEEF STEW
Carolyn's Version

5–6 pounds sirloin steak, cut into
  1-inch cubes
2 tablespoons unbleached flour
1 cup onion, chopped fine
1 garlic clove, minced

2 tablespoons sugar
3 quarts canned beef consommé
1 cup Burgundy wine
Salt and pepper

Dust meat with flour; sauté with onions and garlic until well browned. Add sugar; cook one minute. Add consommé and wine; cook over low heat for 3½ hours, or until done. Season with salt and pepper. If you like a thick gravy, slightly thicken with mixture of water and flour.

Serves 12.

PUMPKIN-PEAR SOUP

3 ripe pears, peeled and sliced thin
¼ cup onions, chopped
2 tablespoons butter
2 cups canned pumpkin
4 cups chicken broth
½ cup water

¼ cup dry white wine
¼ teaspoon salt
1 (3-inch) stick cinnamon
⅓ cup light cream
Sour cream and green onions,
    for garnish

Using a large skillet, cook pears and onion in butter over medium-high heat, stirring constantly until tender. Place in food processor, along with pumpkin; process until smooth. Transfer to a large saucepan; add chicken broth and next four ingredients. Bring to a boil; reduce heat and simmer, uncovered, for 20 minutes. Remove cinnamon stick and stir in cream. Heat thoroughly, but do not boil at this point. Garnish individual servings with sour cream and strips of green onions.

Yield: 6 cups.

JAN'S CHEESE SOUP
A Family Favorite!

1 carrot, finely grated
1 onion, chopped
1 garlic clove, minced
2 tablespoons butter
1 teaspoon dried celery flakes
2 cups chicken broth

2 cups milk
3 tablespoons unbleached flour
½ teaspoon each salt and pepper
⅛ teaspoon garlic salt
1 cup Cheddar cheese, grated

Using a medium saucepan, sauté carrot, onion, and garlic in butter until onions are soft and translucent. Add celery flakes, chicken broth, and milk. Using a small bowl, add enough water to flour to make a smooth paste; slowly stir into soup. Add salt, pepper, and garlic salt. Cook over medium heat until slightly thick; add cheese. Stir until cheese is melted and incorporated. Do not boil.

Serves 4.

Jan shared this recipe with me years ago. I've cut the butter content down, used celery flakes rather than sliced celery, and added garlic, but it's still "Jan's Cheese Soup" to our family!

BLACK BEAN SOUP
with Marinated Rice

1 pound dried black beans	1 teaspoon dried oregano
9 cups water	1½ teaspoons ground cumin
2 garlic cloves, minced	1 tablespoon hot sauce
¼ teaspoon salt	2 tablespoons lemon juice
1½ cups green pepper, chopped fine	Marinated Rice
1½ cups onion, chopped fine	(recipe follows)

Sort and wash beans. Place in a large Dutch oven and cover with water to a depth of two inches above beans; soak for eight hours.

Drain beans. Add the 9 cups water, garlic, and salt; bring to a boil. Reduce heat and partially cover; simmer two hours, or until beans are tender. With the exception of the marinated rice, add all other ingredients. Continue to simmer for an additional 45 minutes, allowing the vegetables to get tender. Ladle into individual soup bowls, and top each with 2 tablespoons marinated rice.

Serves 6.

Marinated Rice

⅔ cup cooked brown rice	1 tablespoon lemon juice
½ cup tomato, chopped fine	1 teaspoon olive oil
¼ cup green onions, chopped fine	

Combine above ingredients in a medium-sized bowl; stir well to blend. Cover and chill for at least three hours. Use as an accompaniment for Black Bean Soup.

Serves 6.

I'm so happy the black bean finally made it to Texas—or did we Texans get this going? Hmmm . . .

NEW ENGLAND CLAM CHOWDER

1 cup onion, chopped
2 garlic cloves, minced
1 rib celery, sliced thin
1 carrot, grated fine
2 tablespoons butter
1 cup potatoes, chopped
  into small cubes
2 cups milk
2 cups light cream

3 tablespoons unbleached flour
2 teaspoons salt
1 teaspoon ground white pepper
¼ teaspoon each, tarragon, basil,
  thyme, and rosemary (dried)
2 tablespoons lemon juice
2 cups cooked clams
  (or flaked fish)
½ cup crisp cooked bacon pieces

Using a large saucepan, sauté onion, garlic, celery, and carrot in butter until onions are translucent and tender. Remove from pan; set aside.

Add potatoes to the saucepan and barely cover with water; bring to a boil. Reduce heat and simmer until just tender. Add milk and cream. Using a small bowl, add just enough water to the flour to make a smooth paste. Slowly pour into the potato mixture; mix well. Add salt, pepper, and dried spices. Continue to cook until thickened; add lemon juice, clams, and bacon pieces. Adjust seasonings to preferred taste.

Serves 6.

WHITE WINE SOUP

3 cups tomato juice
3 cups orange juice
1½ cups white wine
Juice of 1½ lemons
1½ teaspoons sugar

2¼ teaspoons salt
Cayenne pepper, to taste
Hot sauce, to taste
Worcestershire sauce, to taste
Chopped parsley, for garnish

Mix all ingredients except parsley; chill. Serve in individual demitasse cups. Garnish with chopped parsley.

SPICY AFRICAN PEANUT SOUP
Simple's Recipe

1 tablespoon vegetable oil
1 onion, chopped
1 sweet potato, diced
2 garlic cloves, minced
4 (14.5 ounce) cans chicken broth
1 teaspoon ground thyme
½ teaspoon ground cumin

1 cup whole grain rice (uncooked)
2 cups picante sauce (thick and chunky)
2 (14.5 ounce) cans garbanzo beans
2 cups broccoli florets
⅔ cup creamy peanut butter

Place oil, onion, potato, and garlic in a four-quart saucepan; sauté over medium heat until garlic starts to brown slightly. Add broth, spices, and rice. Bring to a boil; cover and decrease heat to simmer for 15 minutes. Add picante sauce, beans, and broccoli; cook until broccoli is tender. Add peanut butter; stir until well blended.

Serves 8.

MEXICAN GOULASH

1 (10 ounce) package small shell macaroni
1 pound lean ground beef
1 onion, chopped
½ green bell pepper, chopped

1 garlic clove, minced
1 (10 ounce) can tomatoes & green chiles
1 pound Mexican pasteurized cheese
Salt and pepper to taste

Cook macaroni according to package instructions. After cooking, drain all but 3 cups water; set aside.

Place ground beef, onion, bell pepper, and garlic in large skillet. Cook over medium-high heat until meat is well browned. Drain; return to skillet. Add chopped tomatoes & green chiles, cheese, salt, and pepper. Mix well to blend and melt the cheese. Add macaroni and water to skillet; stir well (if mixture seems too thick, add a little more water). Serve hot with cornbread!

Serves 8.

SHRIMP CREOLE
For Ricky

¼ cup vegetable oil
1 onion, chopped
1 garlic clove, minced
1 green bell pepper, chopped
3 ribs celery, sliced thin
2 tablespoons unbleached flour
1 (16 ounce) can chopped
   tomatoes
1 (6 ounce) can tomato sauce

¼ teaspoon garlic powder
1 bay leaf
1 teaspoon salt
2 teaspoons chili powder
8 dashes hot sauce
1½ pounds medium shrimp,
   precooked
1 cup tomato juice
10 cups hot cooked rice

Using a large skillet, combine oil, onion, garlic, bell pepper, and celery. Sauté over medium heat until onion is just tender and translucent. Add flour; stir until smooth. Add tomatoes, tomato sauce, and seasonings; simmer for 15 minutes. Add shrimp and tomato juice; cover and simmer 10 minutes. Remove bay leaf and serve over hot cooked rice.

Serves 6.

SHRIMP GUMBO

2 tablespoons butter
1 onion, chopped
½ green bell pepper, chopped
3 tablespoons filé powder
2 cups chicken broth
1 (14.5 ounce) can chopped tomatoes
3 cups water
1 tablespoon hot sauce

1 tablespoon parsley, minced
1 tablespoon dried thyme leaves
1 teaspoon each, salt and pepper
½ teaspoon garlic powder
1 bay leaf
2 cups okra, sliced into halves
2 cups small shelled shrimp
6 cups hot cooked rice

Place butter in a large skillet; add onion and bell pepper. Sauté over medium heat until onion is soft and translucent. Remove from heat; stir in filé powder. Slowly add chicken broth and next nine ingredients. Return to heat and simmer for 30 minutes. Add okra; cook for an additional 8 minutes. Add shrimp. Bring to a simmer; remove from heat and allow to stand, covered, for an additional 10 minutes. Adjust seasonings to taste. Serve over hot cooked rice.

Serves 8.

Variation: *You may substitute chunks of cooked chicken breasts or sliced hot link sausage for the shrimp.*

GREEN CHILE CHOWDER

4 large potatoes, peeled and cut
    into ½-inch cubes
1 large onion, chopped
3 roasted Anaheim chiles, seeded
    and chopped (see index for roasting)
1 jalapeño, seeded and minced
4 cups chicken broth

1 teaspoon each, salt and
    white pepper
4 tablespoons butter
¼ cup unbleached flour
3 cups milk
Cheddar cheese, grated

Using a large saucepan, combine potatoes, onion, prepared chiles, jalapeño, and chicken broth. Bring to a boil over medium heat; reduce heat. Add salt and pepper; simmer until potatoes are tender (approximately 20 minutes). Reserving liquid and vegetables, drain and set aside.

Using a medium skillet, melt butter over low heat; add flour, stirring constantly to make a light colored roux. Stirring continuously, slowly pour 3 cups of the reserved liquid into the roux mixture. Add milk; raise heat to bring to a simmer. Mash one-half of the reserved potato mixture, and add along with the remaining potato mixture; gently stir to blend. Continue to cook over medium heat, stirring constantly, until thoroughly heated. Serve in individual soup cups; garnish with cheese.

Serves 6.

GREEN CHILE CHILI

1 pound dried navy beans
8 cups chicken broth, divided
1 onion, chopped
2 garlic cloves, minced
1 tablespoon white pepper
1 tablespoon ground cumin
1 tablespoon dried oregano
½ teaspoon ground cloves
5 cups chicken breasts, cooked
    and chopped

2 (4 ounce) cans chopped
    green chiles
1 cup water
1 teaspoon salt
1 jalapeño, seeded and minced
Monterey Jack cheese, grated
Purchased chunky salsa
Sour cream
Green onions, chopped fine

In a large Dutch oven, cover washed, sorted beans with water two inches above beans; soak overnight. Drain; add 6 cups of the chicken broth, and next six ingredients. Bring to a boil; reduce heat, cover, and simmer two hours, or until beans are tender. Once beans are tender, add the remaining 2 cups chicken broth, chicken, green chiles, water, salt, and jalapeño. Return to a boil; cover and reduce heat to simmer for one hour, stirring occasionally. Serve in individual bowls; garnish with cheese, salsa, sour cream, and chopped green onions.

Serves 8.

HUNGARIAN CHILE PEPPER SOUP

5 cups tomatoes, peeled and chopped
3 cups chicken broth
1 medium onion, chopped
1 garlic clove, minced
3 Hungarian wax chiles, seeded
    and chopped
1 chipotle chile in adobo sauce,
    (drain)

2 tablespoons unbleached flour
1 tablespoon vegetable oil
½ teaspoon each, salt and pepper
½ teaspoon paprika
Sour cream, for garnish
2 roasted Anaheim chiles, seeded
    (see index for roasting)

Combine tomatoes, broth, onion, garlic, Hungarian chiles and chipotle chile; stir well. Divide; pureé in a food processor. Place in a large saucepan; bring to a boil over medium heat. Reduce heat and simmer, uncovered, for approximately 20 minutes.

    Combine flour and oil in a small skillet; stir well. Cook over medium heat until slightly brown, stirring continuously. Remove from heat; gradually stir in one cup of the tomato mixture. Continue stirring as this mixture is reincorporated into the remaining tomato mixture; add salt, pepper, and paprika. Continue to cook, stirring frequently, until slightly thickened. Serve in individual serving bowls. Garnish with piped swirls, or "Z" figure, of sour cream, topped with thin strips of Anaheim chiles.

Serves 4.

WINTER SQUASH STEW

1 tablespoon oil
1 red onion, chopped
1 teaspoon sugar
2 teaspoons cumin seeds,
    slightly toasted, divided
2 tablespoons unbleached flour
1 tablespoon chili powder
1 garlic clove, minced

4 cups winter squash (I use
    butternut)
2 cups water
1 (15.5 ounce) can yellow hominy
1 (10.5 ounce) can beef broth
½ cup green bell pepper, chopped
¼ cup fresh cilantro, minced
Salt and pepper, to taste

Using a large skillet, place oil, onion, sugar, and 1 teaspoon of the cumin seeds in oil. Sauté over medium heat until onions are lightly browned. Stir in flour, chili powder, and garlic. Add squash, water, hominy, and broth; bring to a boil. Cover and reduce heat; simmer 10 minutes. Uncover, and simmer an additional 8 minutes, or until squash is tender and stew has thickened. Stir in the remaining cumin seeds, bell pepper, and cilantro. Season with salt and pepper.

Serves 4.

TORTILLA SOUP

8 medium tomatoes
1 onion, peeled and quartered
¼ cup vegetable oil
1 roasted poblano chile, seeded
  (see index for roasting)
2 garlic cloves, minced
12 corn tortillas, cut into thin strips
2 teaspoons ground cumin
1 teaspoon chili powder
1 bay leaf
6 cups chicken broth

4 cups beef broth
1 (8 ounce) can tomato sauce
½ teaspoon salt
¼ teaspoon red pepper
½ teaspoon black pepper
4 smoked chicken breasts, chopped
1 cup Colby Jack cheese, grated
1 avocado, peeled and sliced
Fresh cilantro sprigs, for garnish
Sour cream, for garnish

Combine tomatoes, onion, and 1 tablespoon oil; toss to coat. Place in a roasting pan, and broil in oven until tomatoes look blistered, stirring often. Transfer to food processor. Process until smooth, in two different batches. Pour into a Dutch oven; add poblano chile, garlic, half of the tortilla strips, cumin, chili powder, bay leaf, and next three ingredients. Bring to a boil over high heat; reduce heat to low, and simmer for 30 minutes. Stir in salt, red pepper and black pepper. Pour mixture through a large wire-mesh strainer into a large container, discarding solids. Return to Dutch oven. Adjust seasonings to preferred taste and continue to keep warm over low heat.

Pour 2 tablespoons oil into a large skillet. Fry the remaining half of the tortilla strips over high heat until crisp. Drain on paper towels.

To serve, place small amounts of crisp tortilla strips, chicken, cheese, and avocado into individual bowls. Ladle soup into bowls, and garnish with a bit of sour cream and cilantro.

Serves 6.

When planning to prepare this recipe, I substitute whole canned tomatoes for fresh if the season doesn't allow for tasty tomatoes.

SQUASH CHOWDER

1 cup celery, chopped fine
1 cup onion, chopped fine
2 tablespoons butter
3 tablespoons unbleached flour
1½ cups milk
2 cups chicken broth
½ teaspoon fresh ground pepper

1½ cups yellow squash, chopped
1½ cups zucchini, chopped
1 tablespoon prepared mustard
1 (17 ounce) can whole kernel corn
1 (2 ounce) jar diced pimiento,
    drained
2 cups Cheddar cheese, grated

Using a large saucepan, sauté celery and onion in butter over medium heat until onion is soft and translucent. Remove from heat; stir in flour. Add milk slowly, stirring to blend smoothly. Return to heat; add chicken broth and next six ingredients. Continue to cook until hot; reduce heat to simmer. Add cheese; stir well to incorporate.

Serves 4.

LOBSTER CHOWDER

2 lobsters, precooked
1 large baking potato,
    peeled and cubed
3 cups chicken broth
2 ears corn, kernels removed
1 small onion, chopped
1 carrot, chopped
1 tablespoon butter

1 garlic clove, minced
½ cup white wine
1 tablespoon cornstarch
1 cup heavy cream
2 teaspoons each, thyme and chives
1 tablespoon crisp fried bacon
    pieces
Salt and white pepper, to taste

Split lobsters; remove meat and cut into bite-sized pieces. Set aside.

Place potato cubes and chicken broth in large saucepan. Bring to a boil over high heat. Reduce heat and simmer until potatoes are just tender. Add corn kernels.

As potatoes are cooking, sautè onion and carrot in butter until onions are translucent. Add garlic, being careful not to brown. Pour in wine; stir. Add to potato mixture once potatoes are just tender.

Dissolve cornstarch in heavy cream; stir into potato mixture. Add lobster pieces and remaining ingredients. Continue to cook until slightly thickened, stirring frequently, and being careful to not boil.

Serves 6.

CREAM OF BROCCOLI SOUP

2 tablespoons butter
1 onion, chopped
1 garlic clove, minced
3 cups milk
4 tablespoons unbleached flour
2 cups chicken broth

½ teaspoon dried dill weed
½ teaspoon ground mace
1 teaspoon salt
½ teaspoon ground white pepper
4 cups chopped broccoli
4 ounces Swiss cheese, grated

Using a large saucepan, combine butter, onion, and garlic. Sauté over medium heat until onion is soft and translucent; remove from heat. Using a small bowl, add enough milk to the flour to make smooth and thin; add to the onion mixture, along with the remaining milk. Return saucepan to medium heat; add chicken broth, dill weed, mace, salt, pepper and broccoli. Continue to cook, stirring constantly, until heated thoroughly. Just before serving, stir in cheese to melt.

Serves 6.

FRENCH ONION SOUP

4 cups canned beef broth
1 cup sliced carrot
1 garlic clove, crushed
Vegetable cooking spray

1 teaspoon butter
3 onions, sliced thin
4 (½-inch thick) slices French bread
½ cup Swiss cheese, shredded

Combine first three ingredients in a large saucepan; bring to boil. Cover, and reduce heat to simmer for 20 minutes. Strain broth, discarding carrot and garlic. Return broth to saucepan; set aside.

Coat a large skillet with cooking spray; add butter and onion slices. Sauté onion over medium heat until tender and lightly browned. Add onion to beef broth and bring to a boil; reduce heat and simmer 10 minutes, stirring occasionally.

Place bread slices on baking sheet. Bake at 350° for approximately 5 minutes, or until bread slices are lightly toasted. Sprinkle with cheese; bake an additional 2 minutes, or until cheese melts.

Ladle soup into individual bowls and top with cheese toast. Serve immediately.

Yield: 4 cups.

For a short time in my life, I wanted to order French Onion Soup every time we patronized a restaurant. I think my sisters experienced that, too! Did you?

CREAMY GARLIC SOUP
with Shiitake Mushrooms

1 onion, chopped
1 cup button mushrooms, sliced
2 shallots, chopped
4 tablespoons butter, divided
6 garlic cloves, minced
3 cups heavy cream
4 cups light cream
1 cup milk

2 cups chicken broth
1 tablespoon fresh thyme
1 tablespoon fresh parsley, chopped
Salt and White pepper, to taste
½ cup brandy
8 shiitake mushrooms, sliced and
    roasted (see index for roasting)

Using a large saucepan over medium heat, sauté onion, button mushrooms, and shallots in two tablespoons butter until onions are just translucent. Add garlic; sauté for one minute. Remove from heat. Add creams, milk, chicken broth, thyme, parsley, salt, and pepper. Return to low heat; continue to cook, stirring often, until heated thoroughly. Add brandy; continue to heat for 10 minutes. Serve in individual bowls and garnish with roasted shiitake mushroom slices.

Serves 8.

CHICKEN & DUMPLINGS

1 whole chicken
1 onion, quartered
1 stalk celery, cut in half
1 teaspoon each, salt and pepper
2 cups unbleached flour
1 teaspoon each salt and baking soda

4 tablespoons butter, room
    temperature
1 cup buttermilk
1 cup milk
Salt and pepper, to taste

Place chicken, onion, celery, salt, and pepper in Dutch oven; cover with water. Place over medium-high heat; bring to a boil. Reduce heat; simmer until cooked (about one hour). Remove chicken, onion, and celery. Debone chicken and cut into bite-sized pieces; set aside. Reserve broth; place in freezer until cold enough to solidify grease. Remove from freezer; skim off grease.

Place flour, salt, and baking soda in a medium-sized bowl. Add butter; cut in with a pastry cutter (dough will be crumbly). Add buttermilk. Using hands, knead to make a smooth dough.

Return chicken broth to medium-high heat; add milk and re-season with salt and pepper. Bring to a gentle boil. Place dough onto a lightly floured surface. Using a rolling pin, roll to ¼-inch thick. Cut into 1-inch strips. Pinch off, and place in boiling broth; do not stir. Add chicken and serve hot.

Serves 6.

VEGETABLES

FROM POTATO CROQUETTES
TO COLLARD GREENS

SAUTÉED SPINACH

1 tablespoon olive oil
1 small garlic clove, minced
10 cups fresh spinach, stems removed

¼ teaspoon salt
2 teaspoons Balsamic vinegar

Using a large skillet or wok, heat oil over medium-high heat. Add garlic; sauté until color just barely changes. Add spinach, tossing to coat well with oil. Continue to toss until the leaves begin to wilt. Season with salt and Balsamic vinegar; toss well to distribute evenly. Serve immediately.

Serves 6.

SCALLOPED POTATOES

4 tablespoons unsalted butter,
    divided
1 garlic clove, crushed
1 teaspoon salt
1 teaspoon fresh ground white pepper

½ teaspoon dried dill weed
1 cup whole milk
1½ pounds russet potatoes
1 cup heavy cream
Fresh nutmeg, grated

Coat the bottom of a 9 x 13 x 2-inch baking pan with half of the butter; set aside.

Place the crushed garlic, salt, pepper, dill weed, and milk in a small sauce-pan; bring to a simmer over medium heat. Reduce heat, cover, and continue to keep warm while preparing potatoes.

Peel, wash, and slice potatoes into ⅛-inch slices (a hand-slicing device, such as a French mandoline, will give you the best results). Do not wash potatoes once sliced. Line the bottom of the baking dish with a single layer of sliced pota-toes, overlapping by approximately one-third the width of the potato slices. Re-peat with a second row, overlapping the first row in the same manner. Continue layering in the same manner, being careful to neither overcrowd nor overfill.

Remove the crushed garlic from the hot milk; pour milk over the potatoes. Cover with foil; bake at 425° for approximately 12–15 minutes, or until the pota-toes have absorbed most of the milk. In the meantime, place the heavy cream in a small saucepan over medium-low heat. Once the potatoes have absorbed the milk, remove foil and pour hot cream over the potatoes. Dot the top with the remaining butter, and sprinkle with grated nutmeg (approximately ⅛ teaspoon-ful). Return pan to oven; continue to bake, uncovered, for approximately 20 min-utes, or until potatoes have turned golden in color. Remove from oven. Allow to set for about 5 minutes. Cut into serving size and serve immediately.

Serves 6.

STEAMED CARROTS
with Ginger Root and Tarragon

1 pound carrots
1 tablespoon butter
½ teaspoon ginger root, grated

1 teaspoon fresh tarragon,
    chopped fine
1 teaspoon lemon juice
½ teaspoon each, salt and pepper

Peel carrots; cut into diagonal slices. Steam for approximately 10 minutes, or until just tender. Using a glass measuring cup, melt butter in the microwave (approximately 20 seconds). Stir in the ginger root, tarragon, lemon juice, salt, and pepper. Pour over carrots; toss well to coat.

Serves 6.

POTATOES
Wrapped in Phyllo

2 medium russet potatoes, peeled and
    sliced thin
½ cup butter, melted
12 frozen phyllo pastry sheets, thawed
1 onion, chopped
8 slices bacon, cooked and crumbled

⅓ cup Parmesan cheese, grated
1 teaspoon salt
1 teaspoon fresh ground pepper
1 teaspoon dried thyme
¾ cup heavy cream
4 fresh chives

Place potatoes in two-quart saucepan; cover with cold water. Bring to quick boil over high heat; turn burner down to medium-low. Simmer gently until just barely tender. Remove from heat and drain immediately; set aside.

Using a medium-sized skillet, sauté onion in 1 tablespoon butter until just barely translucent. Remove; set aside.

Unfold phyllo; cut into 12-inch squares. (Cover squares with a slightly damp towel, to prevent pastry from drying out.) Place one phyllo square on a flat surface covered with wax paper; brush with butter. Top with two more squares, brushing each with butter. Repeat procedure with remaining phyllo squares, so that you have a total of four phyllo stacks, each three layers high. Layer equal portions of potato, onion, bacon, and cheese in center of each stack of pastry squares. Sprinkle evenly with salt, pepper, and thyme. Pour three tablespoons of heavy cream over each filling. Bring corners of phyllo to center, and pinch/twist to seal; tie with a chive. Using a spatula, place each tart on a baking sheet. Bake at 350° for approximately 30 minutes, or until pastry is golden in color. Serve immediately.

Serves 4.

ASPARAGUS
Wrapped in Turnip Root

1½ pounds fresh asparagus	½ teaspoon salt
4 small turnips	½ teaspoon pepper
¼ cup butter, melted	Baby carrots, for garnish

Asparagus:
Wash and trim top five inches of asparagus (reserving unused stems for another use, if you wish). Using a two-quart saucepan, bring 1 quart of water to a boil; add asparagus. Cook quickly for approximately 5 minutes, or until just barely tender. Drain. Refresh under cold water to retard further cooking; drain again.

Turnips:
Peel turnips smoothly. Slice off ends, leaving center 1½ inches wide. Core centers, leaving outside rim ½-inch thick. Slice one side slightly to make flat, so that the turnips will be balanced, in a napkin ring manner, for presentation. Place rings side by side in a saucepan; add water to cover. Bring to a boil, and immediately turn heat down to a constant simmer. Cook approximately 8 minutes, or until almost tender (place a piece of leftover turnip in with rings for testing). Drain. Refresh in cold water to retard further cooking. Drain again; set aside.

Assembly and final cooking:
Gather five or six pieces of well-drained asparagus in a bundle, with tips all pointing same direction. Slide into turnip rings, and place in a baking dish on the previously prepared flat slide. Repeat procedure per each serving. Using pointed end of a paring knife, gently cut a small, shallow hole on top side of each turnip, and place a small sliced circle of baby carrot inside (for garnish). Melt butter; add salt and pepper. Using a pastry brush, baste each bundle with butter mixture. Place in 350° oven for approximately 15 minutes. Using a spatula to lift from baking dish, serve immediately.

Serves 4.

FRESH GARDEN VEGETABLES

1½ cups each miniature zucchini, acorn squash, and carrots

Place all veggies in steamer and steam for approximately 15 minutes, or until just tender.

Serves 6.

I personally enjoy the flavor of the veggies alone, but, if you prefer, add a little salt and pepper!

ASPARAGUS
with White Sauce and Almonds

2 pounds asparagus
2 tablespoons butter
2 tablespoons unbleached flour
1 cup milk
2½ tablespoons Parmesan cheese

White Wine Worcestershire sauce*
½ teaspoon each, salt and
   white pepper
¼ cup roasted, slivered almonds

Using top five inches of asparagus only, place in a medium-sized saucepan and cover with water. Bring to a quick boil over high heat; cook until just crisp-tender (approximately 5 minutes). Arrange on a serving platter and keep warm.

Melt butter in a medium-sized skillet over medium heat. Stir in flour to make a smooth roux; remove from heat. Gradually stir in milk, being careful to avoid lumping. Return to heat and continue to cook until thickened and bubbly. Stir in cheese, 1 tablespoon white wine Worcestershire sauce, salt, and pepper. Pour over center of asparagus, leaving top and bottom uncovered for a pretty presentation. Sprinkle with roasted almonds.

Serves 6.

*White wine or lemon juice may be substituted for White Wine Worcestershire sauce.

ASPARAGUS
My Favorite Way

2 pounds fresh asparagus
1 tablespoon butter

½ teaspoon salt
Juice of half a lemon (optional)

Using top five inches only, place in a medium-sized saucepan and cover with water. Bring to a quick boil over high heat; cook until just crisp-tender (approximately 5 minutes). Drain; refresh under cold water to retard further cooking. Drain well. (At this point, you may place in a zip-closure bag and refrigerate until ready to use.)

Melt butter in a large skillet or wok, over medium heat. Add asparagus, and toss gently to heat thoroughly; sprinkle with salt and fresh-squeezed lemon juice.

Serves 4–6.

CREAMED POTATOES
For David

10 large russet potatoes
4 tablespoons butter
2 teaspoons salt
1 teaspoon fresh ground pepper
1 cup milk

1 small onion, chopped and
   sautéd (optional)
3 garlic cloves, sliced and
   sauté (optional)

Peel and wash potatoes; slice medium-thin. Place potatoes in saucepan and cover with cold water; bring to a boil. Reduce heat and simmer over medium heat until tender; drain. Add butter, salt, pepper and milk in saucepan. Mix with an electric mixer on medium-high until smooth in consistency.

Serves 8.

For onion-flavored potatoes, add sautéed onion after adding all ingredients; mix well. Follow in same manner for garlic-flavored potatoes, using roasted garlic pulp.

TWICE-BAKED POTATOES

3 large baking potatoes
Vegetable oil
4 tablespoons butter, softened
¼ cup milk
¼ cup sour cream

2 tablespoons chopped green onions
1 teaspoon parsley flakes
½ teaspoon salt
½ teaspoon fresh ground pepper
¼ cup grated Cheddar cheese

Scrub potatoes thoroughly; allow to dry, then rub skins with oil. Bake at 400° for one hour, or until done. Cut potatoes in half lengthwise. Carefully scoop out pulp, leaving shells intact. Spoon pulp into mixing bowl, and add remaining ingredients. Beat on medium speed with an electric mixer until smooth. Refill shells with mixture; garnish with a little grated cheese, if desired. Return to oven, and bake at 350° for approximately 15 minutes.

Serves 6.

ROASTED POTATO FANS

6 large russet potatoes   1 teaspoon each, salt and pepper
6 tablespoons butter, melted   1 teaspoon dried dill weed

Being careful to not cut all the way through, make crosswise slices every quarter-inch in potatoes. Place in a 13 x 9 x 2-inch baking dish. Mix butter, salt, pepper, and dill weed. Using a pastry brush, baste between potato slices. Bake in 400° oven, basting occasionally, for approximately one hour. Potatoes will be fanned out slightly, and lightly browned.

Serves 6.

SPINACH-STUFFED TOMATOES

6 medium tomatoes   ½ teaspoon salt
2 tablespoons butter   ½ teaspoon fresh ground pepper
¼ pound mushrooms, sliced   1 cup soft breadcrumbs
10 ounces frozen spinach,   3 large eggs, slightly beaten
   thawed and drained

Cut tops from tomatoes about one-third of the way down. Scoop out pulp, leaving approximately a quarter-inch shell. Turn shells upside down on paper towels to drain.

Using a medium-sized skillet, melt butter over medium heat; add mushrooms and sauté for two minutes. Stir in spinach, salt, and pepper; cook for an additional two minutes. Remove from heat and stir in breadcrumbs and eggs. Fill tomato shells with mixture, and place in a slightly oiled 13 x 9 x 2-inch baking dish. Bake at 350° for approximately 25 minutes. Garnish tops with buttered breadcrumbs, if you choose!

Serves 6.

GREEN BEAN BUNDLES

2 (14½ ounce) cans whole green   ½ cup butter, melted
   beans, drained   1 teaspoon garlic powder
6 slices bacon   1 cup brown sugar

Divide beans into six bundles; wrap a slice of bacon around each. Place in a 13 x 9 x 2-inch baking dish. Combine remaining ingredients and pour over top. Bake at 350° for 25 minutes.

Serves 6.

GREEN BEANS
with Roasted Red Peppers and Pearl Onions

1 roasted red bell pepper,
  seeded and peeled
½ pound pearl onions
1½ cups water
3 tablespoons balsamic vinegar
3 tablespoons olive oil
½ teaspoon each, salt and pepper

1½ cups water
1½ pounds fresh green beans
3 tablespoons balsamic vinegar
1 tablespoon olive oil
½ tablespoon Dijon mustard
½ teaspoon dried thyme
½ teaspoon each, salt and pepper

Cut red pepper into ⅓ inch strips; set aside.

Using a large saucepan, place onions in 1½ cups water. Bring to a boil over high heat. Cook for one minute. Drain. Refresh with cold water to retard further cooking; drain. Peel onions; set aside.

Combine 3 tablespoons balsamic vinegar, oil, salt, and pepper; pour over onions, tossing well to coat evenly. Place on a baking sheet, and bake at 400° for 30 minutes, stirring every 10 minutes. Set aside.

Using a large saucepan, bring 1½ cups water to a boil over high heat. Add beans and cook 5 minutes. Drain; refresh with cold water to retard further cooking. Combine beans, onions, and pepper strips in a large bowl; set aside.

Combine 3 tablespoons balsamic vinegar and remaining ingredients; pour over vegetable mixture, tossing gently to coat evenly. Place in a 13 x 9 x 2-inch baking dish. Cover and bake at 350° for 30 minutes.

Serves 6.

FRESH GREEN BEANS
with Toasted Almonds

1 pound fresh green beans
1 quart water
1 tablespoon butter

½ teaspoon each, salt and pepper
⅓ cup sliced almonds, toasted

Wash beans; trim ends and remove strings. In a large saucepan, bring one quart of water to a boil over high heat; add beans. Cook uncovered for approximately 8 minutes (until just barely cooked). Drain. Refresh under cold water to retard further cooking; drain. (At this point, the beans can be placed in a zip-closure bag and refrigerated until ready to use.) Melt butter in a large skillet or wok; sauté over medium heat until thoroughly heated. Season with salt and pepper; toss in almonds!

Serves 6.

PUMPKIN & SPINACH AU GRATIN
Seasonally Delicious

10 cups fresh pumpkin, peeled,
    seeded, and cubed
Cooking oil spray
2½ cups onion, sliced thin
½ cup unbleached flour
4 cups chicken broth

1 teaspoon salt
½ teaspoon fresh ground pepper
½ teaspoon ground nutmeg
1½ cups Swiss cheese, grated
2 (10 ounce) packages frozen
    spinach

Place pumpkin in a Dutch oven; add enough water to just cover. Bring to a boil over high heat; reduce heat to medium, and simmer until just tender (approximately 10 minutes). Drain; set aside.

Coat a large skillet with cooking oil spray. Add onion, and sauté over medium heat until it begins to brown. Remove onion; set aside.

Add flour to skillet; gradually add broth, stirring with a whisk to prevent lumping. Cook over medium heat until thick and bubbly, stirring constantly. Add salt, pepper, and nutmeg. Remove from heat; set aside.

Combine pumpkin, onion, ½ cup of cheese, and spinach into a large bowl; toss gently. Spoon mixture into a gratin dish coated with cooking oil spray. Pour sauce over pumpkin/spinach mixture, and sprinkle with the remaining cup of cheese. Bake at 350° for 30 minutes, or until bubbly.

Serves 6.

OVEN-ROASTED ASPARAGUS

2 pounds fresh asparagus
2 garlic cloves, minced
2 tablespoons olive oil

1 teaspoon salt
½ teaspoon fresh ground pepper
½ teaspoon dried thyme

Trim asparagus, using top five inches only. Place in a 13 x 9 x 2-inch baking dish, along with the minced garlic; coat with olive oil. Sprinkle with salt, pepper and dried thyme; toss gently to coat. Bake at 400° for 15–20 minutes; gently stirring once. Serve immediately.

Serves 4–6.

MUSHROOMS
Grilled, Sautéed, or Oven-Roasted

20 mushrooms
½ cup butter

1 tablespoon Worcestershire sauce
Sour cream (optional)

For sautéing:
Clean and trim stems of mushrooms. Place in a saucepan, along with the butter and Worcestershire sauce. Simmer over medium heat, stirring often, for approximately 15 minutes. These may be served as an entrée accompaniment, or as an appetizer with sour cream.

For grilling:
Slide clean mushrooms onto metal skewers. Baste thoroughly with melted butter. Grill at 350° on an outdoor grill, basting and turning often. These are best served with grilled steak. Many times I slice mushrooms, and cook them in a "nest" made with foil as I'm grilling other foods—especially burgers!

For oven roasting:
Dip clean and trimmed mushrooms into melted butter, and place on baking pan. Bake at 400° for 15 minutes, or until doneness preferred (depends on type, and size of mushrooms.) Our favorite oven-roasted mushrooms are Shittake mushrooms. They go great with so many entrées!

GRILLED VEGETABLES
For Various Dishes

1 eggplant, sliced
1 zucchini squash, sliced
1 yellow (garden) squash, sliced
3 portabella mushrooms, sliced

1 onion, sliced
1 red bell pepper, seeded and sliced
2 poblano peppers, seeded and sliced
½ cup butter, melted

Prepare outdoor grill: Using heavy-duty foil, cover grill rack, leaving the outer edge free from foil. Using a paring knife, slice small slits sporadically in foil; coat slightly with cooking oil spray. Heat grill, and bring to 350. Make certain that flames are not reaching prepared foil!

Slightly baste vegetables with butter. Place on grill, and cook for approximately five minutes; turn and re-baste (being careful to not let butter come in contact with fire.) Cook an additional five minutes, or until done.

BROCCOLI
Seasoned With Zesty Butter

3 pounds broccoli, florets only
½ cup orange juice
4 tablespoons butter, unsalted

¼ cup shallots, minced
2 teaspoons grated orange peel

Steam the broccoli until just tender. In a small saucepan, bring the orange juice to a boil over medium-high heat; reduce to 2 tablespoons. Meanwhile, melt butter in a large skillet over medium-high heat. Add shallots and orange peel; cook until shallots are tender. Stir in orange juice and broccoli; increase heat and toss until broccoli is heated thoroughly.

Serves 6.

ZUCCHINI
(Ordinaire)

½ cup onion, halved and sliced thin
3 tablespoons butter
3 medium-sized zucchini, sliced thin

½ teaspoon salt
½ teaspoon white pepper
½ teaspoon sugar

Place butter and onion in large skillet or wok. Cook over medium-high heat until onion starts to become translucent; add zucchini. Sauté, stirring frequently, for approximately 5 minutes (zucchini doesn't take long to cook; it will turn bright green). Sprinkle with salt, pepper, and sugar; toss gently to coat.

Serves 6.

JULIENNE CARROTS

6 cups carrots, julienned
2 cups onions, halved and sliced thin
½ cup butter

2 cups water
Salt and pepper, to taste
¼ cup fresh parsley, chopped

Using a large skillet or wok, sauté carrots and onions in butter over medium heat for 5 minutes. Add water, salt, and pepper. Continue to cook until just tender; drain. Add parsley; mix well.

Serves 6.

VEGGIE STIR FRY

4 tablespoons butter, divided
1 cup small shallots
18 oyster mushrooms, stems
    trimmed
2 cups sugar snap peas, stringed
1 teaspoon sugar

2 cups asparagus, cut in 2-inch pieces
1 cup carrots, sliced thin on diagonal
4 green onions, sliced ½-inch on
    diagonal
3 cups fresh spinach
3 tablespoons balsamic vinegar

Place 2 tablespoons butter, shallots, and mushrooms in wok; stir fry 3 minutes. Add peas and sugar; stir fry 2 minutes. Add remaining butter, asparagus, and carrots; stir fry 4 minutes. Add green onions, spinach, and vinegar; fry until spinach wilts.

Serves 6.

ISABELLE'S HUNGARIAN NOODLES

3½ cups unbleached flour
4 eggs, slightly beaten
2 teaspoons salt, divided
1½ cups water
1 teaspoon vegetable oil

4 tablespoons butter
1 small onion, chopped
½ cup milk
1 cup Gruyère (or Gouda)
    cheese, grated
Salt, to taste

Place flour, eggs, one teaspoon salt, and water in work bowl of electric mixer; mix well to blend (dough must be smooth, not firm). Using a Dutch oven, bring 8 cups water to a boil; add the remaining salt and oil. Spoon dough into *spätzle maker,* allowing the dough to "drain" into the water. When noodles swim on top, they are ready! Remove from water; drain and rinse. Set aside. Combine butter and onions in a large skillet. Sauté over medium heat until lightly browned. Stir in noodles, milk, and cheese. Season to taste!

Serves 6.

Thank you, Isabelle, for teaching me to make this!

CURRIED CARROTS & PINEAPPLE

1 cup pineapple juice	1½ teaspoons curry powder
¼ cup water	1½ cups pineapple chunks
1½ tablespoons cornstarch	8 medium carrots, sliced and
4 tablespoons butter	precooked
	Salt and pepper, to taste

In a small bowl, combine juice, water, and cornstarch; stir until smooth. Set aside. Using a large skillet, melt butter over medium heat. Stir in curry and cornstarch mixture. Cook, stirring continuously, until smooth and thick. Stir in pineapple, carrots, and seasonings just before serving.

Serves 6.

CARROTS IN MUSTARD SAUCE

5 cups baby carrots	½ teaspoon fresh ground pepper
4 tablespoons butter	2 cups light cream
2 tablespoons unbleached flour	2 teaspoons prepared mustard
1 teaspoon salt	¼ cup green onions, chopped

Place carrots in a large saucepan and cover with water. Bring to a boil over high heat; reduce heat to medium. Continue to cook until tender; drain and set aside. Using the same saucepan, add butter and melt over low heat. Stir in flour, salt, and pepper; mix until smooth. Slowly whisk in cream and mustard. Continue to cook, stirring often, over medium heat until thickened and smooth. Stir in carrots, and adjust seasonings to preferred taste. Sprinkle with chopped green onions.

Serves 6.

CARROTS IN TRIPLE SEC SAUCE

5 cups baby carrots	1 teaspoon orange zest
4 tablespoons butter	¼ cup triple sec
2 tablespoons brown sugar	Chopped parsley (for garnish)

Place carrots in a large saucepan and cover with water. Bring to a boil over high heat; reduce heat to medium. Continue to cook until tender; drain and set aside. Using the same saucepan, add butter and sugar. Cook over low heat until sugar melts; add orange zest and cook 1 to 2 minutes to extract the oil. Add triple sec; mix well. Add carrots; toss gently until coated with glaze. Heat thoroughly; sprinkle with parsley to garnish.

Serves 6.

BAKED RICE

4 tablespoons butter
1 cup uncooked rice
4 cups chicken broth

½ cup mushrooms, chopped
1 (3 ounce) can water chestnuts
1 onion, chopped

Melt butter in large skillet; add rice and brown over medium-high heat. Add broth, mushrooms, water chestnuts, and onion; stir well. Remove from heat; pour into a lightly oiled casserole dish. Bake at 350 for approximately 35 minutes (or until liquid is all absorbed).

Serves 6.

VEGETABLE RICE MEDLEY

¼ cup butter
1 cup onions, minced
1 cup celery, chopped fine
2 garlic cloves, minced
6 cups chicken broth

2 cups long-grain brown rice
½ teaspoon salt
½ teaspoon fresh ground pepper
1 cup carrots, diced small
½ cup green bell pepper, diced small

Melt butter in large skillet; add onions, celery, and garlic. Cook over medium-high heat until onion is just translucent. Add broth, rice, salt, and pepper; stir well. Transfer to a lightly oiled casserole dish, and bake at 350 for approximately 35 minutes. Carefully remove from oven, and stir in carrots and bell pepper; cook an additional 10–15 minutes.

Serves 6.

This is especially tasty served as a bed for baked chicken or fish!

WILD RICE
with Mushrooms and Apples

1 cup wild rice
3 cups mushrooms, chopped
1 onion, chopped
2 garlic cloves, minced
6 tablespoons butter

½ cup sliced almonds, toasted
3 apples, peeled and chopped
3 cups chicken broth
½ teaspoon salt
½ teaspoon fresh ground pepper

Soak rice in water for two hours; drain well. Using a large skillet, sauté mushrooms, onion and garlic in butter over medium-high heat until onions are translucent. Add remaining ingredients; stir well. Transfer into a large, lightly oiled casserole dish. Bake covered at 350° for one hour.

Serves 6.

SPICY SWEET POTATOES
(Creamed)

5 medium sweet potatoes, peeled
    and cubed
1 small russet potato, peeled and cubed
½ cup butter, room temperature

1 teaspoon salt
½ teaspoon cayenne powder
2 teaspoons pure chili powder
¼ cup maple syrup

Place potatoes in a large saucepan; cover with cold water and bring to a boil over high heat. Reduce heat to medium-low, and simmer until tender. Drain water off potatoes; add remaining ingredients. Mix, using an electric mixer, on medium-high speed until smooth in consistency. Adjust seasonings to preferred taste.

Serves 6.

HOLIDAY SWEET POTATOES
(Whole)

6 medium sweet potatoes, peeled
2 cups brown sugar
1 tablespoon lemon juice

4 tablespoons butter
1 cup miniature marshmallows

Place sweet potatoes in a large saucepan and barely cover with water. *(I cut mine in half because my mom does . . . and they're less likely to break.)* Bring to a boil; reduce heat to a gentle boil. Cook until potatoes are just tender; drain one half of the liquid. Return to heat; add brown sugar, lemon juice, and butter. Cook until tender, being careful to not overcook. Transfer to an appropriate-sized, shallow, casserole dish; top with miniature marshmallows. Cover and bake at 350° for approximately 10 minutes; remove cover and cook an additional 5 minutes.

Serves 6.

BAKED BEANS
(Barbecue-style)

1 (31 ounce) can pork and beans
¼ cup brown sugar
1 cup ketchup
4 tablespoons prepared mustard

2 tablespoons white vinegar
4 tablespoons Worcestershire sauce
1 small onion, diced
2 strips of bacon (optional)

Combine all ingredients, excluding bacon, into a large bowl (remove pork from beans). Mix well to blend. Pour into a lightly oiled casserole dish and place bacon strips on top. Bake at 350° for approximately one hour.

Serves 8.

POTATO WEDGES
(Oven-Fried)

6 large russet potatoes
3 tablespoons peanut oil
1 teaspoon salt

1 teaspoon fresh ground black pepper
½ teaspoon red pepper
1 teaspoon dill weed

Scrub potatoes clean; cut into halves, lengthwise. For each half, cut four wedges lengthwise. Place in a large bowl and mix well with the remaining ingredients. Place on baking sheet, skin-side down. Bake at 400 for approximately 45 minutes, or until golden brown.

Serves 6.

SUMMER VEGETABLE SKEWERS
with Cumin Butter

3 each red and yellow bell peppers
2 purple onions
6 small ears of fresh corn

18 medium mushrooms
Cumin Butter (recipe follows)

Cut bell peppers and onions into 1½-inch squares, separating onions. Husk and cut corn into rounds, one inch thick. Clean and trim stems of mushrooms to ¼ inch. Alternate vegetables onto skewers. Brush with Cumin Butter and grill on outdoor grill, basting and turning occasionally, until cooked just crisp-tender.

Serves 6.

Cumin Butter

1 cup butter, melted
1½ teaspoon ground cumin

1 teaspoon dried red pepper flakes
1 teaspoon each, salt and pepper

Combine all ingredients; mix well to blend.

Yield: 1 cup.

NEW POTATO HASHBROWNS
For Allan

4 large new potatoes, diced
1 small onion, chopped
¼ cup butter

½ teaspoon each, salt and pepper
1 teaspoon dried parsley
⅛ teaspoon garlic salt

Place all ingredients in a large, covered casserole dish. Microwave for approximately 10 minutes, stirring every 2 minutes or, until just tender. Transfer to a large skillet. Brown over medium-high heat, stirring continuously.

Serves 6.

FRESH VEGETABLES
Tossed in Olive Butter

4 small red potatoes, unpeeled
   and sliced
1 pound fresh asparagus, cut
   into 2-inch pieces
1 sweet red pepper, cut into
   julienne strips

2 carrots, sliced thin on diagonal
1 pound fresh mushrooms, sliced
1 (7 ounce) jar baby corn ears
1 zucchini, sliced ½-inch thick
Olive Butter (recipe follows)

Using a steamer, steam potatoes for approximately 5 minutes. Add asparagus, red pepper, and carrots; steam 5 minutes. Add mushrooms and corn; steam 5 minutes. Add zucchini; steam 5 minutes. Transfer vegetables to a bowl; toss with Olive Butter.

Yield: 6 servings.

Olive Butter

⅓ cup butter, melted
3 tablespoons lemon juice

⅓ cup sliced ripe olives
1 tablespoon lemon zest

Combine all ingredients; mix well to blend.

Yield: ¾ cup.

WINTER SQUASH
Wrapped in Parchment

1–2 cups butternut squash	½ teaspoon sage
¼ cup green onions, chopped	3 tablespoons olive oil
1 teaspoon garlic, chopped fine	4 pieces parchment (12 x 15-inch)
Salt and pepper, to taste	¼ cup butter

Peel and slice squash crosswise; remove seeds and fibers. Keep four of the smaller, "O"-shaped slices, and dice the remainder into ½-inch cubes. Place the squash cubes, onions, garlic, salt, pepper, sage, and olive oil in a medium-sized bowl; toss well to coat evenly. Take one piece of parchment paper, and fold in half to make a crease; reopen it. Generously butter the bottom half, covering all but an inch from the edge. (It is important to coat the surface thoroughly, otherwise the sugars in the squash will stick to the parchment paper and burn.) Place one "O"-shaped piece of squash in the middle of the buttered part of the paper, and top with ¼ cup of cubed squash. Lay a few small pieces of butter on top (approximately 1 teaspoon total). Fold top half of paper down, and tightly roll the edges over onto themselves to make a half-circle. Twist the end of the packet firmly to seal closed. Repeat procedure with the remaining three. Bake at 425° for approximately 25 minutes.

Serves 4.

JULIENNE CARROTS AND ZUCCHINI

4 medium carrots, peeled	1 teaspoon chives, minced
2 firm, medium zucchini	½ teaspoon salt
4 tablespoons butter, melted	¼ teaspoon ground white pepper

Use a julienne blade on food processor, or slice carrots and zucchini lengthwise into ¼-inch slices. Stack slices, and cut into ¼-inch strips. Cut strips approximately three inches long. Place carrots in steamer basket, and layer zucchini on top. Steam for 6 minutes, or until just tender. Combine butter, chives, salt, and pepper; pour over vegetables and toss gently.

Serves 6.

POTATO CROQUETTES

3 cups creamed potatoes

1 egg, beaten

3 tablespoons buttermilk

3 tablespoons green onion
tops, chopped

1 teaspoon each, salt and white pepper

1 cup round butter crackers, crushed

¼ cup melted butter

½ teaspoon paprika

Combine potatoes, egg, buttermilk, onions, salt, and pepper; mix well. Divide mixture into six equal portions, and shape into patties; pat on cracker crumbs. Place on a baking sheet; cover and refrigerate for up to 4 hours. Just before cooking, combine butter and paprika; drizzle on top. Bake at 375° for 20 minutes, or until golden.

Serves 6.

PINTO BEANS

2½ cups dried pinto beans

2 slices bacon, OR ham bone

1 bay leaf

1 tablespoon chili powder

Salt and pepper, to taste

1 onion, chopped (optional)

Sort beans. Wash, and place in a four-quart saucepan. Cover with water two inches above beans; allow to stand overnight. Drain; refill saucepan with water, and bring to a boil. Place bacon in a microwave-safe cup, and cook until brown. Add to beans, along with the bay leaf. Reduce heat and continue to cook at a gentle boil for 1½ hours, or until tender. (Add water as needed.) Season with chili powder, salt, and pepper. (If you choose, sauté onion in a medium-sized skillet, and add to beans when adding seasonings—or add raw onion just before reducing heat to a gentle boil.)

Serves 6.

We enjoy topping our beans with chopped onions and dill pickles—and, of course, cornbread!

COLLARD GREENS

12 cups collard greens,
    stems removed
1 slice bacon

Salt and pepper, to taste
Hot pepper sauce, optional

Place greens in a Dutch oven with 4 cups water. Bring to boil over high heat, stirring to wilt greens quickly. Reduce heat, and continue to cook at a gentle boil. Place bacon in a microwave-safe cup, and cook until brown; add to greens. Continue to cook for 45 minutes, or until tender. Season with salt and pepper. When served, offer hot pepper sauce to sprinkle on top!

Serves 6.

SPICY PEPPER SLAW

1 red bell pepper, cut matchstick size
1 jalapeño, seeded and minced
¼ cup olive oil
⅓ cup red wine vinegar

2 tablespoons sugar
6 cups green cabbage, sliced thin
2 cups purple cabbage, sliced thin
⅓ cup green onions, chopped fine

Place pepper strips and minced jalapeño in a large bowl. Using a small saucepan, bring oil, vinegar, and sugar to a boil over medium heat, stirring often. Once the sugar is dissolved, remove from heat and pour over the peppers. Toss to coat; allow to cool. Add cabbage and onions; gently toss to coat evenly. Season with salt and pepper. Chill for one hour.

Serves 6.

HERBED BASMATI RICE

6 cups chicken broth
4 cups Basmati rice
4 tablespoons parsley, chopped fine

1 tablespoon butter
½ teaspoon crushed saffron
1 teaspoon salt

Pour the chicken broth into a medium-sized saucepan; bring to a boil over medium-high heat. Add the remaining ingredients, and reduce heat to low. Place lid on the saucepan, and continue to cook for approximately 15 minutes, or until the liquid is absorbed. Remove pan from heat; allow to stand for an additional 5 minutes before serving.

Serves 6.

STIR-FRY RICE

3 tablespoons peanut oil
½ small chicken breast, chopped
2 green onions, chopped
1 carrot, peeled and chopped fine

3 cups long grain rice, cooked
1 scrambled egg, chopped fine
¼ cup light soy sauce

Heat oil in wok to 350°. Add chopped chicken, onions, and carrots; stir fry quickly to cook, but not brown. Add rice, egg, and soy sauce. Quickly stir fry for approximately 2 minutes.

Serves 6.

BROCCOLI CASSEROLE

4 tablespoons butter
¼ cup celery, sliced thin
½ cup onion, chopped
1 (10½ ounce) can cream of
    mushroom soup

1 (10½ ounce) can cream of
chicken soup
4 ounces pasteurized cheese
10 ounces cooked broccoli
1½ cups cooked rice
1 cup butter crackers, crushed

Using a large saucepan, melt butter over medium heat. Add celery and onion; sauté until onion is translucent. Add soups and cheese; continue to cook until cheese is melted. Add broccoli and rice; mix well. Pour into a two-quart casserole dish and sprinkle cracker crumbs on top. Bake at 350° for 15 minutes.

Serves 8.

SQUASH CASSEROLE

4 cups stuffing mix, unseasoned
8 tablespoons butter, melted
2 pounds summer squash, sliced
1 carrot, grated

1 onion, chopped fine
1 can cream of chicken soup
1 cup sour cream

Mix stuffing mix and butter in a medium-sized bowl. Place half of mixture in a 13 x 9 x 2-inch baking dish; set aside. Place squash in a medium-sized saucepan; cover with water. Bring to a boil over medium- high heat. Reduce heat and gently boil until squash is just tender; drain in colander and set aside. Using the same saucepan, combine carrot, onion, soup, and sour cream. Heat thoroughly over medium heat, stirring to blend well. Remove from heat; add squash and gently mix. Pour into prepared baking dish; top with remaining stuffing mixture. Bake at 350° for 30 minutes.

Serves 6.

CORN CASSEROLE

1 onion, chopped
2 tablespoons butter
2 tablespoons unbleached flour
½ cup milk
2 cups whole kernel corn, drained

2 cups cream corn
½ teaspoon salt
4 tablespoons sugar
1 egg, slightly beaten
1 cup cracker crumbs, crushed

In a medium-sized saucepan, sauté onion in butter until onion is translucent. Stir in flour; mix well. Add milk, stirring well to blend. Add corn, salt, sugar, and eggs; mix well. Pour into 13 x 9 x 2-inch baking dish; top with cracker crumbs. Bake at 350° for 30 minutes, or until knife inserted in middle comes out clean.

Serves 6.

SPANISH RICE

1 cup uncooked rice
2 tablespoons butter
1 garlic clove, minced
1 small onion, chopped

1 teaspoon cumin
1 teaspoon salt
1 (14½ ounce) can diced tomatoes
2 cups chicken broth

Brown rice in butter in a large skillet over medium-high heat. Add garlic and onion and cook for one minute. Reduce heat to low; add remaining ingredients and mix well to blend. Cover, and cook until liquid is absorbed (approximately 25 minutes).

Serves 4.

MINNESOTA WILD RICE

1 cup wild rice
2 cups chicken broth
1 teaspoon salt
3 tablespoons butter

¼ cup mushrooms, chopped
3 tablespoons onion, chopped
1 garlic clove, minced
Toasted slivered almonds, optional

Soak rice in water 2 hours; drain. Place in a medium saucepan with broth and salt. Bring to a boil; reduce heat, cover, and simmer for 40 minutes, or until liquid is absorbed. Place butter in a medium skillet; sauté mushrooms, onion, and garlic until onions are translucent. Add to rice; fold in almonds.

Serves 4.

WILD RICE
with Apples and Water Chestnuts

1 cup wild rice
2 cups chicken broth
1 tablespoon butter
¼ cup each, red and green
    apples, chopped
¼ cup pecans

2 teaspoons grated orange peel
¼ cup water chestnuts, chopped
½ teaspoon each, basil and
    thyme (dried)
½ teaspoon each, salt and pepper

Soak rice in water 2 hours; drain. In a large saucepan, bring broth and butter to a boil; add rice. Reduce heat and simmer for about 45 minutes, or until liquid is absorbed. Remove from heat; add remaining ingredients to rice; mix well.

Serves 4.

To use the above recipe for a stuffing, such as for Cornish hens, don't soak rice in the beginning. Increase chicken broth to 4 cups. Gently boil for 1 hour; drain. Add remaining ingredients; mix well. Fill cavities of hens; baste with butter. Bake at 350° for about 1 hour, basting with a glaze such as Apricot Glaze (see index) during the last 20 minutes.

GRANDMOTHER'S DRESSING

1 small (7-inch) pan cornbread
2 dozen biscuits, cooked and dried
1 tablespoon salt
2 teaspoons fresh ground black pepper
⅛ teaspoon red pepper

2 tablespoons sugar
4 eggs
3 boiled eggs, chopped fine
4 onions, chopped fine
6 cups chicken broth, hot

Crumble cornbread and biscuits into a large Dutch oven. Add all ingredients, except broth. Slowly add boiling hot broth, stirring constantly to blend ingredients. Adjust seasonings. Place, uncovered, into 400° oven for 10 minutes. Reduce heat to 350°; cover and bake for 1–1½ hours.

Serves 12.

Sometimes I add a small amount of ground sage—it depends on my mood. However, Grandmother never did—I don't think! This year Grandmother will celebrate her ninety-first birthday. She's not actually my grandmother, she's my mother-in-law!

Entrées

From Cornish Hens to
Church Chicken

SAUTÉED TURKEY BREAST
with Ancho Mole Sauce

6 lean, fresh turkey breasts
½ cup lime juice

½ teaspoon ground cumin
½ teaspoon fresh ground pepper

Place the above ingredients in a large zip-closure bag. Refrigerate two hours, turning once. Using a large skillet, sauté turkey in a small amount of butter over medium heat until cooked thoroughly. Serve with Ancho Mole Sauce (recipe follows).

Serves 6.

Ancho Mole Sauce

8 dried ancho chiles
1 cup tomato, peeled and chopped
2 tablespoons vegetable oil, divided
1 corn tortilla
¼ cup cashews, broken
¼ cup sesame seeds
1 small onion, chopped
1 garlic clove, minced
1 slice pumpernickel bread, toasted

¼ cup raisins
1 tablespoon pitted prunes, chopped
¼ teaspoon aniseeds, crushed
½ teaspoon ground cinnamon
¼ teaspoon ground coriander
⅛ teaspoon ground cloves
1 teaspoon sugar
½ teaspoon salt
4 cups chicken broth, divided

Discard stems and remove seeds from chiles, reserving two tablespoons seeds. Tear chiles into pieces, and place in a large skillet over medium heat. Cook until thoroughly heated, turning pieces to keep from burning. Add 4 cups water; bring to a boil. Remove from heat; cover and let stand one hour. Drain. Place chiles and tomato in food processor; set aside.

Place one tablespoon of the oil in medium skillet. Sauté tortilla over medium-high heat until heated thoroughly, turning once. Place in food processor with chiles and tomato. Using the same skillet, combine the remaining tablespoon oil and cashews. Cook over medium heat for 2 minutes. Add sesame seeds and reserved chile seeds; continue to cook until browned. Add onion and garlic; cook until onion is translucent. Place in food processor with the chile/tomato mixture. Add remaining ingredients. Use just enough broth to maintain a smooth consistency when processing. Purée, and carefully mix in the remaining broth. Using a wire strainer, pour back into skillet. Cook over medium-low heat until thickened, stirring occasionally to keep from sticking. Serve warm.

Yield: 4 cups.

PASTA PRIMAVERA

½ cup butter
1 onion, minced
2 garlic cloves, minced
1 pound asparagus, cut in
    1½-inch pieces
½ pound mushrooms, sliced thin
1 zucchini, cut in ¼-inch rounds
1 carrot, cut ⅛-inch diagonally
1 cup heavy cream

½ cup chicken broth
2 teaspoons dried basil
2 ounces prosciutto, chopped
⅓ cup green onion, chopped
Salt, to taste
Fresh ground pepper, to taste
1 pound cooked fettuccine, drained
1 cup Parmesan cheese, freshly grated

Using a wok (or deep skillet) over medium-high heat, add butter, onion, and garlic. Sauté until onion is just translucent. Add asparagus, mushrooms, zucchini, and carrot; stir-fry 2 minutes. (Remove some of the asparagus tips, and reserve for garnish.) Increase heat to high; stir in cream, broth, basil, prosciutto, green onion, salt, and pepper. Cook 3 minutes. Add fettuccine and cheese, stirring gently but quickly. Mix and heat thoroughly; remove from heat. Serve on individual serving plates; garnish with reserved asparagus tips.

Serves 6.

HOMEMADE PASTA
For Glenda

1½ cups unbleached flour
1 egg
1 egg white

1 tablespoon olive oil
1 teaspoon salt
Few drops of water

Place the flour in a heap on a pastry board. Make a well in the center of the board and put the egg, egg white, oil, and salt in the middle. Using your fingers, mix well to form a ball. (The dough will be a bit dry, so this is where the "few drops of water" come in.) Work the dough until you've formed a smooth ball (about 10 minutes). Divide dough and wrap in plastic wrap. Allow to rest for 15 minutes before rolling it.

Working with one piece of dough at a time, place on floured pastry board. Flatten it with the palm of your hand into an oblong, about one inch thick. Dust the top lightly with flour. Using a heavy rolling pin, start at one end of the oblong and roll it out lengthwise away from yourself. Turn the dough crosswise and roll across its width. Repeat, turning and rolling the dough, until it is paper thin, using flour to keep from sticking. To make fettuccine, use a sharp knife and slice crosswise into even strips, ¼-inch wide. Cook in six quarts boiling, salted water for 5–8 minutes, or until just tender. Drain. (May also refrigerate the uncooked pasta in plastic wrap for up to 24 hours.)

Serves 4.

SPAGHETTI SAUCE
with Meatballs

Sauce:

1 pound beef short ribs, separated	1 (46 ounce) can tomato juice
1 large onion, chopped	4 tablespoons dried basil
4 garlic cloves, minced	2 teaspoons dried oregano
2 cups mushrooms, sliced	¼ teaspoon ground red pepper
1 (12 ounce) can tomato paste	1 teaspoon each salt and pepper
1 (15 ounce) can tomato sauce	2 tablespoons brandy

In a large Dutch oven over medium-high heat, sear the short ribs (use no-stick spray or about 2 tablespoons of vegetable oil). Brown on all sides. Add onion, garlic, and mushrooms; cook until onion is translucent. Add remaining ingredients. Reduce heat, cover, and simmer while making meatballs.

A friend who owns a restaurant in Wyoming shared the following meatball recipe with me about twenty years ago. Thank you, Kay!

Meatballs:

2 pounds ground beef	¾ cup Parmesan cheese
1 pound hot pork sausage, ground	3 tablespoons dried parsley
3 eggs	½ teaspoon garlic powder
3 cups breadcrumbs	Salt and pepper, to taste

Place the above ingredients in a very large bowl. Using your hands, mix thoroughly. Shape into balls that are the size of golf balls. Place them, one by one, into the sauce, making sure they are covered with the sauce. Cover and bake at 250° for at least 4 hours . . . no peeking, either! Serve with freshly cooked spaghetti.

Serves 8, generously.

Variation: *For meat sauce, substitute 2 pounds lean ground beef for the short ribs, browning thoroughly beforehand. Adjust seasonings, for the meatballs add flavor to the sauce!*

GERMAN PASTA SAUCE

4 garlic cloves, minced	1½ cups crème fraîche, or sour cream
3 cups sweet white wine	¼ teaspoon each, salt and pepper

Sauté garlic in skillet; add wine. Bring to a boil over medium heat; cook one minute. Whisk in crème fraîche or sour cream, salt, and pepper. Serve over freshly cooked noodles.

Yield: 4 cups.

CANNELLONI
with Spinach and Goat Cheese

The Sauce:

1 whole garlic, roasted (see index)	3 tablespoons brandy
4 cups (canned) chopped tomatoes	1 teaspoon oregano
1 tablespoon oil	1 bay leaf
1 onion, chopped fine	Salt and pepper, to taste

After roasting the garlic, cut in half and squeeze the pulp into food processor or blender. Add the tomatoes; purée. Place the oil and onion in a large saucepan; sauté until onion is just tender. Add the tomato mixture and remaining ingredients. Cook over medium-low heat, stirring often, for approximately 30 minutes. If mixture seems too thick, add some tomato juice; adjust seasonings.

The Filling:

1 tablespoon oil	¼ cup toasted slivered almonds
1 red onion, chopped fine	1 egg, slightly beaten
4 garlic cloves, minced	1¼ cup ricotta cheese
18 cups spinach, shredded	1 cup Parmesan cheese, divided
½ cup fresh herbs: basil, marjoram,	½ teaspoon each, salt and pepper
parsley, thyme	1 cup goat cheese, crumbled
1 teaspoon lemon zest	

Combine the oil, onion, and garlic in a large skillet or wok. Sauté over medium-high heat until onion is translucent; add spinach and ¼ cup herbs, and lemon zest. Continue to cook, wilting the spinach (may need to cook in two separate batches and combine after wilted). Remove from heat; add slivered almonds. Set aside until ready to stir into cheese mixture, listed below.

In a large bowl, combine egg with ricotta cheese; mix well. Add ½ cup of the Parmesan cheese, salt, and pepper. Add spinach mixture; stir in goat cheese. Set aside, covered, until ready to assemble.

The Cannelloni, Assembly, and Cooking:
Prepare Homemade Pasta (see index). If not overly anxious to prepare your own pasta, use dried pasta shells and cook just short of being done.

Ladle a small amount of sauce into a 13 x 9 x 2-inch baking dish; set aside. Roll pasta into thin sheets, and cut into 12 four-inch squares. Working one at a time, spread approximately ¼ cup filling alongside one edge of pasta. Roll up cigar style, loosely (filling will expand during baking). Place the cannelloni side by side in the baking dish; pour remaining sauce over top, making sure to cover completely. Cover and bake at 350° for 25 minutes. Serve on individual plates; sprinkle with remaining Parmesan cheese and herbs.

Serves 12.

LASAGNA

1 pound lean ground beef
1 onion, chopped
2 garlic cloves, minced
1 (28 ounce) can diced tomatoes
1 (14½ ounce) can diced (Italian
    Seasoned) tomatoes
1 (6 ounce) can tomato paste
1 (8 ounce) can tomato sauce
1 tablespoon dried parsley
2 teaspoons dried oregano

1 teaspoon dried basil
¼ teaspoon fresh ground pepper
2 cups low-fat cottage cheese
½ cup Parmesan cheese, grated
2 cups no-fat ricotta cheese
1 tablespoon dried parsley
1 egg, slightly beaten
12 lasagna noodles, precooked
2 cups provolone cheese, grated

The Sauce:
Using a large skillet, combine ground beef, onion, and garlic. Cook over medium-high heat until meat is browned; drain well. Return to skillet and add next eight ingredients. Bring to a boil. Reduce heat to low; cover, and simmer for 30 minutes.

The Cheese:
Combine cottage cheese, Parmesan, ricotta, parsley, and egg in a large bowl; mix well.

Assembly: Spread a thin layer of sauce in a 13 x 9 x 2-inch baking dish. Arrange four lasagna noodles on top, followed with half of the cheese mixture, 2 cups tomato mixture, and ½ cup of the provolone. Repeat layers, ending with noodles. Cover and bake at 350° for 45 minutes. Remove from oven. Uncover, and sprinkle remaining provolone on top. Return to oven for 10 minutes, or until cheese melts. Remove; allow to stand 10 minutes before serving.

Serves 8.

CORNISH HENS
with Wild Rice and Orange Sauce

Cornish Hens:

4 Cornish hens
½ cup butter, softened

Salt and pepper, to taste

Spread butter on hens; season with salt and pepper. Place in a shallow roasting pan and bake at 350°, basting frequently with pan juices. Bake for 50–60 minutes. Remove from oven; keep warm. Reserve pan and juices for preparing Orange Sauce.

Orange Sauce:

Zest of 1 orange
2 oranges, peeled and sectioned
4 tablespoons Grand Marnier

1 cup chicken broth
1 tablespoon butter, softened
1 tablespoon unbleached flour

Using a small saucepan, place zest in one cup water. Bring to boil over high heat; reduce heat and simmer 10 minutes. Drain; return to saucepan, and set aside. Peel oranges, removing all white covering, and freeing of connecting membranes. Place in pan with zest.

Discard excess butter from roasting pan; add Grand Marnier and ignite. When flame burns out, stir in chicken broth. Cook over medium-high heat, stirring to deglaze pan. In a small bowl, mix butter and flour together to make a smooth paste. Spoon a little of the broth into the mixture, until thin enough to pour into the broth without lumping. Add the orange zest and orange sections; simmer over medium-low heat for 2 minutes. Keep warm until ready to serve.

Wild Rice:

2 cups wild rice
½ cup walnuts, chopped

¼ cup butter, room temperature
Salt and pepper, to taste

Cook rice according to package directions; season with walnuts, butter, salt, and pepper.

Presentation: In four equal portions, spoon rice slightly off-center onto individual plates. Place hen in center of rice, and spoon the orange sauce over the hens; reserve any remaining sauce to offer upon request. Serve a vegetable of choice opposite the hen.

Serves 4.

CORNISH HENS
Glazed with Apricot Sauce

Cornish Hens:

4 Cornish hens
½ cup butter, softened

Salt and pepper, to taste
Paprika, to taste

Spread butter on hens; season with salt, pepper, and paprika. Place in a shallow roasting pan and bake at 350°, basting frequently with pan juices, for 40 minutes. Continue to cook for an additional 20–30 minutes, basting with apricot sauce. Remove from oven; keep warm.

Apricot Sauce:

¾ cup apricot preserves
2 teaspoons orange rind, grated

2 tablespoons orange juice

Combine the above ingredients in a small bowl; set aside.

Wild Rice:

½ cup cashews, chopped fine
2 tablespoons butter, melted
½ cup green onions, chopped

6 ounces long grain wild rice mix
2⅓ cups chicken broth

Using a large saucepan, sauté cashews in butter until cashews are golden. Remove cashews; set aside. Place onions in saucepan and sauté until just tender. Add rice mix, and prepare according to package directions, substituting chicken broth for water. Once cooked, add the cashews and mix well to distribute evenly.

Presentation: In four equal portions, spoon rice off-center onto individual plates. Place hen in center of rice, and spoon some more apricot sauce on top. Serve a vegetable of choice opposite the hen.

Serves 4.

CORNISH HENS
with Mushroom-Wine Sauce

1 teaspoon vegetable oil
½ cup green onions, minced
¼ cup carrots, minced
1 tablespoon unbleached flour
¾ cup dry white wine
¾ cup water
½ teaspoon chicken bouillon
    granules
½ teaspoon dried rosemary

¼ teaspoon dried thyme
½ teaspoon garlic powder
1 bay leaf
1 cup fresh mushrooms, sliced
4 Cornish hens, skinned
1 teaspoon fresh ground pepper
2 cups baby carrots
2 stalks celery, cut 1-inch thick
    on diagonal

Place oil, onions, and carrots in a large skillet. Sauté over medium-high heat until onions are translucent. Remove from heat; stir in flour. Add enough wine to smooth, then continue to add all the wine and next seven ingredients. Bring to a boil; reduce heat and simmer 5–10 minutes, stirring often.

Using an electric knife, split hen in half lengthwise. Sprinkle with pepper. Place in a lightly oiled roasting pan, cut side down, and spoon mushroom sauce over top. Cover and bake at 350 for 45 minutes, basting frequently. Add baby carrots and celery. Cover and bake an additional 20 minutes, or until vegetables are crisp-tender and hens are done. Remove bay leaf.

Serves 8.

LEMON-ROSEMARY CHICKEN BREAST

12 boneless, skinless chicken breasts
1½ cups olive oil
1 cup lemon juice
8 garlic cloves, pressed

6 tablespoons fresh rosemary,
    minced
1 teaspoon salt
1 teaspoon fresh ground pepper

Combine ingredients in a large glass container, mixing well to coat chicken. Divide into two zip-closure bags, and marinate for eight hours. Grill chicken 10 minutes on each side, or until cooked thoroughly.

Serves 12.

SOUTHWEST CHICKEN

6 boneless, skinless chicken breasts
1 garlic clove, pressed
1 tablespoon canola oil

6 thin slices Monterey Jack cheese
1 cup tomatoes, chopped
½ cup green onions, chopped

Place chicken, garlic, and oil in large zip-closure plastic bag; mix well. Refrigerate six hours.

When ready to cook, grill on an outdoor grill over medium-high heat for approximately 20 minutes, turning once. Just before taking off grill, place a slice of Monterey Jack cheese on top of each; allow to melt. Remove from grill, and place on individual serving plates. Top each with equally divided tomatoes, followed with chopped green onions. Serve immediately.

Serves 6.

HAWAIIAN CHICKEN

6 boneless, skinless chicken breasts
1 cup teriyaki sauce

1 garlic clove, pressed
12 slices pineapple

Place chicken, teriyaki sauce, and garlic in large zip-closure plastic bag; mix well. Refrigerate 6 hours.

When ready to cook, grill on an outdoor grill over medium-high heat for approximately twenty minutes, turning once. Place pineapple slices on grill during the last 7 minutes of grilling. Remove from grill. Serve chicken on individual plates, and top each with two slices of grilled pineapple.

Serves 6.

SAUTÉED CHICKEN BREAST

4 boneless, skinless chicken breasts
Purchased poultry seasoning mix
¼ cup butter

Cream Gravy (see index for recipe)
Shiitake mushrooms, roasted
   (see index for roasting)

Coat chicken in poultry seasoning. Using a large skillet, sauté in butter over medium heat until cooked, turning once (about 8–10 minutes per side). Remove from heat. Make cream gravy with drippings.

Place chicken on individual serving plates. Spoon a small amount of gravy over each, and top with roasted shiitake mushrooms.

Serves 4.

SOUTHERN FRIED CHICKEN
with Cream Gravy

3 cups flour
2 teaspoons salt
1 teaspoon fresh ground pepper
1 teaspoon paprika

1 teaspoon ground sage
2 each: chicken legs, thighs, breasts
1 egg, beaten with 2 cups buttermilk
Canola oil, for deep frying

Combine flour, salt, pepper, paprika, and sage in large bowl; mix well to blend. Lightly dust chicken pieces in flour mixture. Dip chicken into egg and buttermilk mixture, and re-coat with flour. Fry chicken in a large, heavy skillet with approximately 1–1½ inches of oil, preheated to 375 (adjust cooking temperature, as needed). Cook, turning once with tongs, until light golden brown. As chicken pieces are cooked, transfer to paper towels and drain. Reserve oil for gravy.

Cream Gravy

⅓–½ cup reserved oil and drippings
¼ cup flour
2 + cups milk

½ teaspoon salt
¼ teaspoon fresh ground pepper

Using skillet and oil from fried chicken, stir in flour. Mix well to make a very smooth roux; add more oil or flour, if needed, to make a smooth, creamy paste. Over medium heat and stirring constantly, cook roux to a light golden brown. Remove from heat and gradually whisk in milk, working quickly to prevent roux from lumping. Return to heat; continue to cook until slightly thick. If gravy seems to thicken too much, add more milk. Season with salt and pepper.

If you're going to serve gravy, then you need to make sure that it's seasoned properly, so check out the salt and pepper, and make sure you cook the roux to light golden, too!

ORANGE-GINGER CHICKEN

4 boneless, skinless chicken breasts
3 tablespoons peanut oil
1 cup orange marmalade
¼ cup light soy sauce

1½ tablespoons ginger, minced
3 tablespoons water
3 garlic cloves, minced

Using a large skillet, sauté chicken in oil over medium heat until cooked, turning once (about 8–10 minutes per side). Add remaining ingredients; mix well. Cover and cook over medium-low heat until thick and bubbly. Serve with rice.

Serves 4.

CHICKEN CRABMEAT SUPREME

12 boneless, skinless chicken breasts
½ cup butter
1 cup unbleached flour
1 cup milk
1 cup chicken broth
½ cup dry white wine
2 onions, chopped
2 tablespoons butter
1 cup fresh crabmeat

1 cup mushrooms, sliced
¾ cup cracker crumbs
3 tablespoons parsley
1 teaspoon salt
1 teaspoon pepper
1½ cups Swiss cheese, grated
Paprika, to taste
Parsley, for garnish

Pound chicken thin; set aside. In a medium-sized saucepan, melt ½ cup butter and blend in flour. Slowly add milk, making a smooth paste. Stirring constantly, add chicken broth and wine. Stir and heat over medium heat until mixture is thickened; set aside. Using a large skillet, sauté onion in 2 tablespoons butter until translucent. Stir in crabmeat, mushrooms, cracker crumbs, parsley, salt, and pepper. Add 2 tablespoons of the reserved sauce; stir to blend. Spoon mixture onto one chicken breast; starting at the long end, roll up. Repeat for remaining breasts. Place seam side down in a 13 x 9 x 2-inch baking dish and pour remaining sauce over all. Cover and bake at 350° for one hour. Uncover, sprinkle with cheese and paprika. Bake until cheese melts. Garnish with fresh parsley sprigs.

Serves 8.

CHICKEN CASSEROLE
with Avocado and Cream Sauce

6 boneless, skinless chicken breasts
3 tablespoons butter
1 onion, chopped
1 stalk celery, sliced thin
1 teaspoon salt
1 teaspoon fresh ground pepper
4 tablespoons unbleached flour
1 cup chicken broth

1 cup light cream
½ cup sharp cheese, grated
1 teaspoon salt
½ teaspoon hot pepper sauce
1½ cups mushrooms, sliced thin
2 avocados, sliced
½ cup slivered almonds, toasted

Place chicken in a large saucepan and barely cover with water. Bring to a boil over medium-high heat; reduce heat and gently simmer for approximately 30 minutes, or until done. Drain, cover, and set aside.

Place butter, onion, and celery in a large saucepan; sauté over medium-high heat until onions are just translucent. Add salt, pepper, and flour; stir until smooth. Slowly add chicken broth, stirring constantly to prevent lumping. Add cream, and continue to cook until thickened. Add cheese, salt, and hot pepper sauce; stir well to blend. Place meat and mushrooms in a lightly buttered 13 x 9 x 2-inch baking dish; pour sauce over top. Cover, and bake at 350° for 25 minutes. Add avocado slices and return to oven until avocados are warmed. Sprinkle toasted almonds on top.

Serves 6.

CHURCH CHICKEN
For Ruth

8 boneless, skinless chicken breasts
8 slices bacon
4 ounces dried beef

2 cans mushroom soup
1 cup dairy sour cream

Wrap chicken with bacon. Lightly oil, and cover bottom of 13 x 9 x 2-inch baking dish with beef; top with chicken. Mix soup and sour cream; pour over all. Bake at 275° for 3 hours, uncovered. *(Notice I said "3" hours?!)*

Serves 8.

CHICKEN & VEGETABLE STIR FRY

4 boneless, skinless chicken breasts

2 tablespoons oil

1 teaspoon garlic powder

½ teaspoon red pepper

¼ cup oyster sauce

1 onion, quartered and separated

2 stalks celery, sliced thin on diagonal

4 carrots, sliced thin on diagonal

1 bunch fresh broccoli, florets only

1 cup mushrooms, quartered

1 zucchini, sliced (¼-inch thick)

1½ cups bean sprouts

Slice chicken breasts into ¼-inch slices. Place chicken and oil in wok; stir fry at 350° until just done. Add garlic powder, red pepper, and oyster sauce; stir fry. Add onion, celery, carrots, broccoli, and mushrooms; stir fry until onions are barely tender. Add zucchini; continue to cook for two more minutes; add bean sprouts. Cook until sprouts are tender, about one minute.

Serves 4.

GRILLED LOBSTER TAILS

6 lobster tails

1 cup butter, melted

4 limes, juiced

Split whole lobster tails down the middle and open. Mix butter and lime juice; divide in half. Brush lobsters with one-half the mixture of lime juice and butter. Place on a covered grill, shell side down, and baste again. Cover with lid and cook for 10 minutes over full hot coals. After 10 minutes, baste with butter mixture, and cook an additional 2 minutes. Serve with lime and butter sauce.

Serves 6.

Over Italian food and a fine bottle of wine, we sat clueless, thinking that the Gourmet Club was to meet on the following night. This is one of the dishes we missed—I vote for a repeat!

STIR-FRY LOBSTER
in Orange Sauce

4 lobster tails
2 tablespoons butter
1 tablespoon ginger root, grated
1 garlic clove, minced
2 tablespoons cornstarch
1½ cups orange juice

2 tablespoons honey
2 teaspoons orange rind, grated
½ teaspoon curry powder
6 cups long-grain cooked rice
½ cup green onions, chopped

Using a Dutch oven, place lobster tails in boiling water for 6 to 8 minutes, or until done; drain. Rinse under cold water; split and clean tails. Cut lobster meat into bite-sized pieces; set aside. Place butter, ginger, and garlic in wok or large skillet; sauté one minute over medium-high heat. Dissolve cornstarch in ½ cup orange juice, then incorporate into remaining orange juice along with honey, orange rind, and curry powder. Add juice mixture to wok, and stir constantly until thickened and bubbly. Stir in lobster, and cook until thoroughly heated. Spoon lobster over cooked rice on individual serving plates; sprinkle green onions on top.

Serves 6.

MIXED GRILL OF SHRIMP
with Sausage and Mushrooms

¾ cup olive oil
1 tablespoon dried thyme leaves
2 garlic cloves, minced

½ teaspoon dried red pepper, crushed
32 large shrimp, peeled and deveined

Place the ingredients (above) in a large zip-closure bag; marinate one hour at room temperature.

32 button mushrooms, stems trimmed   2 pounds andouille sausage, sliced

Remove shrimp from marinade. Thread one mushroom, horizontally, onto one skewer. Hold one sausage piece in curve of one shrimp; thread together on a skewer next to mushroom. Repeat, alternating, for a total of four mushrooms, four shrimp, and four sausage pieces per skewer. Arrange skewers on grill. Cook turning once until shrimp are cooked through, about 8 minutes.

Serves 8.

PEEL & EAT SHRIMP

1½ cups water or beer
1 tablespoon prepared shrimp boil mix
1 pound fresh shrimp

Prepared cocktail sauce
Prepared horseradish, to taste

Using a large saucepan, bring water and seasonings to a boil. Allow to simmer for awhile to ensure a good, seasoned liquid. Return liquid to a boil; add shrimp. Continue to cook approximately 3 more minutes, or until shrimp curls and turns pink. Drain and chill thoroughly. Serve with cocktail sauce mixed with desired amount of horseradish.

Serves 2.

SHRIMP & MUSHROOM SAUTÉ
with Creole Seafood Seasoning

1½ pounds large shrimp
Creole Seafood Seasoning
Flour, for dusting shrimp
½ cup butter
1 cup green onions, chopped

4 garlic cloves, minced
2 tablespoons parsley, minced
2 cups mushrooms, chopped
1 teaspoon unbleached flour
1 cup white wine

Peel and devein shrimp. Sprinkle lightly with Creole Seafood Seasoning and flour. Using a wok or a large saucepan, place butter, onions, garlic, parsley, and mushrooms. Sauté over medium-high heat for approximately 2 minutes, stirring continuously. Stir in one teaspoon each of the Creole Seafood Seasoning and flour; gradually stir in wine. Continue to cook, stirring gently, until shrimp are done, approximately 3 to 5 minutes. Serve over hot cooked rice.

Serves 6.

Creole Seafood Seasoning

⅓ cup salt
¼ cup garlic powder
½ cup fresh ground pepper
2 tablespoons cayenne pepper

2 tablespoons dried thyme
2 tablespoons dried oregano
⅓ cup paprika
3 tablespoons onion powder

Combine the above ingredients in a large zip-closure bag; mix thoroughly.

Yield: 2 cups.

PORK TENDERLOIN
with Apple and Mushroom Sauce

1 (3 pound) pork tenderloin	½ teaspoon salt
2 teaspoons dried thyme	½ teaspoon fresh ground pepper

Sprinkle tenderloin with thyme, salt, and pepper; place in a lightly oiled 13 x 9 x 2-inch baking pan. Bake, uncovered, at 450° for 20 minutes. Reduce heat to 325° and bake one hour, or until a meat thermometer reaches 160°. Remove tenderloin from oven; allow to stand 10 minutes before slicing. To serve, place three slices tenderloin onto eight individual plates; spoon approximately ¼ cup Apple and Mushroom Sauce (recipe follows) on top, and garnish with fresh thyme sprigs.

Serves 8.

Apple and Mushroom Sauce

4 tablespoons butter, divided	⅓ cup apple cider
3 cooking apples, peeled and	1 cup chicken broth
sliced into eighths	1 cup heavy cream
1½ cups fresh mushrooms, sliced	Fresh thyme sprigs, for garnish
1 tablespoon brandy	

Place 2 tablespoons of the butter in a large skillet. Over medium-high heat, sauté apple slices until just barely tender, turning once; remove and set aside. Using the same skillet, add the remaining 2 tablespoons butter and mushroom slices. Sauté until mushrooms are just tender; remove and set aside.

Over medium-high heat, deglaze the 13 x 9 x 2-inch pan with brandy and apple cider, stirring to loosen drippings. Pour into skillet used for sautéing apples and mushrooms. Add chicken broth and heavy cream to mixture. Cook, stirring constantly, over medium-high heat until hot and bubbly. Continue to cook until mixture thickens slightly, stirring to keep from sticking. Add apples and mushrooms; stir well to blend and heat thoroughly.

This is a good entrée to serve when dinner may be delayed for various reasons— it holds over well!

JAMAICAN JERKED PORK
Wrapped in Green Chiles

Tenderloin:

1 (2½ pound) pork tenderloin	¼ cup orange juice
2 teaspoons dried thyme	½ teaspoon orange zest
¼ teaspoon ground sage	2 tablespoons lime juice
1 teaspoon ground red pepper	½ cup balsamic vinegar
1 teaspoon fresh ground black pepper	2 tablespoons light soy sauce
½ teaspoon grated nutmeg	2 tablespoons pineapple juice
½ teaspoon ground cinnamon	1 cup onion, chopped fine
1 teaspoon allspice	1 medium-sized garlic clove, pressed
3 teaspoons salt	1 jalapeño chile, seed and mince
1½ tablespoons brown sugar	¼ cup olive oil

Combine the above ingredients in a large zip-closure bag; mix well. Place in refrigerator overnight.

At this point, plan ahead to have sauces ready for completion of entrée (as well as the roasted poblano chiles called for in the filling section). If you aren't certain of how to prepare roasted chiles, see index. The chiles are to be slightly split lengthwise in the center in order to remove seeds, and place the filling inside.

When ready to grill, remove tenderloin, reserving marinade for basting. Grill on an outdoor grill over medium heat, turning and basting often, until internal temperature reaches 160° on a meat thermometer. Remove from grill. Cover, and allow to rest 10 minutes. (This may be prepared in oven, rather than over an outdoor grill. Bake at 450° for 20 minutes; reduce heat to 325° and continue to cook for approximately one hour, or until internal temperature reaches 160° on a meat thermometer.) Dice meat for the final preparation.

Tomato Sauce:

3 tablespoons butter	2 cups Chicken Stock (see index)
4 tablespoons onions, chopped	¼ cup white wine
1 garlic clove, minced	½ teaspoon salt
4 tomatoes, seeded and chopped	¼ teaspoon ground white pepper

Place butter, onions, and garlic in a large saucepan. Sauté over medium-high heat until onions are translucent. Add remaining ingredients and continue to cook until liquid is reduced by half; remove from heat. Pour into a food processor or blender, and process until smooth. Strain through a wire strainer and return to skillet. Continue to cook over medium heat until slightly thickened. Adjust seasonings. Set aside or refrigerate until ready to use; reheat before serving.

Turmeric Cream Sauce (Optional):

¼ cup chicken stock	1 teaspoon ground turmeric
1 jalapeño chile, seeded and diced	½ cup crème fraîche, or sour cream

Place the chicken stock and chile in a small saucepan; bring to a boil over medium-high heat. Add turmeric, and cook an additional one minute. Remove from heat and allow to reach room temperature; strain. Slowly whisk in crème fraîche or sour cream, blending well. Spoon into a pastry bag, using a small tip for drizzling onto prepared entrée.

The Filling:

2 tablespoons butter	½ cup red wine vinegar
1 small onion, chopped fine	1 teaspoon light soy sauce
2 garlic cloves, minced	1 teaspoon dried basil
½ cup red bell pepper, chopped fine	1 teaspoon cilantro, minced
¼ cup green bell pepper, chopped fine	¼ teaspoon each, salt and pepper
3 tablespoons pineapple tidbits, halved	Prepared diced pork tenderloin
3 tablespoons pumpkin seeds, roasted	8 roasted poblano chiles, centers
¼ cup white wine	slightly slit, seeds removed
½ cup brown stock (see index)	(see index for roasting)
¼ cup brown sugar	

Place butter in large skillet. Over medium-high heat, sauté onion, garlic, and bell peppers until onions are just translucent. Add the pineapple, pumpkin seeds, and wine; cook until absorbed. Add the brown stock, sugar, vinegar, and soy sauce; continue to cook over medium heat for approximately 5 minutes. Add remaining ingredients (excluding chiles). Cook an additional 5 minutes. Spoon into prepared chiles, being careful to not overfill, but making them full enough to expose the filling.

Presentation: Spoon a small amount of the tomato sauce onto individual plates. Place one filled chile on top. Drizzle each with Turmeric Cream Sauce. Serve immediately.

Serves 8.

When I make this recipe, I prepare enough to have leftovers for freezing. Of course, everything tastes better when it hasn't been frozen—but it sure is nice to have this on hand when other things take priority over cooking . . . and it's still delicious!

PORK TENDERLOIN
with Black Olive Tapenade

1 pork tenderloin, trimmed
Black Olive Tapenade (recipe follows)
Salt and pepper, to taste
3 tablespoons olive oil

½ cup dry red wine
1 cup fresh mushrooms, sliced
½ cup butter

Butterfly tenderloin. Using a meat mallet, pound one side flat. Spread Tapenade on surface of tenderloin; roll up (lengthwise) and secure with cooking string. Season with salt and pepper. Place in a large skillet with oil. Over medium-high heat, sear on all sides; place in 350° oven. Bake for approximately 20 minutes, or until thermometer shows an internal temperature of 140°. Remove from oven; loosely wrap tenderloin in foil and allow to rest 10 minutes before slicing. Return skillet to cooktop; over medium-high heat, add red wine to deglaze the skillet. Add mushrooms, and continue to cook until wine is reduced to one half. Remove from heat, and slowly whisk in small amounts of butter, being careful to blend, and not melt butter. Continue to add butter until all is incorporated, returning to heat as needed. Slice tenderloin and place on individual plates. Spoon a small amount of sauce over top.

Serves 4.

Black Olive Tapenade

1 cup Niçoise or Kalamata olives,
   pitted
2 tablespoons capers
2 garlic cloves, minced
¼ teaspoon dried thyme

1 tablespoon Dijon mustard
1 tablespoon lemon juice
½ teaspoon fresh ground pepper
2 tablespoons olive oil
3 tablespoons cilantro, chopped fine

Excluding cilantro, place all ingredients in a food processor or blender. Process until chopped fine, but not smooth. Stir in cilantro.

FRENCHED RACK OF LAMB
with Sweet Cherry Sauce

3 frenched lamb racks

4 tablespoons olive oil

3 garlic cloves, minced

2 tablespoons fresh rosemary

2 teaspoons fresh ground pepper

Place ingredients in a large, heavy-duty plastic bag; seal tightly. Marinate overnight in refrigerator. When ready to cook, prepare grill, using mesquite wood. Over low fire, place lamb fat-side down. Grill slowly until light golden brown, or a quick-read thermometer reaches 135°. Remove from grill; cover well, and allow to rest for 10 minutes. Slice between ribs, and return to a medium-hot grill to cook for an additional 3–5 minutes. (After first grilling, the ribs could be sliced and returned to marinade until ready to grill the second time.) Serve three ribs of lamb per person, placed in an upright position to display the golden browned bones nicely. These are delicious with Sweet Cherry Sauce (recipe follows), or mint jelly.

Serves 8.

Sweet Cherry Sauce

2 cups dried tart cherries

1½ cups sugar

1 cup water

¾ cup red wine vinegar

½ cup onion, chopped fine

¼ cup raspberry vinegar

3 teaspoons ginger, peeled and grated

1 tablespoon jalapeño pepper, minced

1 teaspoon ground coriander

½ teaspoon ground cumin

½ teaspoon ground cardamom

1 teaspoon orange zest

¼ teaspoon ground cloves

¼ teaspoon ground cinnamon

Combine above ingredients in a medium-sized saucepan. Bring to a boil over medium heat. Reduce heat; simmer for approximately one hour, or until thickened. Serve warm, or at room temperature, with rack of lamb or a variety of pork dishes.

PRIME RIB
with Mousseline Sauce

1 prime rib roast (size you desire)   **Salt, pepper, garlic powder, to taste**
½ cup unbleached flour

Sprinkle prime rib with flour and seasonings. Place in a lightly oiled 13 x 9 x 2-inch baking pan. Cook for 5 minutes per pound at 500°. Turn oven off, and leave roast for 2 hours. Do not open oven door during this time! (If you don't trust this method, insert a meat thermometer in the middle of prime rib, and cook to degree of doneness indicated. In this case, don't turn the oven off; instead, reduce the temperature to 300°.) Be sure to save the juices to serve alongside, or for making prime rib soup . . . yum! Allow 2 servings per pound.

Mousseline Sauce

3 egg yolks   **½ cup butter, melted**
1 tablespoon lemon juice   **2 tablespoons prepared horseradish**
½ teaspoon salt   **1 cup heavy cream, whipped**
½ teaspoon ground white pepper

Combine egg yolks, lemon juice, salt, and pepper in food processor or blender. Process until well-blended. As machine is running, add hot butter in slow stream. Transfer to a medium-sized bowl; mix in horseradish and fold in whipped cream. Adjust horseradish to preferred taste. Serve as a condiment with prime rib.

ITALIAN POT ROAST

1 (5 pound) beef roast   **½ cup sherry**
2 tablespoons oil   **½ cup red wine vinegar**
1 tablespoon each, salt and pepper **2½ cups tomatoes, chopped**
3 tablespoons onion, minced   **1 teaspoon each, dried basil**
1 garlic clove, minced   **   and oregano**
                                     3 tablespoons unbleached flour

In a large Dutch oven, brown meat in oil over medium-high heat. Add next 7 ingredients. Cover and cook in 300° oven for 5 hours. Add basil and oregano; cook an additional 10 minutes. Add flour to a small amount of water to make a smooth paste (approximately ⅓ cup). Remove roast from Dutch oven; gradually stir paste into pan gravy. Cook until gravy is of desired thickness.

COUNTRY-STYLE ROAST BEEF
with Onion, Carrots, Potatoes, and Gravy

1 chuck roast (4 pound)
Browning and seasoning sauce
Salt and pepper
3 tablespoons oil
6 cups water

1 onion, halved
4 russet potatoes, peeled and halved
6 carrots, peeled and halved
1–1½ cups milk or buttermilk
½ cup flour

Baste roast in browning and seasoning sauce; season with salt and pepper. Pour oil into pan of a six-quart pressure cooker. Over medium-high heat, sear roast on both sides. Remove from heat; add 6 cups water and onion. Place lid on pressure cooker, and continue cooking according to manufacturer's instructions for your particular pressure cooker (I cook mine at ten pounds of pressure for approximately 45 minutes, continuously monitoring the pressure gauge and amount of heat I'm using.) When finished cooking, remove cooker from heat; allow to cool completely, and remove lid only after checking pressure gauge to be certain there is no longer any pressure in the cooker. Carefully remove meat and onion; cover to keep warm.

Strain leftover liquid into a clean container. Wash cooker. Once again, strain the liquid back into the cooker. Add potatoes and carrots to liquid. Bring to a boil over medium-high heat; reduce heat to low. Continue to cook at a steady simmer, until potatoes are just tender. Remove from heat. Using a large slotted spoon, gently remove; cover to keep warm.

Return cooker and liquid to medium heat; add milk (I like to use buttermilk, for it gives this gravy a really nice flavor). Using a small bowl, mix flour with enough water to make a smooth sauce consistency. Using only amount needed to thicken to your preference, slowly strain into hot liquid, stirring constantly to prevent lumping. Season with salt and pepper. Remove from heat; pour into serving bowl.

Serves 4.

STANDING RIB ROAST OF BEEF
with Madeira Sauce

1 standing rib of beef   **1 teaspoon dried thyme**
2 teaspoons each, salt and pepper

Order beef ahead of time, allowing two servings per pound. Roast should be prepared in this manner: Trimmed, fat scored, chine removed and tied onto roast. When ready to prepare, add spices together to blend; rub into roast, covering the entire surface. Transfer to a large roasting pan, and allow to stand at room temperature for one hour. Place roast in 500° oven for 10 minutes. Reduce oven temperature to 350°. Continue roasting until meat thermometer inserted into thickest portion of meat (without touching bone) registers desired degree of doneness, about 130° for rare (this is cooking approximately 17 minutes per pound). Do not baste. Transfer roast to serving platter. Tent with foil to keep warm.

Serves 12.

Madeira Sauce

⅔ cup water   **4 tablespoons butter**
1½ tablespoons butter   **½ cup minced shallots**
Juice of ½ lemon   **1 cup beef stock**
¼ teaspoon salt   **½ cup Madeira wine**
½ pound small white mushrooms,   **1 tablespoon tomato paste**
  trimmed

Combine water, butter, lemon juice, and salt in medium-sized saucepan; bring to boil over medium-high heat. Reduce heat to low and stir in mushrooms. Cover and cook gently for approximately 5 minutes. Uncover, and set aside.

Discarding as much fat as possible from roasting pan, add butter and melt over medium-high heat. Stir in shallots and sauté until tender. Drain mushroom cooking liquid into measuring cup and add water, if necessary, to equal one cup. Pour into roasting pan with beef stock, Madeira and tomato paste; blend well. Reduce heat to low and cook, stirring to loosen any browned bits, until liquid is reduced to two cups. Stir in mushrooms and cook just until heated through. Adjust seasonings of salt and pepper. Transfer to heated sauceboat. Carve roast at table and serve immediately with sauce.

CHATEAUBRIAND
Accompanied with Sauce Anita

1 beef tenderloin, 3–4 pounds
2 tablespoons butter, melted

1 teaspoon salt
1 teaspoon fresh ground pepper

Spread the tenderloin generously with butter; coat with salt and pepper. Place on baking sheet, and broil in oven for 7 minutes on each side (three sides). Cook 15 minutes at 350°, for rare steak, or 20 minutes for medium-rare (use meat thermometer to accurately cook to desired doneness). Remove from oven; cover and allow to rest for 5 minutes. Slice two steaks from center of tenderloin at thickness desired, approximately two to three inches thick, reserving leftover for another use. Serve immediately, with sauce placed to the side. Garnish with sprig of fresh thyme.

Serves 2.

Sauce Anita

3 shallots, chopped fine
1 cup butter, unsalted, divided
1 cup mushrooms, chopped
1 bay leaf
¼ teaspoon dried thyme

¾ cup dry white wine
1 cup brown stock (see index)
1 teaspoon dried tarragon
1 tablespoon fresh parsley, chopped
Salt and pepper, to taste

Using a medium-sized skillet over medium heat, sauté shallots in 3 tablespoons butter until soft and translucent; add mushrooms and sauté until tender. Add bay leaf, thyme, and white wine. Bring to a boil; reduce heat and simmer until liquid has evaporated. Remove bay leaf. Add stock, tarragon, and parsley. Season with salt and pepper. Bring to a boil, remove from heat, and whisk in the remaining butter, bit by bit, being careful to incorporate and not melt butter. Taste and adjust seasonings. Serve immediately, or hold in a pan of warm water until ready to serve.

BEEF TENDERLOIN
with Spinach, Prosciutto, and Mushrooms

1 well-trimmed tenderloin (7 pounds)	Mushroom Filling (recipe below)
1 teaspoon fresh ground pepper	4 tablespoons olive oil
Spinach Filling (recipe follows)	Fresh cracked pepper, for coating
3 ounces Prosciutto, sliced very thin	

Place the tenderloin smooth side down on cutting board. Make a lengthwise incision down center, stopping about one inch from bottom. Gently pull the center open, and cut the sides in the same manner, stopping about one inch from bottom. (Tenderloin will lay a little lumpy at this point, but flat.) Cover meat with plastic wrap, using a meat mallet, pound to smooth and flatten to about ½-inch thick. This will prepare the tenderloin to roll up nicely. (Do this on only one side.) Sprinkle pepper over meat and spoon on a thin layer of spinach filling, keeping one inch from edge. Add a layer of prosciutto ham, maintaining the same border distance. Layer the chunky mushroom mixture on top of the prosciutto, being careful to spread, but not pack down. Fold short ends in just far enough to hold. Using both hands, gently roll into a long roll, being careful to keep short ends tucked. Tie end with cooking string (cut twelve 14-inch pieces of string; slide one piece under meat and tie. Repeat for length of tenderloin; trim loose ends). Rub the meat with olive oil, and coat with cracked pepper. Place meat, seam side down, in appropriate-sized roasting pan. Bake at 450° until desired doneness is reached. Using a quick-read thermometer inserted into the thickest part of the meat and taking several readings is the most accurate method of measuring the temperature. (For rare: Remove from oven at 115°. For medium-rare: Remove from oven at 120°. For medium: Remove from oven at 130°.) Once removed from oven, allow to rest for 10 minutes; temperature should rise another 5–7 degrees. Slice to desired thickness, and serve on individual plates; top with brown sauce.

Serves 12.

Spinach filling:

4 tablespoons olive oil	½ teaspoon lemon juice
10 cups fresh spinach, chopped	½ teaspoon salt
3 tablespoons creamy goat cheese	

Place oil and spinach in a large skillet. Sauté over medium-high heat until spinach wilts; remove and press to drain through a colander. Add the goat cheese, lemon juice, and salt; mix well by hand. Refrigerate until ready to use.

Mushroom filling:

2 tablespoons butter	½ cup Marsala wine
1 cup shallots, minced	½ teaspoon salt
4 cups mushrooms, chopped	⅛ teaspoon red pepper
2 garlic cloves, minced	½ cup breadcrumbs

Place butter and shallots in a large skillet; sauté over medium-high heat until light brown. Add mushrooms and garlic; continue to cook until tender. Add wine, salt, and red pepper; continue to cook until liquid is almost gone. Place mushroom mixture and breadcrumbs in food processor. Pulse just a few times to chop, leaving mushrooms about the size of peas. Refrigerate until ready to use.

Brown Sauce

¼ cup butter	6 cups Brown Stock (see index)
2 shallots, chopped	½ bunch parsley
1 carrot, chopped	1 bay leaf
1 long stalk of celery, chopped	1 teaspoon fresh ground pepper
½ leek (green part only), chopped	2 sprigs thyme
2 cloves garlic, pressed	¼ cup butter
2 tablespoons tomato paste	½ cup flour
½ cup dry red wine	

Using a large saucepan, combine butter, shallots, carrot, celery, leek, and garlic. Cook over medium-high heat until vegetables are slightly caramelized (10–15 minutes). Stir in tomato paste and cook for approximately 3 minutes. Add wine; continue to cook until almost evaporated. Add brown stock, parsley, bay leaf, pepper, and thyme. Reduce heat to low and simmer for 2 hours, or until liquid is reduced to three cups. Remove from heat. Strain through a wire mesh strainer, allowing it to filter naturally. (At this point you may refrigerate for up to a week.) Melt butter over medium heat in a large saucepan. Slowly stir in flour to make a fine paste, stirring continuously to prevent lumping. Continue to cook until browned slightly. Remove from heat; slowly add sauce, stirring constantly to prevent lumping. Return to heat and continue to cook, stirring continually until thickened.

Yield: 3 cups.

Another choice of sauce, using the above recipe for Brown Sauce, is Sauce Diable (see index). It goes wonderfully with grilled chicken, roasted red meats, or wild game.

TENDERLOIN OF BEEF
Wrapped in Pancetta

2 tablespoons butter, softened
1 (2 pound) beef tenderloin, trimmed
2 teaspoons fresh ground pepper
4 (⅛-inch thick) slices pancetta
    (or bacon)
1 tablespoon butter
4 slices pancetta (or bacon), chopped
⅓ cup shallots, chopped fine

¼ cup cognac
1½ cups dry red wine, divided
4 sprigs fresh marjoram
1½ cups beef stock (see index)
2 teaspoons tomato paste
4 tablespoons butter, cut into pieces
1 teaspoon fresh ground pepper
Fresh marjoram, minced, for garnish

Spread 2 tablespoons butter over tenderloin, and sprinkle with pepper. Wrap pancetta slices around tenderloin, and secure each slice with a wooden pick. Place in appropriate-sized roasting pan, and bake at 450° until a meat thermometer inserted in middle reaches doneness desired. Remove from oven, and place tenderloin onto a platter; lightly cover with foil.

Place roasting pan over medium-high heat; add one tablespoon butter and chopped pancetta. Cook for one minute; add shallots and cook until tender. Remove from heat and pour off fat. Return to medium-high heat. Add cognac and cook to deglaze pan. Add ¾ cup of the wine and marjoram; continue to cook for 5 minutes, reducing liquid somewhat. Add the remaining ¾ cup wine, and cook an additional 5 minutes. Add beef stock, tomato paste, and any excess drippings from tenderloin. Bring to a boil, and cook until reduced to ¾ cup mixture. Remove from heat, and strain through a wire strainer, pressing to extract as much liquid as possible. Return to heat just long enough to barely simmer. Whisk in butter, bit by bit, being careful to incorporate and not melt. Season with pepper.

Slice tenderloin into desired thickness for servings. Divide equally onto four individual plates and spoon sauce on top. Sprinkle with minced marjoram for garnish!

Serves 4.

LOBSTER-STUFFED TENDERLOIN
For Dorthy

3 (4 ounce) lobster tails	6 slices bacon
1 (6 pound) beef tenderloin, trimmed	½ cup green onions, chopped
1 tablespoon butter, melted	½ cup butter
2 teaspoons lemon juice	½ cup white wine
1 teaspoon each, salt and pepper	⅛ teaspoon garlic salt

Using a large Dutch oven, boil lobster tails in salted water for approximately 5 minutes, or until done. Drain; remove lobster from shell. Set aside.

Place the tenderloin smooth-side down on cutting board. Make a lengthwise incision down center, stopping about ½-inch from bottom. Place lobster, end to end, inside tenderloin. Slice lobster, if necessary, to extend length of tenderloin. Combine the butter, lemon juice, salt, and pepper; drizzle over top of lobster. Fold tenderloin up over lobster, and tie with cooking string (cut ten 14-inch pieces of string; slide one piece under meat and tie. Repeat for entire length of tenderloin; trim loose ends.) Place bacon slices on top of tenderloin, and bake at 450° until desired doneness is reached. Using a quick-read thermometer inserted into the thickest part of the meat (and taking several readings) is the most accurate method of measuring the temperature. (For rare: Remove from oven at 115°. For medium-rare: Remove from oven at 120°. For medium: Remove from oven at 130°.) Once removed from oven, allow to rest for 10 minutes; temperature should rise another 5–7 degrees.

Using a small saucepan over medium-high heat, sauté onions in butter until onions are slightly browned. Add wine, and continue to cook for an additional 5 minutes. Add garlic salt; mix well.

Slice tenderloin to desired thickness; serve on individual plates. Drizzle with butter sauce.

Serves 10.

GRILLED STEAKS
with Green Chiles

6 rib-eye steaks	6 whole green chiles (canned)
Salt and pepper, to taste	6 slices Monterey Jack cheese

Grill steaks over medium-hot coals (and mesquite wood chips) for 6–8 minutes per side, or to preferred doneness. Approximately 4 minutes before removing from grill, season with salt and pepper. Spread open one chile and place on top of steak. Place one slice of cheese on top of chile, and allow to melt. Repeat for remaining steaks.

Serves 6.

PAN-SEARED TENDERLOINS

½ cup dry red wine
⅓ cup beef stock
2 tablespoons brown sugar
2 garlic cloves, pressed

2 tablespoons balsamic vinegar
2 teaspoons coarse ground pepper
6 beef tenderloins, 1 inch thick
Salt to taste

Combine above ingredients, excluding salt, in a large zip-closure bag. Mix well, coating meat evenly. Place in refrigerator and marinate for 4 hours, turning once. Remove from marinade. Over medium-high heat, sear in large skillet coated with cooking oil for about 3 minutes per side, or until reached preferred doneness is reached. Season with salt just before cooking is completed.

Serves 6.

GREEN CHILE BURGER

1 pound lean ground beef
Salt, pepper, garlic salt, and
    lemon pepper, to taste
Barbecue Sauce (see index)

4 whole green chiles (canned)
4 slices Monterey Jack cheese
Choice of condiments (suggestions
    follow)

Using ¼ pound meat each, shape hamburger meat to your own preferred style. Sprinkle with desired amount of seasonings, and baste both sides with barbecue sauce. Cook on an outdoor grill over medium-hot coals to desired doneness, turning once. Just before taking off grill, place one (split) green chile atop meat. Add one slice of Monterey Jack cheese over chile, and allow to melt. Serve immediately with your choice of condiments.

Serves 4.

Suggested condiments: Mustard, mayonnaise and ketchup, of course! Iceburg lettuce (I feel green leaf lettuce is too dry for burgers), tomatoes, pickles, red onions, caramelized onions, fresh mushrooms, avocado, alfalfa sprouts, grilled veggies, barbecue sauce, fried bacon, onions, etc., etc., etc.!

QUICK & EASY MEATLOAF

2 pounds lean ground beef
1 package onion soup mix
½ cup ketchup

1 cup water
2 slices sandwich bread,
   torn bite-sized
½ cup ketchup

Mix first five ingredients in a large bowl. Place in a lightly oiled bread pan, and spoon the remaining ½ cup ketchup on top. Bake at 350° for 45 minutes.

Serves 6.

BRAISED VEAL
with Mushroom Cream Sauce

6 veal cutlets, ¼-inch thick
Salt and pepper, to taste
½ cup butter
2 tablespoons green onion, chopped
1 cup mushrooms, sliced thin
2 tablespoons lemon juice
¼ cup orange juice
2 teaspoons lemon zest

2 teaspoons orange zest
1 tablespoon fresh parsley, chopped
2 tablespoons unbleached flour
1 cup milk
1 cup chicken broth
½ cup crème fraîche (see index) or
   sour cream

Cover the cutlets with plastic wrap; tenderize using a meat mallet. Season lightly with salt and pepper. Melt butter in a large skillet over medium-high heat, being careful not to burn butter. Add cutlets, and sauté on both sides until lightly browned. Remove and drain. Arrange the cutlets in a shallow baking dish with ¼ cup water; bake, covered, at 300° for 20 minutes.

Add the green onion to the skillet, and sauté until tender. Add mushrooms, and continue to cook until mushrooms are tender. Stir in lemon juice, orange juice, lemon zest, orange zest, and parsley; continue to cook and deglaze skillet. Place flour in a small bowl; add a small amount of milk and stir, making a smooth paste. Add the remaining milk, and pour into the skillet along with the chicken broth, stirring constantly to prevent lumping. Continue to cook until slightly thickened. Stir in crème fraîche; mix well. Adjust seasonings. Spoon over veal just before serving.

Serves 6.

BAKED RED SNAPPER
with Seasoned Tomatoes and Roasted Poblano Sauce

6 red snapper fillets
Salt and pepper
4 tablespoons olive oil, divided
6 green onions, minced
3 garlic cloves, minced
6 roma tomatoes, peeled, seeded,
    chopped and drained

¼ cup Monterey Jack cheese, grated
Fresh basil and thyme, chopped,
    for garnish
Poblano Sauce (recipe follows)

Season fillets with salt and pepper. Heat 2 tablespoons oil in large skillet over medium-high heat. Sauté fillets until lightly browned, about 2 minutes each side. Arrange fillets in single layer on baking pan lined with parchment paper. Set aside.

Heat the remaining 2 tablespoons oil in large skillet. Sauté onions and garlic until just tender, add tomatoes, and continue to cook for 2 minutes, stirring as needed. Spoon mixture equally over the fillets. Place in 400° oven and bake for 20 minutes. Lightly sprinkle each fillet with Monterey Jack cheese and allow to melt. Remove from oven and sprinkle each with chopped herbs.

Prepare individual plates by lightly spooning Poblano Sauce onto plate. Place fish on top of sauce. Serve immediately.

Serves 6.

Poblano Sauce

3 roasted poblano peppers,
    seeded, stems removed
3 tablespoons roasted garlic pulp
1 cup light cream

¼ cup chicken broth
3 teaspoons lemon juice
1½ teaspoons Liquid Smoke
¾ teaspoon salt

Place ingredients in food processor or blender; process until smooth.

Makes 1½ cups.

This sauce is delicious served on salads and grilled chicken, as well as on fish! I generally increase this recipe and freeze in small portions. It's nice to have on hand!

RED SNAPPER VERACRUZ

4 red snapper fillets
½ cup butter, divided
Salt and pepper, to taste
1 cup mushrooms, sliced
1 jalapeño, seeded and chopped fine

¼ cup onions, chopped
5 cups spinach, chopped
2 tablespoons cilantro, chopped
2 tablespoons pimiento, chopped
Spanish Rice (see index)

Grill fillets over medium heat until they reach desired doneness (about 5 minutes per side.) Baste with half the butter called for in recipe; season with salt and pepper. Place the remaining butter in a large skillet and sauté vegetables in order listed above. Serve topped with vegetables, with Spanish Rice on the side.

Serves 4.

PAN-SEARED TUNA STEAKS

12 sun-dried tomato halves,
    packed without oil
1 cup dry white wine, divided
1 tablespoon orange juice
4 tablespoons black olives, chopped

2 (6½ ounce) tuna steaks
2 tablespoons olive oil
2 garlic cloves, pressed
1 teaspoon salt
1 tablespoon fresh ground pepper

Drain tomato halves. Place in a large glass measuring cup; add ½ cup wine. Cover with plastic wrap and microwave on high for one minute, or until it starts to boil. Allow to cool to room temperature. Add the remaining ½ cup wine, orange juice, and olives; set aside.

Pat the tuna steaks with a paper towel to remove excess moisture. Coat the tuna with olive oil, pressed garlic, salt, and pepper. Sear in a large, non-stick skillet over medium-high heat, turning once, for about 10 minutes, or until done. Serve immediately. Garnish tops with tomato mixture.

Serves 2.

POACHED FILLET OF BABY SALMON
with Beurre Blanc Sauce

2 cups dry white wine	1 bay leaf
1 cup water	2 green onions, chopped
1 tablespoon butter	1 stalk celery, chopped
1 teaspoon each, salt and pepper	1 carrot, chopped
1 tablespoon lemon juice	2 baby salmon fillets, divided
1 teaspoon lemon zest	Golden caviar, for garnish (optional)

Excluding salmon, place the above ingredients in a large skillet. Bring to a boil over medium-high heat. Reduce heat to medium, and simmer for 20 minutes. Add salmon fillets; bring to a boil. Reduce heat to low. Poach for 5 minutes; turn, and poach for an additional five minutes, or until done. Remove, and place on individual plates. Spoon a small amount of Buerre Blanc Sauce on top (recipe follows). Place one-half teaspoon of caviar on side.

Serves 4.

Beurre Blanc Sauce

½ cup dry white wine	1 cup butter, cut into small pieces
½ cup white wine vinegar	Salt and white pepper, to taste
3 tablespoons shallots, chopped fine	

In a small saucepan, combine wine, vinegar, and shallots. Bring to a boil over medium-high heat. Reduce heat and continue to cook until reduced to ¼ cup. Remove from heat and whisk in butter, bit by bit, making sure that the butter is incorporated, but not melted. Return to heat as needed, but remove when it appears to melt rather than thicken. Season to taste with salt and white pepper.

OVEN-ROASTED SALMON

2 tablespoons fresh ginger, grated	½ teaspoon each, salt and pepper
2 tablespoons white wine vinegar	4 pearl onions, halved
½ cup maple syrup, divided	2 (6½ ounce) salmon fillets
2 tablespoons parsley, chopped fine	

Combine the ginger, vinegar, ¼ cup syrup, parsley, salt, and pepper in small bowl; mix well. Place onions and salmon on baking sheet; pour mixture evenly over all. Bake at 450° for 10 minutes. Baste with the remaining syrup and bake an additional 5 minutes, or until flaky.

Serves 2.

POACHED SALMON
on Beds of Wilted Spinach

1 garlic clove, minced
½ cup onion, chopped fine
4 tablespoons olive oil
½ teaspoon each, salt and pepper
6 cups fresh spinach
2 cups fresh basil leaves

2 cups dry white wine
2 salmon fillets, divided
¼ cup light soy sauce
3 tablespoons honey
3 tablespoons lemon juice
Fresh basil leaves, for garnish

Place garlic, onion, and olive oil in a large skillet. Over medium-high heat, sauté until onions are translucent. Add salt and pepper; stir. Add spinach and basil leaves; stir quickly to wilt. Remove and divide equally onto four individual plates, keeping warm. Add wine to skillet, stirring to deglaze pan. Add salmon fillets; bring to a boil. Poach for five minutes; turn, and poach for an additional five minutes, or until done. Remove, and place salmon on top of spinach mixture. Mix soy sauce, honey, and lemon juice in a small bowl; drizzle on top of salmon. Garnish with basil leaves.

Serves 4.

COLD POACHED SALMON
with Mustard-Lime Sauce

2 cups water
2½ cups dry white wine
2 salmon fillets, divided
1 teaspoon each, salt and white pepper
1 cup sour cream

¼ cup Dijon mustard
4 teaspoons lime juice
4 teaspoons honey
½ teaspoon lime zest
Fresh basil, for garnish

Place water and wine in a large skillet; bring to boil over medium-high heat. Add salmon fillets; bring to a boil. Reduce heat to low. Poach for 5 minutes; turn, and poach for an additional 5 minutes, or until done. Season with salt and white pepper. Using slotted spatula, transfer salmon to platter. Cover and refrigerate until cold. (May be prepared one day in advance.)

Combine sour cream, mustard, lime juice, honey, and zest in a small bowl. Mix well and chill for at least one hour.

Presentation: Arrange fillets on individual plates; drizzle with Mustard-Lime Sauce. Top with basil leaves.

Serves 4.

ROAST DUCKLING
with Lemon and Ginger Sauce

6 ducks, 5 to 6 pounds each   ½ cup vegetable oil

Duck Stock:

Reserved necks, giblets, and wing tips from ducks (do not use livers)

4 tablespoons vegetable oil	1 cup dry white wine
2 onions, sliced	¼ cup parsley
2 carrots, sliced	2 bay leaves
2 ribs celery, sliced	12 peppercorns
8 cups chicken broth	1 teaspoon salt
1 cup water	1 teaspoon dried thyme leaves

In a large saucepan over medium-high heat, sear the reserved duck pieces in the 4 tablespoons vegetable oil until lightly browned (approximately 15 minutes). Add the onion, carrots and celery; cook until onions are slightly browned. Add the remaining ingredients; bring to a boil. Reduce heat to low, and simmer for approximately 2 hours. Strain the stock into a large bowl and allow to stand for 10 minutes. Skim fat that rises to the top, or place in freezer until cooled enough for fat to set up, then remove. This may be prepared up to two days in advance; keep refrigerated.

Lemon and Ginger Sauce:

4 cups duck stock	4 tablespoons red currant jelly
4 tablespoons ginger root, peeled and chopped fine	1 tablespoon lemon zest
	⅛ teaspoon salt
2 tablespoons lemon juice	⅛ teaspoon white pepper
4 teaspoons cornstarch	

Using a medium-sized saucepan over medium-high heat, bring duck stock, ginger root, and lemon juice to a boil. Cook until reduced to 2 cups. In a small bowl, dissolve the cornstarch in about ½ cup of the stock and currant jelly. Slowly incorporate this mixture into the stock, whisking continuously to prevent lumping. Add lemon zest, salt, and pepper. Reduce heat to medium-low, and continue to cook until thickened. Remove from heat. Set aside and keep warm. (May be made ahead of time and refrigerated. When ready to use, reheat over low heat to prevent burning or sticking.)

Roasting the ducks:

Rinse the ducks and pat dry. Cut off any excess neck skin and remove the excess fat from inside the cavities. Using tines of a roasting fork, pierce the duck's skin all over, being careful not to pierce the meat. Truss the ducks with cooking string and rub them with vegetable oil.

Place the ducks, breast-side up, on roasting racks in roasting pan. Bake at 400° for 30 minutes; reduce heat to 325° and continue to cook for 1½ hours, or until meat thermometer inserted into the thickest part of the thigh reads 180°, or the drumstick slides easily in its socket (you will need to prick the skin some more during the cooking time, also). Remove from oven; cover loosely with foil, and allow to rest 10 minutes. Using a heavy knife, split the ducks lengthwise, discarding the backbones. Remove the duck legs at the thigh joint; remove the thigh bones. Cutting against the breast bones and ribs, remove the breast sections in whole pieces. Slice each breast section crosswise on the diagonal into three pieces. Discard the carcasses and bones.

Serves 12.

Presentation: Divide lemon and ginger sauce equally onto twelve dinner plates. Place three slices of duck onto each plate. A little bit of Pineapple and Pecan Chutney is a nice addition on the side (see recipe below).

Pineapple & Pecan Chutney

3 cups pineapple chunks
1 cup sugar
½ cup malt vinegar
¼ cup ginger root, peeled and chopped

1 jalapeño, chopped, seeds removed
2 garlic cloves, minced
1 cup pecan halves, roasted (see index)

Excluding pecan halves, combine the remaining ingredients in a medium-sized saucepan. Bring to a boil over medium-high heat, stirring continually. Reduce heat to medium-low; continue to cook until liquid is reduced by half and syrupy. Remove from heat; stir in pecan halves. Allow to cool; cover and refrigerate. Serve at room temperature.

SAVORY QUAIL
For Kelly

8 quail (ready to cook)
¼ cup unbleached flour
1 teaspoon each, salt and pepper
¼ cup butter
½ cup dry white wine

2 tablespoons green onions, sliced
½ cup light cream
2 egg yolks
¼ teaspoon salt
Dash of pepper

Tie legs of each quail together with string. Using a bag, mix flour, salt, and pepper. Add quail, a few at a time, and shake to coat well. Melt butter in a large skillet over medium-high heat. Add quail, and brown well on both sides, adjusting heat as needed. Add wine and onions. Cover and simmer until birds are tender, approximately 30 minutes. Remove quail to a warm platter; keep warm. Reserve ½ cup pan juices in skillet. Beat cream with egg yolks, ¼ teaspoon salt, and dash of pepper; slowly stir in pan juices. Cook and stir until thickened (do not boil). Serve sauce over quail.

Serves 4.

SMOKED CHICKEN ENCHILADAS
Green or Red

4 boneless, skinless chicken breasts	1 tablespoon butter
10 tomatillos, husks removed	1 tablespoon cornstarch
2 cups chicken broth	¼ cup sour cream
1 cup cilantro, stems removed	1 tablespoon honey
1 onion, chopped	⅛ teaspoon salt
1 clove garlic, minced	8 corn tortillas
½ jalapeño pepper, chopped	2 cups Monterey Jack cheese, grated

Prepare an outdoor grill, using some mesquite wood for smoke flavor. Grill chicken over medium-low heat until cooked through. Remove from grill; allow to rest for 10 minutes. Slice into thin strips; set aside.

Place tomatillos and chicken broth in a medium-sized saucepan. Bring to a boil over medium-high heat; cook until tomatillos are just tender (about 8 minutes). Add cilantro, allowing it to wilt. Turn off heat. Using a medium-sized skillet, sauté onion, garlic, and jalapeño in butter until slightly browned. Add to tomatilla mixture, and transfer all to food processor or blender. Process by pulsing until tomatillas are very small, almost smooth. Add cornstarch, sour cream, and honey; pulse to blend. Return to saucepan; season with salt, and continue to cook until thickened to your preference. Set aside.

Wrap tortillas in foil, and heat in 350° oven until softened (about 15 minutes). Or dip in hot tomatillos sauce, working quickly so that tortillas won't fall apart. Place smoked chicken pieces in middles of tortillas (a bit off-center). Top with cheese, and roll up. Pour enough sauce in bottom of a 13 x 9 x 2-inch baking dish to just cover bottom. Place filled tortilla, seam side down, in dish; repeat procedure with remaining enchiladas. Pour remaining sauce over all enchiladas, and top with leftover grated cheese. Bake, covered, for 25 minutes in 350 oven. Remove from oven, uncover, and allow to stand while preparing individual plates. Using a spatula, gently place two enchiladas on each plate, spooning on extra sauce—and just a dollop of sour cream! Garnish with extra cilantro sprigs.

Serves 4.

Red Enchilada Sauce

½ onion, chopped	½ teaspoon cumin
1 garlic clove, minced	2 tablespoons unbleached flour
1 tablespoon butter	2 cups chicken broth
¼ cup red chili powder	1 (14½ ounce) can tomatoes, diced small

In a large skillet, sauté onion and garlic in butter over medium-high heat until tender. Remove from heat; stir in chili powder, cumin, and flour. Slowly pour in broth, making a smooth paste. Continue to pour, being careful to not lump. Return to heat; add tomatoes, and cook until thickened.

MOM'S ENCHILADAS
For David

The Meat:

1 pound lean ground beef

1 onion, chopped

1 garlic clove, minced

1 teaspoon each, salt and pepper

Combine ingredients in a large skillet; cook over medium-high heat until browned. Drain; set aside.

The Sauce:

1 (12 ounce) can tomato paste

2 cans water

2 heaping tablespoons chili powder

½ teaspoon each, salt and pepper

Combine ingredients in a medium saucepan. Cook over medium heat until bubbly and thick, stirring.

Assembly:

1 pound Cheddar cheese, grated

12 corn tortillas

Place one tortilla at a time in sauce; lift and place flat in a 13 x 9 x 2-inch baking dish. Spoon a scant ¼ cup ground beef mixture onto one half the tortilla, 3 tablespoons cheese on top of meat, and 2 tablespoons extra sauce on top of cheese. Fold remaining half of tortilla over the filling. Repeat procedure for remaining enchiladas, placing them side by side. When completed filling tortillas, pour remaining meat on top of all, followed by the sauce and cheese. Bake, covered, at 350° for 30 minutes. When ready to serve, use a spatula to remove from baking dish onto individual plates.

Serves 6.

My mother has made these enchiladas for her family and friends for as long as I've known her. Mom likes to fry the tortillas before dipping them in the sauce— I don't, and she says that's why hers taste better! She also makes a wonderful iceberg salad for an accompaniment, filled with every salad vegetable she can manage to fit in, especially tomatoes. The cold iceberg lettuce, along with the tomatoes, provides just the right amount of moisture to go alongside these enchiladas. We actually place the salad on top of the enchiladas, and we never use a salad dressing. Hope you will enjoy them as much as her family and friends do!

JALAPEÑO CRÊPES
Filled with Crab and Dressed with Butter Sauce

Jalapeño Crêpes:

6 jalapeño chiles, stems and seeds
  removed
4 sprigs cilantro (or parsley)
4 eggs
2 cups unbleached flour

2 cups milk
1 teaspoon salt
¼ teaspoon sugar
5 tablespoons butter, melted

Place the above ingredients, excluding butter, in a food processor or blender. Mix until smooth; add butter and pulse a few times to blend. Allow to stand for one hour before making crêpes. Follow instructions on crêpe maker, or if you prefer: Slightly butter a 7- to 8-inch skillet; heat over medium-high heat. Ladle a scant ¼ cup batter in middle and tilt to spread, coating bottom of skillet. Cook one minute, or until bottom is slightly brown; turn over and cook second side until brown. (Keep batter stirred, and adjust heat as needed.) Cover cooked crepes lightly to prevent drying out.

Yield: 15 crêpes.

Crab Filling:

4 tablespoons butter, chilled, divided
1 tablespoon white wine vinegar
4 green onions, chopped

3 tablespoons cilantro, chopped
1 large tomato, seeded and chopped
1½ pounds lump crabmeat, cooked

Place one tablespoon butter, vinegar, onions and cilantro in a medium-sized skillet. Cook over medium- high heat until onions are tender (about 3 minutes). Remove from heat and whisk in the remaining butter, one tablespoon at a time, being careful to incorporate the butter rather than melt it. Mix in crabmeat. Keep warm until ready to assemble.

Butter Sauce:

1 cup butter, chilled
2 tablespoons white wine vinegar
6 green onions, chopped
4 roasted poblano chiles, seeded
  and sliced thin

1 large tomato, seeded and chopped
12 pimiento-stuffed olives, sliced thin
1 tablespoon Mexican capers
Fresh cilantro sprigs, for garnish

Melt ½ tablespoon butter with vinegar in a medium-sized skillet over low heat. Add onions and cook until soft, about three minutes. Whisk in remaining butter, bit by bit, making sure to incorporate rather than melt. (If at some point it begins to melt, remove from heat and whisk in more cold butter.) Add chiles, tomato, olives, and capers; mix well. Keep warm in thermos or double boiler.

Assembly: Fill crêpes with crab filling; fold sides together over filling. Place seam side down in a lightly oiled 13 x 9 x 2-inch baking dish; bake 10 minutes at 350°. Serve with warm Butter Sauce on top.

WARM LOBSTER TACO

2 pounds lobster meat, cooked
1 tablespoon butter
4 cups spinach, shredded

3 cups jalapeño jack cheese
6 (10 inch) flour tortillas, warmed

Using a large skillet over medium-high heat, sauté lobster meat in butter until heated thoroughly. Spoon equal portions of lobster, spinach, and cheese onto centers of warm tortillas. Roll and serve immediately with salsa on the side.

Serves 6.

The butter sauce used in the Jalapeño Crepes recipe would be great with these tacos (see previous recipe).

CHICKEN TACOS

2 roasted poblano chiles, seeds
   removed
3 boneless, skinless chicken breasts
2 large tomatoes, chopped
1 onion, sliced, rings separated

1 teaspoon fresh ground pepper
1 cup sour cream
6 (10-inch) flour tortillas, warmed
1½ cups Monterey Jack cheese,
   grated

Slice chiles into strips; set aside. Cut chicken breasts into ¼-inch strips; place in a large skillet coated with just a bit of oil. Cook over medium-high heat for four minutes; add tomatoes, onions, and pepper. Continue to cook until onion is translucent and chicken is cooked through (about 5–6 minutes). Spread 2–3 tablespoons sour cream down middle of each warm tortilla. Equally divide the green chile strips, chicken mixture, and cheese on top of sour cream. Roll up and serve warm with salsa.

Serves 6.

SHRIMP QUESADILLAS

¾ pound shrimp, peeled, deveined,
    and chopped
3 tablespoons butter
1 onion, chopped
2 garlic cloves, minced
1 jalapeño pepper, seeded and
    chopped fine

1 cup fresh corn kernels
2 tomatoes, chopped fine
3 tablespoons lemon juice
¼ cup cilantro, chopped fine
¼ teaspoon each, salt and pepper
8 (7 inch) flour tortillas
1 cup Monterey Jack cheese

Using a medium-sized skillet, stir-fry shrimp in butter over medium-high heat until barely done (about 4 minutes). Remove, and set aside. Place onion, garlic, jalapeño, and corn kernels in skillet. Cook until onion is tender; add shrimp, tomatoes, lemon juice, cilantro, salt, and pepper. Heat thoroughly. Divide mixture equally onto four tortillas and top with ¼ cup cheese. Place remaining tortillas on top. Place in a skillet, and grill over medium heat until cheese melts.

Serves 4.

Quesadillas are one of my favorite foods to eat, and they can be prepared in so many wonderful ways—be creative!

CHILES RELLENOS
(Vegetarian)

1 large onion, chopped
4 garlic cloves, minced
1 jalapeño, seeded and minced
1 (1 pound, 12 ounce) can tomatoes
½ teaspoon dried oregano
¼ teaspoon each, salt and pepper
1 cup corn kernels
1 cup zucchini, chopped

½–1 cup dry breadcrumbs
Salt and pepper, to taste
⅓ cup green onions, chopped
3 tablespoons cilantro, chopped fine
4 roasted poblano chiles, centers slit,
    seeds removed, stems intact (see
    index for roasting)

Place onion, garlic, and jalapeño in lightly oiled large skillet. Cook over medium-high heat until lightly browned. Transfer to work bowl of food processor, or a blender. Add tomatoes; blend until smooth. Strain through a wire mesh strainer into a medium-sized saucepan. Season with oregano, salt, and pepper; reduce mixture over medium heat until thickened. Set aside.

Combine Corn, zucchini, breadcrumbs, salt, pepper, green onions, and cilantro; mix well. Spoon into prepared green chiles. Bake at 350° for 20 minutes, or until hot.

Pour a small amount of tomato mixture onto individual serving plates. Top with a chile relleno.

Serves 4.

CHICKEN & GREEN CHILES
Wrapped in Flour Tortilla

2 roasted poblano chiles, seeds removed

1 large onion, sliced and separated

2 garlic cloves, minced

1 large tomato, chopped fine

2 tablespoons cilantro, chopped

Salt and pepper, to taste

4 (10-inch) flour tortillas

2 cups refried beans

1 cup Monterey Jack cheese

4 chicken breasts, cooked and sliced thin

Slice chiles; set aside. Place onion and garlic in lightly oiled large skillet. Cook over medium-high heat until lightly browned; add chiles and cook an additional minute. Remove from heat; gently stir in tomato, cilantro, salt, and pepper. Set aside.

Spread centers of flour tortillas with refried beans. Sprinkle with cheese, then chicken strips. Top with green chile mixture. Fold both sides of tortilla over center. Serve immediately.

Makes 4.

TRLICA'S PUMPKIN-STUFFED SHELLS
With a taste of Mexico!

16 large pasta stuffing shells, dried

2 cups prepared pumpkin

½ cup Italian breadcrumbs

1 teaspoon allspice

¼ cup Parmesan cheese

2 cups picante sauce

½ cup spicy Monterey Jack cheese, grated

Cook pasta shells according to instructions on package, stopping just before they are completely cooked. Drain; set aside. Combine pumpkin, bread crumbs, allspice, and Parmesan cheese in a large bowl; mix well. Spread a small amount of picante sauce on the bottom of a 13 x 9 x 2-inch baking dish. Spoon mixture into shells, being careful not to tear them (this is why you stop short of cooking completely!). Place side by side atop of picante sauce. Pour remaining sauce on top. Cover and bake at 350° for 25 minutes. Uncover, and top with Monterey Jack cheese; bake additional 5 minutes.

Serves 8.

MEXICAN CASSEROLE

1 whole chicken	1 (10½ ounce) can cream of
1 onion, chopped	chicken soup
1 garlic clove, minced	1 (10 ounce) can tomatoes
1 bell pepper, chopped	and green chiles
1 tablespoon butter	1 small bag (taco flavored)
1 (10½ ounce) can cream of	tortilla chips
musroom soup	2 cups Cheddar cheese, grated

Place chicken in a Dutch oven; cover with water and bring to a boil over medium-high heat. Reduce heat to medium-low and simmer until done (approximately 35 minutes). Remove chicken; drain and allow to cool. Once cool enough to handle, remove skin and bones. Chop into bite-sized chunks. Set aside.

Place onion, garlic, bell pepper, and butter in a medium-sized saucepan. Sauté over medium-high heat until onions are just tender. Add soups and tomatoes with green chiles; continue to cook, stirring constantly, until heated thoroughly. Remove from heat.

Assembly: In a large casserole dish, layer ingredients in this order: tortilla chips, chicken, soup mixture, cheese. Repeat, ending with cheese. Place in 350° oven for approximately 20 minutes, or until heated thoroughly.

Serves 6.

This casserole is best when served with a cold iceberg salad that's loaded with chopped tomatoes!

MEXICAN LASAGNA

1 pound lean ground beef	1 package taco seasoning mix
1 onion, chopped	8 flour tortillas, cut into strips
1 (10 ounce) can tomatoes with chiles	1 cup sour cream
1 (10 ounce) can tomatoes, chopped	1½ cups Monterey Jack cheese, grated
1 cup tomato sauce	¾ cup Parmesan cheese

Place ground beef and onion in large skillet. Cook over medium-high heat until browned; drain. Add tomatoes, tomato sauce, and seasoning mix. Cook 30 minutes over medium-low heat. Place half of meat mixture into a 13 x 9 x 2-inch baking dish. Place tortilla strips over the meat sauce; top with sour cream, followed by the cheese. Add remaining sauce; top with Parmesan cheese. Bake at 350° for 30–40 minutes, uncovered.

Serves 6.

Karen, you always have good recipes . . . thanks for sharing!

GRILLED FAJITAS

Flank steak (2 pounds), trimmed
6 (boneless, skinless) chicken
　　breasts
1 pound shrimp, peeled and
　　deveined
1½ cups lime juice
1 (12 ounce) can of beer
1 tablespoon chili powder
3 teaspoons ground cumin
3 teaspoons dried oregano
1 teaspoon salt
2 teaspoons fresh ground pepper

4 garlic cloves, minced
Cooking spray
2 onions, halved and sliced
2 poblano chiles, seeded and julienned
2 red bell peppers, seeded
　　and julienned
2 yellow bell peppers, seeded and
　　julienned
2 cups mushrooms, sliced
2 cups pepper jack cheese, grated
12 (10-inch) flour tortillas, warmed
Condiments: guacamole, sour cream,
　　pico de gallo, and salsa of choice

Place steak, chicken and shrimp into three separate (large) zip-closure plastic bags. In a glass measuring cup (4-cup or larger) mix lime juice through minced garlic. Dividing equally, pour into the three zip-closure bags; place in refrigerator and marinate for 6–8 hours.

Prepare outdoor grill, using some mesquite wood for smoke flavor. Heat grill to medium-high. Place steak, chicken, and shrimp on grill. Cook steak about 15 minutes per side, chicken 10 minutes per side, and shrimp about 3 minutes per side. Remove; allow steak and chicken to rest for 10 minutes, then slice into thin strips.

Return to grill; carefully cover rack with heavy-duty foil, being careful to keep sides free for air. Using a paring knife, make small slits on foil, and lightly coat with oil. Add chiles, peppers, and mushrooms. Stir-fry until onions are transparent and slightly browned; remove. Serve warm, by layering meat, veggies, cheese, and desired condiments in middle of warm tortilla.

Serves 6.

Like veggie fajitas? Well, first of all, eliminate the meat, then allow your imagination to run wild! Try julienned zucchini, squash, carrots, eggplant, spinach, asparagus, goat cheese—just whatever you have on hand that you think you would enjoy combining—there's no rule to this! (Is there?)

SOUR CREAM NOODLE BAKE

2 pounds lean ground beef
1 onion, chopped
2 garlic cloves, minced
2 cups tomato sauce
1 tablespoon sugar
2 teaspoons salt
½ teaspoon garlic salt

¼ teaspoon black pepper
1 (8 ounce) package noodles
1 cup green onions, chopped
8 ounces cream cheese, softened
2 cups sour cream
1½ cups Cheddar cheese, grated

Place ground beef, onion, and garlic in large skillet. Cook over medium-high heat until browned; drain. Add tomato sauce, sugar, salt, garlic salt, and pepper. Reduce heat and simmer for 20 minutes. Pour into a 13 x 9 x 2-inch casserole.

Cook noodles according to package directions, stopping just before they are completely cooked; drain. Add green onions, cream cheese, and sour cream; mix well. Pour on top of meat in casserole. Top with grated Cheddar cheese. Bake at 350° for 30 minutes. Serve hot!

Serves 6.

CHICKEN SPAGHETTI

2 cups chicken broth
1 (10 ounce) package spaghetti
1 tablespoon butter
1 onion, chopped
2 garlic cloves, minced
1 (10½ ounce) can cream of
   mushroom soup

1 (10½ ounce) can cream of
   chicken soup
1 cup milk
1 cup sour cream
Salt and pepper, to taste
2 cups cooked chicken breast, cut
   bite-sized
1 cup Provolone cheese, grated

Using a Dutch oven, bring chicken broth to a boil over medium-high heat; add spaghetti. Reduce heat and continue to simmer until tender. Drain; return to Dutch oven and set aside.

Over medium-high heat, cook butter, onion, and garlic in a medium saucepan until onions are translucent. Add soups, milk, sour cream, salt, and pepper. Continue to cook over medium-low heat until heated thoroughly, stirring often. Add chicken, and pour mixture over spaghetti; mix well. Place in a lightly oiled casserole dish; sprinkle cheese on top. Cover and bake at 350° for 20 minutes, or until thoroughly heated.

Serves 6.

Appetizers: Pineapple & Water Chestnuts Wrapped in Bacon, page 14; Roasted Sweet
Peppers with Cheese and Herbs, page 15;
Stuffed Cherry Tomatoes, page 20; Stuffed Jalapeños, page 3;
Paula's Shrimp with an Attitude, page 13.

Habitual Spinach Salad, page 42.

Mandarin Orange Tossed Salad, page 48.

Tortilla Soup, page 74.

Spaghetti Sauce with Meatballs, page 104.

Southern Fried Chicken, page 111.

Grilled Steaks with Green Chiles, page 129;
Asparagus Wrapped in Turnip Root, page 81;
Roasted Potato Fan, page 84.

Jamaican Jerked Pork Wrapped in Green Chiles, page 118.

Grilled Veggie Sandwiches, page 147; Potato Wedges, page 93.

Jalapeño Cornbread, page 167.

Cinnamon Rolls, page 173

Kolaches, page 174.

Blueberry Cheesecake, page 188.

Cranberry Cake with Hot Butter Sauce, page 198.

Strawberry Pie, page 215.

Peanut Brittle, page 234.

CRAB CAKES

¼ cup mayonnaise
4 tablespoons heavy cream
2 tablespoons Dijon mustard
2 eggs, lightly beaten
½ cup green onion, sliced thin
2 tablespoons celery flakes
1 garlic clove, pressed
½ teaspoon salt

¼ teaspoon ground white pepper
Dash of red pepper
1 tablespoon lemon juice
1¼ cups soft bread (torn into pieces)
1 pound cooked crab, shelled
2 cups fine breadcrumbs
¼ cup butter, divided
4 lemon wedges

In a large bowl, combine first eleven ingredients; mix well. Stir in bread pieces. Gently fold in crab, being careful to leave bite-sized chunks intact (this is what makes the crab cakes so delicious!). Form into patties, about 3 tablespoons each, and dust with fine breadcrumbs. Sauté in half the butter over medium heat in a large skillet, adding more butter as needed. Cook until both sides are browned, about 5 minutes each side. Drain on paper towels. Serve warm with lemon wedges.

Serves 4.

GRILLED VEGGIE SANDWICHES
on Focaccia Bread

1 eggplant, sliced into ¼-inch circles
3 portabella mushrooms, sliced
1 red bell pepper, sliced
1 onion, sliced and separated
2 yellow summer squash, sliced

2 zucchini, sliced
2 tomatoes, sliced
1 cup butter, melted
Focaccia bread (see index)
4 slices Monterey Jack cheese

Place all vegetables onto baking pan; baste with butter. Grill over medium-high heat on outdoor grill (cover rack with foil). Cut bread into serving size you desire; cut in half. Layer with grilled vegetables, topping with cheese; broil to melt.

Makes 4.

MY OMELET

4 tablespoons butter, divided
1 onion, sliced and separated
1 garlic clove, minced
1 red bell pepper, sliced
1 cup mushrooms, sliced
½ cup deli ham, sliced into strips
5 eggs

¼ cup milk
1 teaspoon each, salt and white pepper
1 cup fresh spinach, shredded
½ cup Monterey Jack cheese, grated
Sour cream and chopped tomatoes,
    optional

Combine 2 tablespoons butter, onion, garlic, bell pepper, and mushrooms in large skillet. Cook over medium-high heat until onions and bell pepper are just tender; set aside. Add ham to same skillet; heat thoroughly; set aside.

Place eggs, milk, salt, and pepper in work bowl of electric mixer. Beat on medium speed until smooth. Using two large skillets with non-stick surfaces, place one skillet over low heat. Place second skillet over medium heat; add remaining butter. Once butter is melted, pour egg mixture into skillet. Cook, lifting slightly with a metal spatula to allow uncooked portion to flow underneath. Once the omelet will no longer flow and the underside is slightly browned, flip omelet into the reserved skillet. (By this time, the skillet will be hot enough to cook this side.) Cook for about 2 minutes. Flip omelet back into its original skillet; turn off heat, but leave pan on burner. (The second skillet does not have to be used. I use it because I don't want the eggs in my omelet to be gooey!) Place the onion mixture and ham on one side of the omelet. Place the shredded spinach on top, followed by the Monterey Jack cheese. Fold the remaining half over the filling and press slightly with the spatula. Turn the other skillet over top, creating a lid. Allow to set for 3–4 minutes, allowing enough time for the cheese to melt. Serve warm, topped with a large dollop of sour cream and chopped tomatoes. This is delicious, beautiful . . . and huge!

Serves 2.

TAHOE BRUNCH

12 slices white bread

2 tablespoons butter, divided

½ pound fresh mushrooms, sliced

1½ cups onions, chopped

2 garlic cloves, minced

1½ pounds ground sausage

½ teaspoon white pepper

1 pound Cheddar cheese, grated

8 eggs

2 cups milk

1 teaspoon dry mustard

3 teaspoons Dijon mustard

1 teaspoon ground nutmeg

2 teaspoons dried parsley

1 teaspoon salt

½ teaspoon white pepper

Reserve crust and tear bread into bite-sized pieces; set aside.

Place half the butter in large skillet. Sauté mushrooms over medium-high heat until tender. Transfer to small bowl. Place the remaining butter and onions in same skillet. Sauté until onions are just barely tender; add garlic. Continue cooking until onions are translucent. Transfer to small bowl; set aside. Place sausage in skillet. Cook over medium heat until brown; sprinkle with pepper. Drain well, using paper towels and squeezing to remove as much grease as possible. Set aside. Grate cheese in medium-sized bowl; set aside.

Place eggs in work bowl of electric mixer. Beat over medium speed, gradually adding milk, until smooth. Add remaining ingredients; stir to blend.

Lightly oil a 9 x 13 x 2-inch casserole dish. Layer half the bread, mushroom mixture, sausage, and grated cheese. Pour egg mixture over all. Cover and refrigerate overnight. When ready to cook, bake at 350°, uncovered, for 50–60 minutes.

Serves 8.

Variation: *Omit the sausage and use a variety of fresh vegetables, such as chopped spinach, asparagus, or green beans.*

BREAKFAST PIZZA
with Sausage and Eggs

1 (8 ounce) can crescent roll dough
½ pound ground sausage
1 cup shredded hash brown potatoes
3 eggs, beaten
½ cup Cheddar cheese, grated

3 tablespoons milk
1 (4 ounce) can chopped green
  chilies
Salt and pepper, to taste

Shape crescent roll dough onto lightly oiled pizza pan; set aside.

Brown sausage in large skillet over medium-high heat. Drain well, using paper towels to soak up as much grease as possible. Sprinkle on top of pizza, followed by the hash browns. Combine the eggs and remaining ingredients; mix well. Pour over top. Bake at 375° for 30 minutes.

Serves 6.

BREAKFAST PIZZA
with Fresh Fruit

1 recipe sugar cookie dough
  (see index)
1 (8 ounce) package cream cheese
½ cup powdered sugar
1 tablespoon milk
3 apples, sliced thin
3 bananas, sliced

1 cup pineapple tidbits, juice reserved
4 kiwi fruit, peeled and sliced
1 quart fresh strawberries, sliced
½ cup seedless grapes (or blueberries)
Sweet Whipped Cream (see index)
Mint sprigs (optional garnish)

Roll chilled cookie dough ¼-inch thick into a circle and place on a lightly oiled pizza pan; prick with a fork. Bake at 375° for about 10 minutes, or until lightly brown. Cool.

Combine cream cheese, powdered sugar, and milk; mix well. Spread on top of cooled cookie dough.

Dip apples and bananas in reserved pineapple juice to help prevent browning; drain and set aside.

Starting with outside edge, begin layering fruit in a circular pattern in the order listed above (strawberries will fill the center). Sprinkle grapes and/or blueberries intermittently to create a pretty finished dish. Cover and chill. When ready to serve, cut into eight equal pieces. Place on individual serving plates and top with a dollop of whipped cream. Garnish with a sprig of mint!

Serves 8.

BREADS

FROM CRUSTED FRENCH TO BISCUITS

DINNER ROLLS
A Family Tradition

½ cup lukewarm water   ¼ cup sugar
1 tablespoon dry yeast

Mix together in a glass measuring cup; allow to stand until bubbly.

1 cup water   1 cup milk
¾ cup butter   2 eggs

Bring water and butter to a boil in a small saucepan over medium-high heat; remove from heat. Allow butter to continue melting; add ½ cup milk. In a small bowl, mix remaining milk with eggs; whisk thoroughly with a fork. Strain through a wire mesh strainer into the water mixture. Combine this mixture and the yeast mixture together in electric mixer work bowl.

4 cups unbleached flour   1 tablespoon salt
2 cups whole wheat flour   ½ cup butter, melted

Using the dough hook, slowly begin adding flour. Continue to mix on low speed until the flour is incorporated, scraping sides. Knead for about 3 minutes (if dough seems too sticky, add just a little more flour). Place in a lightly oiled bowl; cover. Allow to rise until double in bulk. Punch down. (At this point, the dough can be placed in a lightly oiled zip-closure plastic bag. Place in refrigerator until ready to use, up to one week.)

Equally divide the melted butter into three 13 x 9 x 2-inch baking pans. Make dough into balls approximately 1½ inches in diameter. Place in baking pans so that they barely touch when doubled in size, turning over once to butter tops. Loosely cover with lightly oiled plastic wrap; allow to double in size (about 1 hour). Bake at 400° for 15 minutes, or until lightly browned.

Yield: 3 dozen rolls.

I find I have better results in baking if I stir the flour to loosen it before spooning it into a measuring cup. I overfill the measuring cup and slide a flat spatula over the top to remove excess. We each have our own method of doing things, so keep this in mind as you work with bread dough, pastries, cookies and cakes.

SOURDOUGH BREAD

Starter:

2 teaspoons dry yeast
1¼ cups water

1¾ cups unbleached flour

Combine yeast and water in a glass jar. Allow to stand for 5 minutes. Using a wooden spoon (never use metal with sourdough bread), stir to dissolve. Add flour; stir to blend thoroughly. Cover with a dishtowel and allow to stand at room temperature for 48 hours. After this time, the starter is ready to use, or you may refrigerate up to five days. The starter will have a pleasantly sweet-sour smell.

To continue having a starter, replenish the remaining starter by stirring in one cup flour and ½ cup water for every cup of starter you remove. Stir to mix well. Cover and allow to stand at room temperature 12–24 hours. It is once again ready to use or refrigerate. Repeat procedure to continue having sourdough starter on hand. As time passes, the starter becomes even better tasting!

Bread Dough:

1 teaspoon dry yeast
¾ cup water
⅓ cup rye flour

2½ cups unbleached flour
1½ teaspoon salt
1 cup starter

Combine yeast and water in glass measuring cup. Allow to stand 5 minutes. Combine rye flour, unbleached flour, and salt together in a large, non-metallic work bowl. Mix thoroughly, leaving a well in the center. Pour in the one cup starter and the yeast mixture. Working the flour from the sides, mix to form a stiff, sticky dough. Should the dough seem too dry, add just a few more drops of water.

Turn the dough onto a lightly floured work surfaces. Knead until smooth, approximately 10 minutes.

Place dough in a lightly oiled bowl. Cover and allow to rise for approximately 2 hours. Punch down; allow to rest for 10 minutes.

Remove dough from the bowl. Shape into a round loaf. Place on a floured baking sheet; cover with a dishtowel. Allow to rinse until double size (approximately 1½ hours).

Place a cast-iron skillet on lower rack in oven. Preheat oven 425°.

Sprinkle dough lightly with unbleached flour. Make three horizontal slashes across the top of the dough, followed by three parallel slashes (about ¼ inch deep.) Add a few ice cubes to cast-iron skillet. Place bread in oven and bake for 1 hour, or until instant-read thermometer reads 200°. Remove from oven. Place on a wire rack to cool.

Makes 1 round loaf.

SWEET WHITE BREAD

This is a sweet bread with a nice, flaky crust. The starter is made in a manner similar to sourdough bread, except that you stop short of allowing the starter to sour. Planning ahead is most important, so muster up a plan of action—it is well worth you time!

First Stage Starter (suggested time 10:00 a.m.):

½ ounce (about walnut-sized) fully risen bread dough (left over from another bread dough recipe)

¼ cup warm water (110°)
⅔ cup unbleached flour

Pinch the dough into small pieces; place in warm water. Allow to soften for 5 minutes. Using your fingers, mix well. Add flour and mix well (the ingredients just need to be well incorporated). Place the dough in a clean bowl. Cover and allow to rise in a warm place (80–85° degrees) for 8 hours.

Second Stage Starter (suggested time 6:00 p.m.):

First Stage Starter (above)
¼ cup warm water (110°)

¾ cup unbleached flour

Repeat above instructions for mixing, and allow this starter to rise for 4 hours. Cover and chill for at least 1 hour, but no longer than 8 hours, before proceeding. (This is where you can adjust the timing during your planning stage.)

Final Dough (suggested times 6:00 a.m., first rise; 8:30 a.m., second rise; 11:00 a.m., baking time):

1¼ cups room-temperature water (78°)
½ teaspoon dry yeast (not rapid-rise)
Second Stage Starter (above)

3½ cups unbleached flour
1 tablespoon salt

Pour water into a large mixing bowl; sprinkle in yeast and stir by hand to mix. Deflate the second-stage starter; break into pieces and add to water. Allow to soften for 5 minutes. Using electric mixer and dough hook, add flour; pulse the machine on and off a few times to start mixing. Continue to mix on low speed until the flour is incorporated, then allow the dough to rest for 10 minutes. With the machine on low, sprinkle salt onto the dough; increase speed to medium-high and knead the dough for 5 minutes (the dough will be soft and moist). Transfer the dough to a clean bowl; cover and allow to rise for 1½ hours. After this rising, fold the dough down on itself a few times in order to deflate and redistribute the yeast (don't punch down—you don't want to lose the bubbly structure that's been developed). Cover and allow to rise for 45 minutes. After this rise, shape the dough. Separate the dough into four pieces. Cut each of these four pieces into thirds. Shape gently into a miniature baguette about four inches long (don't work the dough, or it will loose its bubbly texture). Place on a non-insulated baking sheet. Using a small dowel stick, press gently through center of dough, lengthwise, but not through the dough. Cover loosely with slightly oiled plastic wrap. Allow to rise until double in size (about 1 hour). Preheat oven to 450°. Place cast-iron skillet on lower rack. When ready to bake bread, put a few ice cubes in skillet to add moisture to oven (this aids in forming a hard outer crust). Bake bread for 15–20 minutes, or until a quick-read thermometer reads 200°. (It's best to use a cooking stone for baking, using a metal spatula to transfer.)

Makes 12 rolls.

This recipe may also be used to make baguettes. Cut dough in half; roll gently in palms to form a 14-inch-long baguette with slightly tapered ends. Allow to rise until double in size, following instructions as above. Using a razor blade, make three diagonal slashes across width of bread just before baking.

Makes 2 baguettes.

PIZZA CRUST

2½ teaspoons dry yeast
¼ teaspoon sugar
1 cup warm water (110°)
¼ cup white cornmeal

½ cup whole wheat flour
1 tablespoon salt
2 tablespoons olive oil, divided
2½ cups unbleached flour

Place yeast, sugar, and water in glass measuring cup; mix well and allow to stand until bubbly (about 10 minutes). Pour into electric mixing bowl; add cornmeal, whole wheat flour, salt, and 1 tablespoon of the oil. Using a dough hook, mix on low speed. Add unbleached flour gradually, a little at a time, to form a stiff dough. Knead dough until smooth and elastic (about 5 minutes), adding just a bit more flour if dough is too sticky. Transfer to a large bowl coated with the remaining tablespoon olive oil. Add dough, turning once to coat each side. Cover and allow to rise until double in size, about one hour.

Punch down. Separate, forming two balls. Using a rolling pin, roll into desired shape on floured surface. Transfer to a peel or pizza pan. Dress pizza to your liking! Bake at 450° on cooking stone until lightly browned.

Yield: 2 crusts.

BUTTERMILK BISCUITS

2 cups unbleached flour
4 teaspoons baking powder
¼ teaspoon baking soda
⅛ teaspoon salt

¼ cup butter
¾ cup buttermilk
3 tablespoons butter, melted

Combine first four ingredients in a large bowl. Cut in ¼ cup butter, using a pastry cutter. Mix until crumbly. Add buttermilk slowly, mixing until dry ingredients are moist (if dough seems too dry, add just a bit more milk). Place on a floured work surface. Using a rolling pin, roll ½-inch thick; cut with a 2½-inch biscuit cutter. Pour melted butter into a 13 x 9 x 2-inch baking dish. Arrange biscuits in dish, turning once to baste with butter. Bake at 350° for 18 minutes, or until light golden brown. Remove from oven; serve immediately.

Yield: 12.

DILL BREAD
Nancy's Recipe

1 tablespoon dry yeast
4 tablespoons sugar
½ cup warm water (110°)
2 cups cottage cheese, room temperature
2 tablespoons minced onions
2 teaspoons salt

½ teaspoon baking soda
2 teaspoons dill seed
2 tablespoons butter
2 eggs, beaten
5 cups unbleached flour
Melted butter for basting

Mix yeast, sugar, and water in a glass measuring cup; allow to stand until bubbly. Except for flour, place remaining ingredients in work bowl of electric mixer; add yeast mixture. Using dough hook, slowly add flour. Continue to mix, scraping sides as needed. Place in a lightly oiled bowl and cover with plastic wrap; allow to double in size (about 1½ hours). Punch down; divide dough into two lightly oiled loaf pans. Cover and allow to rise again until double in size. Bake at 350° for 30–40 minutes, or until instant-read thermometer inserted in middle reads 200°. Baste with melted butter.

Yield: 2 loaves.

PARKER HOUSE ROLLS

3½–4 cups unbleached flour, divided
2½ teaspoons dry yeast
1 cup milk, warmed
¼ cup sugar

¼ cup butter
½ teaspoon salt
3 egg yolks, lightly beaten
Melted butter for basting

In the work bowl of an electric mixer, combine 1½ cups flour and yeast; set aside. In a medium saucepan, heat and stir milk, sugar, butter, and salt until butter is just melted. Pour into flour mixture; add the egg yolks. Using a dough hook, mix on low speed, scraping the sides of bowl. Slowly add enough remaining flour until soft and pliable; knead for about 5 minutes. Place in a lightly oiled bowl; cover with plastic wrap. Allow to rise until double in size (about 1½ hours). Punch down.

Place dough on a lightly floured surface; roll ¼-inch thick. Cut with a 2½-inch round biscuit cutter. (Dip the cutter in flour to prevent sticking.) Brush cut rolls with melted butter. To shape, use a small dowel stick (or the back of a dinner knife) to make a slightly off-center crease in each round (press firmly, but don't go completely through). Fold large half over small half, overlapping slightly. Press folded edge firmly. Place rolls 3 inches apart on insulated baking sheets. Cover loosely with plastic wrap. Allow to rise in a warm place until double in size. Bake at 375° for 10 minutes, or until a light golden brown. Lightly re-baste with butter, if desired.

Yield: 24 rolls.

CHEESE-RYE TWIST

Cheese Bread:

2½ teaspoons dry yeast

½ cup warm water (110°)

½ cup milk

3 tablespoons sugar

1 teaspoon salt

1 tablespoon shortening

1 egg, slightly beaten

3½ cups unbleached flour

1 cup Cheddar cheese, grated

Whole Wheat & Rye Bread

  (recipe follows)

Egg wash (see glossary)

Sesame and Caraway seeds,

  for topping

Mix yeast and water in a glass measuring cup; allow to stand until bubbly. Place the milk in a small saucepan and scald over medium-high heat. Remove; add sugar, salt, and shortening. Allow to cool to 110°. Pour yeast mixture and milk mixture into electric mixer work bowl. Using a dough hook, add egg and mix. Slowly begin adding flour, using a little at a time, to form a soft dough. If dough is too sticky, add more flour, a little at a time. Once the flour is incorporated, add cheese and mix well. Place dough in lightly oiled bowl; cover with plastic wrap. Allow to stand until double in size (about 1 hour).

Whole Wheat and Rye Bread:

2½ teaspoons dry yeast

¼ cup warm water (110°)

3 tablespoons molasses

1½ teaspoons salt

2 teaspoons caraway seeds

2 tablespoons shortening

1 cup warm water (110°)

¾ cup rye flour

¾ cup whole wheat flour

2 cups unbleached flour

Mix yeast, water, and molasses in a glass measuring cup; allow to stand until bubbly. Place salt, caraway seeds, shortening, and water in electric mixer work bowl; add yeast mixture. Using dough hook, gradually mix in rye and wheat flour. Slowly add unbleached flour, kneading to form a soft dough. If dough is too sticky, add more unbleached flour, a little at a time. Place dough in a lightly oiled bowl; cover with plastic wrap. Allow to stand until double in size (about 1 hour).

Shaping and baking the bread:
Punch down both doughs; divide each into four parts. Roll each part into a 17-inch rope. Place a cheese rope and a wheat-rye rope side by side on a lightly floured surface. Twist the two ropes together, tucking the ends under to seal. Place on a lightly oiled insulated baking sheet. Repeat procedure for remaining loaves. Cover with plastic wrap; allow to rise until double in size. Once risen, baste with egg wash. Sprinkle sesame seeds on cheese dough and caraway seeds on wheat-rye. Bake at 375° until light golden brown (about 15 minutes), or until instant-read thermometer reads 200°.

Yield: 4 loaves.

TOMATO-WHEAT TWIST

Tomato Bread:

1 (8 ounce) can tomatoes
2½ teaspoons dry yeast
2 teaspoons sugar
¾ cup onion, minced

2 tablespoons butter
1 teaspoon salt
2 teaspoons celery flakes, crumbled
3 cups unbleached flour

Purée tomatoes and their packing juice in food processor. Pour into a small saucepan and heat over medium-low heat to 110°. Remove from heat; add yeast and sugar. Allow to stand until bubbly. Pour into work bowl of electric mixer; add onion, butter, salt, and celery flakes. Using a dough hook, slowly incorporate flour. If dough seems too sticky, add a little more flour. Place dough in a lightly oiled bowl; cover with plastic wrap. Allow to stand until double in size (about 1½ hours).

Whole Wheat Bread:

2½ teaspoons dry yeast
1 teaspoon sugar
¼ cup warm water (110°)
¾ cup water, room temperature
2 tablespoons olive oil

1½ teaspoon dried Italian herbs
1 teaspoon salt
¾ cup whole wheat flour
2½ cups unbleached flour
Egg wash (see glossary)

Mix yeast, sugar, and ¼ cup warm water in a glass measuring cup; allow to stand until bubbly. Pour remaining water, oil, herbs, salt, and yeast mixture into electric mixer work bowl. Using a dough hook, slowly add flour, scraping sides as needed. Knead for about 5 minutes. Place dough in a lightly oiled bowl; cover with plastic wrap. Allow to stand until double in size (about 1½ hours).

Shaping and baking the bread:
Punch down both doughs; divide each into 4 parts. Roll each part into a 17-inch rope. Place a tomato rope and a wheat rope side by side on a lightly floured surface. Twist the two ropes together, tucking the ends under to seal. Place on a lightly oiled insulated baking sheet. Repeat procedure for remaining loaves. Cover with plastic wrap; allow to rise until double in size. Once risen, baste with egg wash for a nice shiny glaze. Bake at 375° until light golden brown (about 15 minutes), or until instant-read thermometer reads 200°.

Yield: 4 loaves.

REFRIGERATOR ROLLS

2½ teaspoons dry yeast
¼ cup sugar
¼ cup warm water (110°)
1 cup milk
3 tablespoons butter

2 eggs, slightly beaten
1 teaspoon salt
3½ cups unbleached flour
½ cup butter, melted (for dipping)
Egg wash (see glossary)

Mix yeast, 1 teaspoon sugar, and water in a glass measuring cup; allow to stand until bubbly. Scald milk in a small saucepan over medium heat; add remaining sugar and butter; allow to cool to room temperature. Pour yeast mixture, milk mixture, two eggs, and salt into work bowl of electric mixer. Using a dough hook, slowly add flour. Knead until smooth and elastic (about 5 minutes). If dough is too sticky, add more flour, a little at a time. Place in a lightly oiled bowl; cover with plastic wrap. Allow to stand until double in size (about 1 hour).

Once dough has risen, punch down. Divide in half; place in a lightly oiled zip-closure bag. Place in refrigerator until well chilled, preferably overnight, punching down as needed. (It will keep for two days at this point.)

Shaping and baking the bread:
Remove dough from refrigerator; allow to stand 2 hours at room temperature. Lightly butter 24 standard-size muffin cups. Cut each dough half into 12 equal pieces. Roll each piece into a ball and dip into melted butter. Pull and stretch ball into a 6-inch rope. Tie into a knot, and place in muffin cup. Repeat. Brush rolls with egg glaze. Cover and allow to rise until double in size. Bake at 400° until lightly browned (12–15 minutes), or until quick-read thermometer reads 220°.

Yield: 24 rolls.

CRUSTED FRENCH BREAD
with Roasted Red Pepper and Garlic

1 tablespoon dry yeast
1½ teaspoons sugar
1½ cups warm water (110°)
3 cups unbleached flour
½ cup whole wheat flour
½ cup dry quick oats
1½ teaspoons salt

5 tablespoons roasted garlic pulp
5 tablespoons Monterey Jack
   cheese, grated
¾ cup roasted red peppers, chopped
Egg wash (see glossary)
Extra Monterey Jack cheese,
   for topping

Using a glass measuring cup, dissolve yeast and sugar in warm water. Allow to sit until foamy.

Combine 2 cups of the unbleached flour, along with the whole wheat flour, oats, and salt, in the work bowl of an electric mixer. Pour yeast mixture into flour mixture. Using a dough hook, mix well. Continue mixing, adding the remaining one cup flour until mixture is no longer sticky. Place dough in lightly oiled bowl, flipping once to coat both sides with oil. Cover with plastic wrap and allow to rise until double in size, approximately one hour.

After dough has doubled in size, punch down and turn out onto a lightly floured surface, and divide into two parts. Shape each portion into a rectangular shape approximately ¾ inch thick and 12 inches in length (I use a rolling pin). Sprinkle center of each portion with equally divided garlic, cheese, and roasted red peppers. Roll lengthwise into the shape of a loaf, pinching edges to seal.

Lightly oil a non-insulated baking pan; sprinkle with cornmeal. Place loaves on pan, seam side down, turning under the ends to form a well-sealed loaf. Cover with a lightly oiled piece of plastic wrap, and allow to rise for approximately 45 minutes in a warm place, or until double in size.

Once bread has risen, remove plastic wrap and make two or three shallow diagonal slices across tops of loaves. Brush each loaf with egg wash, and sprinkle the extra Monterey Jack cheese on top. Bake at 400° for 20–25 minutes, or until a light golden brown.

Yield: 2 loaves.

FRENCH BREAD

1 tablespoon dry yeast
2 tablespoons sugar
2½ cups warm water (110°), divided

1 tablespoon salt
6½–7 cups unbleached flour

Mix yeast, sugar, and ¼ cup of the water in a glass measuring cup; allow to stand until bubbly. Pour the remaining water and yeast mixture into the work bowl of electric mixer. Using dough hook, slowly add salt and flour. Continue to knead until dough is smooth, about 5 minutes. If dough seems too sticky, add more flour, a little at a time. Place in a lightly oiled bowl; cover and allow to rise until double in size (about 1 hour).

Punch down, and divide into four equal pieces. Using a rolling pin on a floured surface, roll each piece into a 7 x 15-inch oblong. Roll up, as for jelly roll. Place seam side down in a buttered 18-inch baguette pan. Repeat with remaining dough. Using a razor blade, make four slashes diagonally across width of each loaf of bread. Cover; allow to stand until double in size. Preheat oven to 450°. Bake loaves 15 minutes. Reduce temperature to 350°. Continue to bake until lightly browned and bread sounds hollow when tapped on bottom (about 30 minutes).

Yield: 4 loaves.

PUMPKIN CRESCENT ROLLS

2½ teaspoons dry yeast
4½ cups unbleached flour
1¼ cup milk
2 tablespoons shortening

2 tablespoons sugar
1 egg, slightly beaten
½ cup canned pumpkin
Melted butter, for basting

Combine yeast and 2 cups of the flour in work bowl of electric mixer. In a small saucepan, combine milk, shortening, and sugar. Heat over medium heat until shortening is melted. Cool to almost room temperature. Pour into dry mixture in mixing bowl. Add egg and pumpkin. Using a dough hook, beat at low speed, scraping sides of bowl as necessary, for about one minute. Increase speed to medium and mix for about 3 minutes. Gradually add more flour to make a soft dough; knead for about 5 minutes. Place in a lightly oiled bowl; cover and allow to rise until double in size (about 1 hour).

Divide dough into thirds, and place on a lightly floured work surface. Using a rolling pin, roll each third into a 12-inch circle. Brush with melted butter, and cut each third into 12 pie-shaped wedges. Roll up, starting with wide end of wedge. Place point side down on lightly oiled insulated baking sheet. Brush with remaining melted butter. Cover, and allow to double in size (about 1 hour). Bake at 400° 10–12 minutes, or until light golden brown.

Yield: 36 crescent rolls.

HERB ONION ROLLS

1½ cups warm water (110°)
1 tablespoon dry yeast
2 teaspoons sugar
4 tablespoons butter
¼ cup onion, chopped
2 garlic cloves, minced

½ teaspoon dried oregano
½ teaspoon diced tarragon
½ teaspoon dried basil
1½ teaspoons salt
4 cups unbleached flour
Egg wash (see glossary)

Mix water, yeast, and sugar in a glass measuring cup; allow to stand until bubbly. Using a small skillet over medium-high heat, melt butter. Sauté onion and garlic until onion is tender; cool to room temperature. Combine yeast mixture, onion mixture, oregano, tarragon, basil, and salt in work bowl of electric mixer. Using a dough hook, slowly add flour. Knead until smooth and elastic, adding more flour a little at a time if it seems too sticky. Place in a lightly oiled bowl; cover with plastic wrap. Allow to rise until double in size (about 1½ hours).

Punch down. Cut dough into 24 equal pieces. Using palms of hands, roll each piece into a smooth ball. Place in a well-buttered 13 x 9 x 2-inch baking pan, turning once to butter both sides; place 1½ inches apart. Cover and allow to rise until double in size. Glaze with egg wash. Bake at 350° until light golden brown, or instant-read thermometer reads 200°.

Yield: 24 rolls.

FOCACCIA

2½ cups warm water (110°)	6½ cups unbleached flour
2 tablespoons dry yeast	1 tablespoon salt
¼ cup olive oil	Fresh herbs or sea salt

Mix water and yeast in a glass measuring cup; allow to stand until bubbly. Pour into work bowl of electric mixer; add oil. Using dough hook, slowly add flour and salt. Knead until dough is smooth. If dough seems too sticky, add more flour, a little at a time. Knead about 5 minutes. (Dough should be in a nice soft ball and not clinging to sides of bowl.) Place in a lightly oiled bowl; cover with plastic wrap and allow to rise until double in size, about 1½ hours. (Don't punch down; rather, fold the dough over on itself to deflate it.) Allow to rise another 45 minutes to one hour. Fold the dough over on itself again, and cut into three separate pieces (handle it carefully—don't mash, for you want to keep the nice bubbles incorporated into the dough!). Place into three separate well-oiled zip-closure bags. Refrigerate 24–36 hours (it's this resting time that gives the bread its nice chewy texture and surface bubbles).

About 1½ hours before baking, gently remove the dough from the bags (you may have to cut the bags away from dough, instead of sliding it out of the bags). Place on a well-floured surface; cover. Allow to rest for about an hour to reach room temperature, or until it feels spongy to the touch. Place a cast-iron skillet on bottom rack in oven, and, if using a cooking stone, place rack in middle of oven. Preheat the oven to 450°.

If not using a cooking stone, prepare three baking sheets lined with parchment paper (place a little bit of cornmeal on top of parchment). Gently place each focaccia dough onto parchment paper. Using palms of hands, gently press down on dough, causing bubbles to appear on the sides. Slit the bubbles with a razor blade to release the gases. Gently pull and stretch into a square of about 8 inches. Cover; allow the dough to relax for about 10 minutes. Cut two horizontal slashes across top of dough, followed by two parallel slashes. Brush focaccias with olive oil and top with fresh herbs and sea salt. Slide onto cooking stone or non-insulated baking sheet. Place a few ice cubes in the iron skillet to create steam (this helps form a nice crunchy crust). Bake about 15–20 minutes, or until light golden brown. Remove from oven; place bread on rack to cool.

Yield: 3 focaccias.

This bread is delicious eaten with a meal or by itself. However, I make it for grilled veggie sandwiches. Time consuming? Yes, but if you plan ahead it's fun to do, and so well worth the extra effort.

PRETZELS

4½ cups unbleached flour
2½ teaspoons dry yeast
1½ cups milk
¼ cup sugar
2 tablespoons olive oil
1 teaspoon salt

1 tablespoon salt
1½ quarts boiling water
Egg wash (see index)
Coarse salt
Sesame seeds or poppyseeds

Measure half of the flour and yeast into work bowl of electric mixer; set aside. Place the milk, sugar, oil, and 1 teaspoon salt in a small saucepan. Over medium heat, cook to dissolve sugar; allow to cool to about 120°. Using a dough hook, combine the milk mixture with flour and yeast. Gradually add the remaining flour. Mix well, and continue to knead for about 3 minutes. (The dough will be soft and won't stick to the side of work bowl. If dough seems too sticky, add just a little more flour.) Place in a lightly oiled bowl; cover and allow to rise until double in size (about 1½ hours).

Punch dough down. Cover and allow to rest for about 10 minutes. Prepare insulated baking sheets by spraying them lightly with cooking spray.

Place the dough on a lightly floured surface. Using a rolling pin, roll into a 10 x 12-inch rectangle. Cut into eighteen ½-inch wide strips. Gently pull each strip to make a 16-inch rope. Shape ropes into pretzel form in this manner: Leaving about 4 inches at each end, cross one end over the other (this will create a circle above where you crossed). Twist one full turn where you just crossed. Fold ends up to the edge of circle and tuck on the underside. Moisten a bit; press to seal. (You'll get it—just practice!) Carefully place on prepared baking sheets, and bake at 475° for about 4 minutes. Remove from oven; reduce oven temperature to 350°.

Using a large skillet, add salt and water. Bring to a boil over medium-high heat. Place 3 or 4 pretzels at a time in boiling water (may have to increase heat to continue boiling). Boil for two minutes, turning once. Drain on paper towels. Place on baking sheets with cooking spray, about an inch apart. Baste with egg wash. Sprinkle with coarse sea salt and sesame seeds or poppyseeds. Return to oven and bake at 350° for an additional 20–25 minutes, or until light golden brown. Remove from oven; place pretzels on a rack to cool.

Yield: 18 pretzels.

My husband Don and I enjoy making these together—it's a fun thing to do!

QUICK & EASY GARLIC TOAST

2 garlic cloves, minced
¼ cup olive oil
1 tablespoon dried parsley

2 teaspoons dried thyme
1 (purchased) loaf sourdough bread
6 thin slices Monterey Jack cheese

Combine garlic and oil in a small skillet. Sauté over medium heat until garlic is barely cooked. Remove from heat; add parsley and thyme. Allow to cool.

Slice bread crosswise, about ¾-inch thick. Using a pastry brush, baste each slice with oil mixture. Place a piece of cheese on top. Place on a baking sheet and broil in oven until cheese melts. Serve warm.

GARLIC FLATBREAD

2¼ teaspoons dry yeast
1 teaspoon sugar
1 cup warm water (110°)
1 teaspoon salt

3 tablespoons butter, softened
3 cloves roasted garlic, mashed
3–3½ cups unbleached flour
Egg wash (see glossary)

Using a glass measuring cup, dissolve yeast and sugar in warm water. Allow to sit until foamy.

Pour yeast mixture into work bowl of electric mixer; stir in salt, butter, and garlic. Using dough hook, mix in one cup flour, adding more flour to make a soft dough. Turn dough onto lightly floured surface; knead until smooth (about 5 minutes). Divide dough into five equal balls; cover and allow to rest 10 minutes.

Place each ball onto a 14-inch piece of parchment paper. Using a rolling pin, roll out as paper-thin as possible. Brush lightly with egg glaze and place on baking sheet, or baking stone. Bake at 400° for 10–15 minutes, or until lightly browned. Cool on wire rack. To serve, break into pieces.

Yield: 5.

PITA BREAD

2½ teaspoons dry yeast
2 teaspoons sugar
1¼ cup warm water (110°)

1 teaspoon salt
4 cups unbleached flour
2 tablespoons olive oil

Combine yeast, sugar, and water in a glass measuring cup; allow to stand until bubbly. Combine salt and flour in a large bowl. Making a well in the middle of the flour, pour in the yeast mixture and oil. Using a wooden spoon, work flour into the liquid. Turn out onto a floured surface; continue to knead for about 10 minutes, or until a nice pliable ball is formed. If mixture seems too dry, add a little water to form a soft dough. Return to bowl; brush top with oil. Cover with dishtowel and allow to stand until double in size (about 1 hour).

Punch down. Separate into eight pieces. Roll into balls, cover, and allow to rest for 5 minutes. Using a rolling pin, roll into thin ovals (keep your purpose in mind—I like to shape mine a certain way for the type of stuffing I will be using). Place on lightly floured non-insulated baking sheets. Allow to rise, uncovered, for about 30 minutes. Gently turn over, and very lightly dust the tops with flour. Place in 475° oven for approximately 7 minutes, or until light brown. Remove; wrap in a dishtowel to soften. Once cooled, cut a small slice from the edge and press sides together slightly to open out the pockets.

Makes 8.

SOPAPILLAS

2 cups unbleached flour
1 tablespoon baking powder
½ teaspoon salt
2 tablespoons butter

⅔ cup warm water
Peanut oil, for deep frying
Honey, for topping

Using a medium bowl, combine the first three ingredients. Using a pastry blender, cut in butter until fine and crumbly (a food processor is good for this as well). Using a fork, gradually stir in water (dough will still be crumbly). Turn dough onto a lightly floured work surface; knead into a smooth ball. Divide in half; allow to stand 10 minutes, covered. Roll each half into a 10-inch square. Cut into 2½-inch squares, or any shape you desire. Deep-fry at 375° until golden, turning once. Drain on paper towels. Serve with honey!

Yield: About 16.

FLOUR TORTILLAS

3 cups unbleached flour
1 teaspoon salt

½ cup vegetable shortening
¾ cup warm water (110°)

Combine flour and salt in large mixing bowl. Using a pastry blender, cut in shortening until it has a blended, course consistency. Using fingers to blend, slowly add water, working the dough into a smooth ball (if dough seems too sticky, add just a bit more flour). Divide dough into 12 equal portions, and roll each into a ball. Place on a baking sheet; cover with a damp cloth.

Working with one ball at a time, place on lightly floured work surface. Using a rolling pin, roll into flat circles approximately 8 inches in diameter. Repeat with remaining balls, stacking one on top of the other, putting plastic wrap or parchment paper between them. Keep covered to prevent from drying out.

To cook, use a large, non-oiled, cast-iron skillet over medium-high heat. Working with one at a time, place prepared dough in skillet and cook approximately 30 seconds. Flip with a spatula and continue to cook for approximately 30 more seconds. (You can judge doneness by the brown spots on the tortilla. If it seems to be cooking too hot, then reduce cooking temperature.) Transfer cooked tortillas to a clean, dry kitchen towel, and cover to retain their warmth. Serve immediately.

Note: *To make appetizer-sized tortillas, shape into one-inch balls. Using a heavy-bottomed glass or a spatula, press flat. These are nice to make ahead of time when you're planning to have visitors!*

JALAPEÑO CORNBREAD

6 tablespoons butter
1 onion, chopped
2 garlic cloves, minced
1 red bell pepper, roasted, peeled,
    seeded, chopped
2 jalapeños, seeded and chopped fine
1 cup whole-kernel corn
1½ cups yellow cornmeal

1 cup unbleached flour
⅓ cup sugar
2 heaping teaspoons baking powder
1 teaspoon salt
1½ cups buttermilk
2 eggs
1½ cups Monterey Jack cheese,
    grated

Place butter, onion, garlic, red pepper (these can be purchased already roasted), jalapeños, and corn in a 10-inch cast-iron skillet; sauté over medium heat until onions are translucent (approximately 7 minutes). Remove from heat. Combine remaining ingredients (adding cheese last) in a large bowl; mix thoroughly. Using a slotted spoon, transfer the sautéed veggies into the cornmeal mixture. Mix thoroughly and pour back into the hot skillet. Place in oven and bake at 350° for 30–35 minutes, or until knife inserted in middle comes out clean.

Serves 6.

CORNBREAD

⅔ cup yellow cornmeal
¼ cup unbleached flour
2 tablespoons sugar
1 rounded teaspoon salt

1 heaping teaspoon baking powder
1 egg
½ cup milk

Combine the above ingredients in a medium bowl; mix well. Place a small well-oiled, cast-iron skillet on cooktop over medium-high heat. Pour batter into hot skillet, and allow to cook for about 30 seconds. Bake in oven at 425° until top is lightly browned (20–25 minutes).

Serves 4.

Variation: *Using this recipe, I make what we call **Indian Cornbread**. This recipe takes practice, but my family loves it, as the results are delicious. Here's how it works: Thin the batter just a bit, and place the following ingredients on counter next to cooktop: ½ cup chopped green chiles, ¼ cup chopped green onions, ½ cup creamed corn, 1 cup grated Cheddar cheese. Over medium-low heat, pour batter onto a hot, lightly oiled skillet to make a 3½- to 4-inch circle. Spoon on top about 1 tablespoon each of: chiles, onions, and creamed corn. Sprinkle lightly with cheese. Spoon a little more batter over the top. Use a fork to lightly spread batter as evenly as possible, so that the toppings are covered. Your 4-inch circle will now be about seven inches across. Continue to cook until the underside is brown. Now for the tricky part . . . using a large metal spatula, quickly flip! This is difficult to do, for there's a lot on top that can make a mess. Continue to cook until brown. (I mash top slightly with the spatula while this side is cooking.) Enjoy!*

Yield: 1–4.

SQUAW BREAD

2 cups unbleached flour
2½ teaspoons baking powder
½ teaspoon salt

2 tablespoons shortening
¾ cup water
Peanut oil, for deep-frying

Combine first five ingredients in work bowl of electric mixer. Using a dough hook, mix to form a soft ball. If dough seems too sticky, add more flour, little by little. Knead for about 3 minutes. Cover with lightly oiled plastic wrap; allow to rise for 45 minutes. Punch down. Pinching off a piece at a time, roll into balls about the size of large walnuts; pull outwards to thin. Deep-fry in hot oil at 375°. Drain well on paper towels. Serve warm with honey or jam. Yum!

Yield: 8 pieces.

BANANA BREAD

8 tablespoons butter, softened	1 teaspoon baking soda
1 cup sugar	2 cups unbleached flour
2 eggs	4 (medium-sized), bananas mashed
1 teaspoon vanilla	1 cup pecans, chopped
½ teaspoon salt	½ cup raisins, optional

Place butter, sugar, eggs, and vanilla in work bowl of electric mixer. On medium speed, beat well, stopping to scrape sides once. Add salt, soda, and flour; mix well. Add bananas; continue to beat on medium speed, stopping to scrape sides twice. Add pecans and raisins; slowly mix to blend. Spoon into lightly oiled muffin tins to three-quarters full. Bake at 375° for 15–18 minutes, or until wooden pick inserted in center comes out clean.

Yield: 2 dozen.

Instead of muffin pans, you may use a loaf pan or bundt pan. Decrease temperature to 325°, and increase cooking time to 55–60 minutes. And, along with all these various pan options, my mother tops it off by sprinkling sugar on top before baking. How much? Quite a little bit!

STRAWBERRY BREAD
Susan's Recipe

3 cups unbleached flour	¾ cup vegetable oil
1 teaspoon baking soda	4 eggs
1 teaspoon salt	2 cups frozen strawberries, thawed
3 teaspoons ground cinnamon	1½ cup pecans, chopped fine
2 cups sugar	

Combine the above ingredients, except pecans, in electric mixer work bowl. Mix on low speed until moist; increase speed to medium and mix well. Turn mixer off and scrape sides of bowl; continue to mix for another minute. Add pecans; mix to blend. Divide into two lightly oiled loaf pans. Bake at 325° for 55–60 minutes, or until wooden pick inserted in middle comes out clean. Remove from oven. Allow to cool 5 minutes in pan, then invert, releasing bread onto cooling rack. Carefully turn upright and allow to cool.

Yield: 2 loaves.

Option: *You may make mini-muffins with this recipe! Increase temperature to 375° and bake 8–12 minutes, depending on doneness desired.*

BLUEBERRY MUFFINS

1 cup butter, room temperature
½ cup vegetable oil
3 cups sugar
4 eggs
6 cups unbleached flour

1½ teaspoons baking soda
6 teaspoons baking powder
3 tablespoons Butavan (see glossary)
2 cups buttermilk
1 (15 ounce) can blueberries

Using work bowl of electric mixer, begin mixing the above ingredients (except blueberries) in order listed, scraping bowl as necessary. Drain blueberries, reserving liquid. Add liquid to mixing bowl; mix well. Using a rubber spatula, gently fold in blueberries. Spoon into lightly oiled mini-muffin tins to three-quarters full. Bake at 400° for 15–20 minutes, or until wodden pick inserted in middle comes out clean. (This batter can be mixed ahead of time and refrigerated for up to a week.)

Yield: 6 dozen.

POPPYSEED MUFFINS

2 cups unbleached flour
4 teaspoons baking powder
½ teaspoon salt
½ cup sugar
¼ cup poppyseeds

1 cup milk
¼ cup butter, melted
1 egg
½ teaspoon vanilla
¼ teaspoon almond flavoring

Combine the above ingredients in work bowl of electric mixer. Mix on medium speed until just blended, scraping sides of bowl one time. (I've heard that over-beating makes muffins tough—did you know that?) Spoon batter into lightly oiled mini-muffin pans, two-thirds full. Bake at 400° for about 15 minutes, or until lightly browned. Serve hot, warm, or at room temperature!

Yield: 2 dozen.

RAISIN BRAN MUFFINS
Mom's, of course!

1 (15 ounce) box bran cereal with raisins	1 tablespoon baking soda
3 cups sugar	1 tablespoon salt
5 cups unbleached flour	1 cup raisins
	1 cup pecans, chopped

Mix above ingredients in very large bowl; set aside.

4 eggs, beaten	1 quart buttermilk
1 cup butter, melted	2 teaspoons vanilla

Mix above ingredients in a medium-sized bowl; add dry ingredients. Mix well, using a strong spoon. (At this point, batter may be covered and stored in refrigerator for two weeks.) To bake, fill lightly oiled muffin tins two-thirds full; sprinkle tops with sugar. Bake at 400° for 15–20 minutes, or until lightly browned. Remove from oven, loosen from tins, and turn on sides to cool.

Yield: 4 dozen.

GINGERBREAD

2½ cups unbleached flour	¼ teaspoon salt
1 cup dark brown sugar	2 teaspoons instant espresso powder
1 teaspoon baking powder	½ cup applesauce
1 teaspoon baking soda	1 cup sour cream
1 teaspoon cinnamon	1 cup molasses
¼ teaspoon ground ginger	1 tablespoon balsamic vinegar
⅛ teaspoon cayenne pepper	⅓ cup canola oil
⅛ teaspoon coriander seed	1 teaspoon ginger root, grated
⅛ teaspoon ground cloves	2 tablespoons crystallized ginger, minced

Combine the above ingredients, except crystallized ginger, in work bowl of an electric mixer. Mix on low speed until moist; increase speed to medium and mix well, stopping twice to scrape sides of bowl. Using a rubber spatula, add crystallized ginger; mix well to blend. Pour into a lightly oiled, floured, 8-inch square pan. Bake at 325° for 60 minutes, or until wooden pick inserted in middle comes out clean. Remove from oven; allow to cool slightly before serving. Serve with Sweetened Whipped Cream, Vanilla Ice Cream, or Pears in Maple Sauce (see index).

Serves 9.

PUMPKIN BREAD
(Seedless)

4 eggs
⅔ cup water
1 cup vegetable oil
1 (16 ounce) can pumpkin
3 cups sugar
1½ teaspoons salt
2 teaspoons baking soda

1 teaspoon each, ground cinnamon
  and allspice
½ teaspoon each, ground nutmeg
  and cloves
1 teaspoon vanilla
3½ cups unbleached flour
1 cup pecans, chopped

Combine the above ingredients, except pecans, in the work bowl of an electric mixer. Mix on low speed until moist; increase speed to medium and mix well (if batter seems too thick at this point, add just a little more water—up to ¼ cup). Turn mixer off and scrape sides of bowl twice; mix well. Add pecans; mix to blend. Pour into two lightly oiled loaf pans dusted with flour. Bake at 350° for 1 hour, or until wooden pick inserted in middle comes out clean. Remove from oven; cool for 5 minutes. Carefully invert pan, placing bread on cooling rack.

Yield 2 loaves.

PUMPKIN BREAD
(Seeds included!)

3 eggs
1 cup sugar
¾ cup vegetable oil
1 cup canned pumpkin
½ teaspoon salt

1 teaspoon baking soda
1 teaspoon baking powder
¾ teaspoon ground cinnamon
1 cup unbleached flour
¼ cup pumpkinseeds, lightly roasted

Place eggs in work bowl of electric mixer; mix well on medium speed. Gradually mix in sugar, a tablespoon at a time, mixing well in between. Add oil and pumpkin; mix well. Add remaining ingredients, except seeds; mix well, stopping twice to scrape sides of bowl. Using a heavy spoon, gently mix in seeds. Pour into a lightly oiled loaf pan dusted with flour. Bake at 350° for 45–50 minutes, or until wooden pick inserted in center comes out clean. Remove from oven; allow to cool 5 minutes. Carefully invert pan, releasing bread onto cooling rack. Turn upright; cool.

Yield: 1 loaf.

Note: *Raw pumpkinseeds are generally found in health food stores. To roast them: Spread onto a baking sheet; bake at 350° for about 5 minutes, or until toasted to desired doneness.*

CINNAMON ROLLS
For a Special Mother's Day

Dough:

2 cups warm milk (110°), divided
1 tablespoon dry yeast
½ cup sugar
½ cup butter, room temperature

2 eggs, slightly beaten
6–6½ cups unbleached flour
1 teaspoon salt

Mix 1 cup of the milk, yeast, and sugar in a glass measuring cup; allow to stand until bubbly. Add remaining milk, yeast mixture, butter, and eggs in work bowl of electric mixer. Using a dough hook, slowly add flour and salt, scraping sides of bowl as needed. Continue to knead on medium speed until soft (about 4 minutes). Place in a lightly oiled bowl; cover. Allow to rise until double in size (about 1 hour).

The Filling:

½ cup butter, melted
1 cup sugar

1 cup brown sugar
1 tablespoon cinnamon

Excluding butter, combine the above ingredients in a small bowl; mix with a fork to blend. The butter will be called for in "making the rolls" section, below.

The Glaze:

3½ cups powdered sugar
4 tablespoons butter, softened

½ teaspoon vanilla
¼ cup milk

Combine the above ingredients in work bowl of electric mixer. Beat on medium speed until well blended.

Making the rolls: Remove dough from bowl; punch down and divide in half. Using half the dough at a time, place on a lightly floured work surface. Using a rolling pin, roll dough into a ¼–½-inch-thick rectangle (about 8 x 12 inches). Using a pastry brush, baste top with a small amount of the melted butter, and sprinkle with half the dry filling. Roll up in a jellyroll fashion, pinch seam to seal, and cut into one-inch slices. (Repeat with remaining half of dough.) Place rolls on a lightly oiled insulated baking sheet, and baste with a small amount of butter. Allow to rise until doubled in size. Bake at 350° for 12–15 minutes, or until light golden brown. Remove from oven and allow to cool slightly. Spoon glaze on top while they're still warm.

Yield: 2 dozen.

KOLACHES
As Low-fat as I Dare!

½ cup warm water (110°)
½ cup sugar
1 tablespoon dry yeast
1 cup light sour cream,
    room temperature

4 tablespoons butter, soft
1½ teaspoons salt
2 eggs, room temperature
4½ cups unbleached flour

Mix water, sugar, and yeast in a glass measuring bowl; allow to stand until bubbly. Place sour cream, butter, salt, and slightly beaten eggs in work bowl of electric mixer; add yeast mixture. Using a dough hook, slowly began adding flour, a little at a time, until flour is incorporated. Scrape sides of bowl as necessary. Increase speed to medium and continue to knead until dough is smooth, about 4 minutes. If dough seems too sticky, add just a bit more flour, a little at a time. (The dough should feel tender and soft to the touch.) Place in a lightly oiled bowl; cover with plastic wrap and allow to stand until double in size (about 1½ hours). Punch down. If you choose to not bake at this point, place in a lightly oiled zip-closure bag. Refrigerate until ready to use. (Nice to have on hand when you expect guests!)

When ready to bake, slightly oil fingertips, and make dough into balls about the size of large walnuts. Place on a lightly oiled insulated baking sheet, and loosely cover with plastic wrap. Allow to rise until double in size. Punch center down flat, leaving a small outside rim around edge. Brush lightly with heavy cream or egg wash to make a pretty glaze once baked. Fill centers with approximately 2 teaspoons filling of your choice. Sprinkle with Sweet Crumb Topping. Bake at 350° for 15–20 minutes, or until lightly browned.

Yield: About 5 dozen.

Sweet Crumb Topping:

1 cup unbleached flour
1 cup sugar

⅓ cup butter, melted (not hot)

Place flour and sugar in food processor or blender. Slowly pulse while adding butter slowly. It is ready when it is sticking together slightly and crumbly. Store in airtight container in freezer.

Pineapple Topping:

1 cup crushed pineapple
2 tablespoons unbleached flour

2 tablespoons butter

Combine pineapple and flour in small saucepan; mix well to smooth flour. Cook over medium heat until thickened. Remove; stir in butter. Cool. Use about 2 teaspoons per kolache.

Apricot Filling:

1 (8 ounce) package dried apricots	**2 tablespoons butter**
1¼ cup sugar	**½ teaspoon vanilla**

Place apricots in medium saucepan; cover with water. Bring to a boil over medium-high heat; reduce heat and simmer for about 25 minutes. Add sugar; boil for 10 minutes, stirring constantly. Drain and reserve juice. Mash apricots and season with butter and vanilla. If consistency seems too thick, add some of the reserved juice. Allow to cool. Use approximately 2 teaspoons per kolache.

Cottage Cheese Filling:

1 pound cottage cheese, mashed	**3 tablespoons (quick) cream of wheat**
¾ cup sugar	**3 tablespoons butter, melted**
2 egg yolks, slightly beaten	**1 tablespoon lemon zest**

Place the above ingredients in top of double boiler. Cook, stirring continuously, over medium heat until somewhat thickened. (If mixture doesn't thicken as you feel it should, add just a little more cream of wheat.) Allow to cool. (Mixture will continue to thicken as it cools, and it must be cool to place onto kolache dough.) Use approximately 2 teaspoons per kolache.

Poppyseed Filling:

3 cups sugar	**½ cup poppyseeds**
1 cup heavy cream	**1 teaspoon vanilla**
½ cup milk	**3 tablespoons butter**

Except vanilla and butter; place above ingredients in a medium-sized saucepan. Cook over medium-high heat, stirring constantly, until candy thermometer reaches 235° (soft ball stage). Remove from heat; add vanilla and butter. Whip with a large spoon to progress cooling. When cool enough to handle, roll into small balls (about ½ inch in diameter). Place on a baking sheet; freeze. Remove; place in zip-closure bag until ready to use.

When ready to make: Place one ball in the center of dough piece (before second rising), and form into a ball. Make sure you have sealed it thoroughly, or it will run while baking . . . this is the trick I haven't completely conquered! I have learned that it's most important to allow dough to rise fully before baking. If tiny holes form, pinch them together. You will have some "runners" anyway, but they are still worth making. My family would be royally grieved if I didn't include these in this book.

Thank you, Pat, for sharing your original recipe with me. I still have it, but this one is lower in fat and the dough holds over well in the refrigerator. I didn't change your fillings, though!

POPOVERS

1 cup unbleached flour	**1 cup milk**
¼ teaspoon salt	**1 tablespoon butter, room temperature**
3 eggs	**1½ tablespoons butter, for pan**

Place flour, salt, eggs, milk, and 1 tablespoon butter in work bowl of electric mixer. Mix on medium speed, stopping twice to scrape sides of bowl. Increase speed to medium-high, and continue to mix until mixture is smooth.

Lightly oil cups of a popover pan. Equally divide the 1½ tablespoons butter into 6 pieces. Put one piece butter in each cup of popover pan. Place pan in 425° preheated oven for about 1 minute to heat pan and melt butter. Carefully remove from oven and fill each cup half full with batter. Bake 20 minutes; reduce temperature to 325° and continue baking 15–20 minutes, or until lightly browned. Remove from oven; serve warm with flavored butters, cream cheese, or jam!

Yield: 6 popovers.

Variation: *Increase salt to 1 teaspoon; add 1 egg, ½ teaspoon baking powder, and 6 pressed garlic cloves.*

HOMEMADE PANCAKES

3 cups unbleached flour	**4 tablespoons sugar**
4 teaspoons baking powder	**2 eggs**
1 teaspoon baking soda	**2 cups buttermilk**
1 teaspoon salt	**¼ cup butter, melted**

Place ingredients in medium-sized bowl. Using a fork, mix until thoroughly blended (batter will be a bit lumpy, and if it seems too thick, add a little more milk). For each pancake, pour ¼ cup batter onto hot griddle. Turn when pancakes are covered with bubbles and edges are looking dry (I peek at the underside to see if browned!). Serve when both sides are brown. (I place them in the oven at 200°, along with the plates, until I have made enough so that everyone can sit down together to eat . . . be that for two or twenty!) No need to serve extra butter—just pass some warm New England maple syrup.

Serves 4.

WHOLE WHEAT PANCAKES

2 cups unbleached flour
2 cups whole wheat flour
4 teaspoons baking powder
1 teaspoon salt
½ teaspoon baking soda

2 cups buttermilk
2 cups milk
2 eggs
¼ cup butter, melted

Place ingredients in medium-sized bowl. Using a fork, mix until thoroughly blended (batter will be a bit lumpy). For each pancake, pour ¼ cup batter onto hot griddle. Turn when pancakes are covered with tiny bubbles and edges are looking dry. Continue to grill, approximately one minute, or until lightly browned.

Serves 6.

ASHLEY'S OATMEAL PANCAKES
Founded in 1997

1 cup unbleached flour
1 cup (quick cook) oatmeal
1½ cups buttermilk
½ cup milk
2 tablespoons sugar

4 tablespoons butter, melted
2 teaspoons baking powder
1 teaspoon baking soda
1 teaspoon salt
2 eggs

Place ingredients in medium-sized bowl. Mix until thoroughly blended (batter will be a bit lumpy). For each pancake, pour ¼ cup batter onto hot griddle. Turn when pancakes are covered with tiny bubbles and edges are looking dry. Continue to cook for one minute, or until lightly browned.

Serves 4.

BELGIAN WAFFLES

3½ cups unbleached flour
3 tablespoons sugar
1½ tablespoons baking powder
1 teaspoon salt

4 cups milk
½ cup butter, melted, cooled
3 eggs

Place ingredients in work bowl of electric mixer. Mix on medium speed until well blended, scraping sides of bowl once. Allow to stand for 3 minutes before cooking. Cook on preheated Belgian waffle iron, following manufacturer's instructions. Best to serve immediately—however, I generally have guests when I prepare waffles and hold them over in a 200° oven until we can all eat together! I enjoy topping with sifted powdered sugar, whipped cream, and strawberries!

Serves 6.

JO ANN'S WAFFLES

2 cups all-purpose baking mix
1 egg

½ cup oil
1 cup club soda

Place the above ingredients in work bowl of electric mixer. Mix on medium speed until well blended, scraping sides of bowl once. Cook on preheated waffle iron, following manufacturer's instructions.

This is a great recipe for people who are allergic to milk products, and the waffles are crispy and delicious!

DESSERTS

FROM CRÈME BRULÉE
TO BROWNIES

RED BERRY GRATIN

8 cups ripe strawberries, quartered
2 tablespoons strawberry liqueur
1½ cups heavy cream

3 egg yolks, whisked
¾ cup powdered sugar, sifted
1 teaspoon vanilla

Gently mix quartered strawberries together with liqueur; equally fill six 2-cup soufflé dishes. Pour cream into work bowl of electric mixer; beat on medium speed until thickened. Gently fold in whisked egg yolks, powdered sugar, and vanilla; mix well to blend. Spoon evenly over berries. Bake at 400° for about 5 minutes. Broil a few seconds only to brown tops lightly. Serve immediately.

Serves 6.

BANANAS FOSTER PRALINE

3 tablespoons butter
¼ cup brown sugar
3 bananas, halved and sliced in
  half lengthwise

1 ounce praline liqueur
½ cup pecans, broken
1½ ounces rum
Vanilla ice cream

Melt butter over medium heat in a large skillet. Add brown sugar, stirring to dissolve until it becomes syrupy. Add bananas, praline liqueur, and pecans; cook until bananas are slightly soft, turning once. Add rum and flambé, if you choose—or cook for about 30 more seconds. Serve immediately over six individually prepared servings of vanilla ice cream or dessert crêpes filled with vanilla ice cream!

Serves 6.

SAUTÉED PEARS
in White Wine Sauce

4 pears, peeled, cored, sliced
  ½-inch thick
3 tablespoons butter
½ cup sugar
¼ cup water

½ cup white wine
1 tablespoon lemon juice
½ teaspoon lemon zest
Brie cheese and dry toast squares

Sauté pear slices and butter over medium heat in a large skillet for about 3 minutes. Add remaining ingredients and continue to simmer until pears are tender. Serve warm with Brie cheese and dried toast squares.

Serves 4.

WHITE CHOCOLATE CRÈME BRÛLÉE

**4 cups heavy cream, divided
(room temperature)
8 ounces white chocolate
2 teaspoons vanilla**

**10 egg yolks, room temperature
1 cup sugar
½ cup brown sugar**

Combine one cup of the cream and the white chocolate in a small, heavy saucepan. Cook over medium heat, stirring constantly, until chocolate melts. Stir in vanilla; set aside.

Place egg yolks in work bowl of electric mixer. Beating on medium speed, slowly add the sugar and the remaining 3 cups of heavy cream until sugar is dissolved (may need to reduce speed if cream seems to spatter out of the work bowl). Add the white chocolate mixture; mix thoroughly. Pour into six individual-sized ramekins. Place ramekins in a 13 x 9 x 2-inch baking pan. Add about two inches of boiling water to the pan, surrounding the ramekins. Place in a 275°, preheated oven. Bake for one hour, or until set. Remove from oven, and allow to cool to room temperature while still in pan. Once cooled, remove ramekins from water in pan. Cover and refrigerate until well chilled (about six hours). When ready to serve, sprinkle tops with 2 teaspoons brown sugar each. Place ramekins on a baking sheet and place under broiler in oven. Broil six inches from heat (leaving oven door partially open) until sugar melts. Let stand for a few minutes, allowing the sugar to harden before serving.

Serves 6.

All ingredients must be room temperature, or cooking time will increase. Also, please note that this rich, smooth custard should be served very cold.

BASIC DESSERT CRÊPES

**4 eggs
1 cup unbleached flour
2 tablespoons sugar**

**1 cup milk
¼ cup water
1 tablespoon butter, melted**

Combine the above ingredients in a food processor or blender. Blend for 15 seconds; scrape down sides. Continue to blend for about 30 seconds, or until well blended and smooth. Refrigerate batter one hour. Cook on upside-down crêpe griddle, or use method you prefer.

Yield: 25 crepes.

CHOCOLATE CRÊPES

3 eggs
1 cup unbleached flour
2 tablespoons sugar

2 tablespoons cocoa
1¼ cups buttermilk
2 tablespoons butter, melted

Combine the above ingredients in a food processor or blender. Blend for 15 seconds; scrape down sides. Continue to blend for about 30 seconds, or until well blended and smooth. Refrigerate batter one hour. Cook on upside-down crêpe griddle, or use method you prefer.

Yield: 25 crêpes.

LEMON CRÊPES

1½ cups unbleached flour
1 tablespoon sugar
Dash of salt
3 eggs

1½ cups milk
1 tablespoon butter, melted
1 tablespoon brandy
1 teaspoon lemon zest

Combine above ingredients (except lemon zest) in a food processor or blender. Blend 15 seconds; scrape down sides. Continue to blend for about 30 seconds, or until smooth. Refrigerate batter one hour. Cook on upside-down crêpe griddle, or use method you prefer.

Yield: 25 crepes.

ALL-PURPOSE CRÊPES

4 egg yolks
4 eggs
1¼ cups unbleached flour

1 cup milk
1 tablespoon vegetable oil

Combine above ingredients in a food processor or blender. Blend 15 seconds; scrape down sides. Continue to blend for about 30 seconds, or until well blended and smooth. Refrigerate one hour. Cook on upside-down crêpe griddle, or use method you prefer.

Yield 25 crêpes.

STRAWBERRY-FILLED CRÊPES

3 cups fresh strawberries, sliced
⅓ cup sugar
1 cup cottage cheese
1 cup sour cream

½ cup powdered sugar, sifted
12 prepared dessert crêpes (see index)
1 cup fresh strawberries, for garnish
Fresh sprigs of mint, for garnish

Combine strawberries and sugar in a medium-sized bowl; set aside. Place cottage cheese in food processor or blender; mix until smooth. Add sour cream and powdered sugar; mix to blend thoroughly. Place ¼ cup sliced strawberries in center of each crêpe; top with cream mixture. Fold two sides of each crêpe over the middle, one side at a time, overlapping. Top with a small amount of remaining cream mixture. Garnish with fresh strawberries and sprigs of mint. Serve very cold.

Serves 6.

PRALINE CRÊPES
with Cinnamon Cream

The Cinnamon Cream:
2 cups light cream, divided
¼ teaspoon ground cinnamon

4 egg yolks
¼ cup sugar

Combine one cup cream with cinnamon in a medium-sized saucepan. Combine the remaining cup of cream with the egg yolks in a two-cup glass measuring cup; whisk well. Strain the egg mixture through a wire mesh strainer into the saucepan containing the milk and cinnamon. Add sugar; stir to blend. Cook over medium-high heat, stirring constantly, until thickened. Remove from heat and allow to cool. Pour into a bowl; cover and refrigerate until cold.

The Grand Finale:
1 cup butter
¼ cup light brown sugar
2 cups praline liqueur

8 prepared dessert crêpes (see index)
¼ cup brandy
Prepared cinnamon cream

Melt butter in large skillet over medium-high heat; add sugar and cook until transparent in color. Add liqueur; continue cooking until mixture reduces to a syrup. Add one crêpe at a time, folding into the syrup. Add brandy; flambé, if you choose, or cook an additional 30 seconds. Place two crêpes on each individual serving plate. Top with Cinnamon Cream. Garnish with pecans if you desire.

Serves 4.

Variation: *Add one cup heavy cream to chilled cinnamon cream, along with an extra ¼ teaspoon ground cinnamon. Freeze in ice cream machine, as per instructions. This is a good dessert ice cream to serve with apple, apricot, peach, and pear dishes.*

CHOCOLATE CRÊPE SOUFFLÉ
with Espresso Sauce

The Soufflé:

3 egg yolks

1 cup milk

2 tablespoons unbleached flour

¼ cup sugar

1 teaspoon vanilla

¼ cup unsweetened cocoa powder

6 egg whites

1 teaspoon lemon juice

½ cup sugar

12 prepared chocolate crêpes (see index)

Powdered cocoa, for garnish

Fresh strawberries or raspberries

Combine egg yolks and milk in a two-cup glass measuring cup; mix well, using a fork. Using a wire mesh strainer, strain egg mixture into a small bowl. Place flour and ¼ cup sugar in a medium-sized saucepan. Slowly add egg mixture to the flour mixture, stirring to blend well; add vanilla. Cook over medium heat until thickened, stirring constantly to prevent lumping. Remove from heat; sprinkle top with cocoa. Whisk to blend. Set aside to cool.

Place the egg whites and lemon juice in work bowl of electric mixer. Beat on medium speed until foamy. Gradually begin adding ½ cup sugar. Continue to beat on medium-high until stiff peaks, but not dry peaks, form. Using a rubber spatula, gently fold the chocolate mixture into this egg mixture; blend thoroughly.

Assembly: Spoon about ⅓ cup soufflé mixture onto the middle of each crêpe. Gently fold two sides of each crêpe over the middle, one side at a time, overlapping. Place on a baking sheet; bake at 400° for about 5 minutes, or until soufflé has set. Remove from oven. Transfer to individual serving plates, using a metal spatula. Dust tops lightly with sifted cocoa, drizzle with Espresso Sauce, and garnish with fresh strawberries or raspberries.

Serves 6.

Espresso Sauce

2 cups heavy cream

2 tablespoons instant espresso powder

16 ounces bittersweet chocolate

Place the above ingredients in top of a double boiler. Heat over medium heat until chocolate melts and blends smoothly.

CHERRIES JUBILEE CRÊPES

2 (16½ ounce) cans pitted dark
   cherries
1 tablespoon cornstarch
4 tablespoons currant jelly
2 tablespoons brandy

6 cups vanilla ice cream
12 prepared dessert crêpes (see index)
½ cup powdered sugar
2 cups prepared whipped cream (sweet)

Drain cherries, reserving liquid in a small bowl. Dissolve cornstarch in a small amount of reserved liquid, adding the remaining liquid and currant jelly. Place in a medium-sized saucepan and heat to thicken over medium heat. Stir in cherries and brandy; heat thoroughly. Keep warm.

Place ½ cup vanilla ice cream in middle of each dessert crêpe. Fold two sides of each crêpe over the middle, one side at a time, overlapping. Place two crêpes onto well-chilled, individual serving plates. Lightly sift powdered sugar on top of crêpes and plate. Spoon hot cherry mixture on top, and garnish with whipped cream.

Serves 6.

Suggestion: *Prepare the ice cream and crêpes ahead of time; freeze until ready to serve.*

LEMON-FILLED CRÊPES

3 tablespoons cornstarch
1 cup sugar
1 cup water
3 egg yolks
1 tablespoon butter

1 tablespoon lemon zest, divided
½ cup lemon juice
12 lemon crêpes (see index)
½ cup powdered sugar
2 cups prepared whipped cream (sweet)

Combine cornstarch and sugar in a medium-sized saucepan. Slowly add ½ cup water, stirring to dissolve cornstarch. Combine the remaining water and egg yolks in a one-cup glass measuring cup; mix well, using a fork. Strain the egg mixture through a wire mesh strainer into the cornstarch mixture. Cook until thickened over medium heat (about 5 minutes), stirring constantly. Remove from heat. Stir in butter, half of the lemon zest, and lemon juice; mix well. Allow to cool; cover and refrigerate until very cold. Fill each crêpe with equally divided amount of filling. Gently fold two sides of each crêpe over the middle, one side at a time, overlapping. Serve two crêpes each on chilled individual serving plates. Lightly dust tops of crêpes and plates with powdered sugar. Top with a small amount of whipped cream and garnish with the remaining half of lemon zest.

Serves 6.

CRÊPE BOWLS
with Lime and Blackberries

6 dessert crêpes, warm
1 egg yolk
½ cup milk, divided
1 tablespoon cornstarch
⅓ cup sugar, divided

½ teaspoon lime zest
2 tablespoons lime juice
3 egg whites
Blackberry Sauce (recipe follows)
½ cup powdered sugar

Lightly spray six 6-ounce ramekins with cooking spray. Place one warm crêpe inside a ramekin, forming a bowl shape. Place another ramekin inside, or fill with some pastry weights until crêpes are cool.

Combine egg yolk and ¼ cup of the milk in a one-cup glass measuring cup. Beat with a fork; pour through a strainer into a large saucepan. Using the same measuring cup, mix the cornstarch with the remaining ¼ cup milk. Stir to dissolve cornstarch; pour into the saucepan, along with the egg mixture and half the sugar. Cook over medium heat until thick. Add zest and lime juice; stir well. Set aside to cool.

Place the egg whites in the work bowl of electric mixer. Beat on medium speed until foamy. Begin adding the remaining sugar, a little at a time. Increase speed to medium-high, and continue to beat until stiff peaks, but not dry peaks, form. Gently fold into the lime mixture with a rubber spatula; blend well.

Remove the inner ramekin, or pastry weights, from the crêpes. Equally spoon lime filling into each crêpe. Place ramekins on a baking sheet, and bake at 375° for 15 minutes, or until filling appears puffy and lightly golden. Remove from oven, and carefully lift crêpe cups from ramekins. Place on individual serving plates that have been prepared with Blackberry Sauce drizzled on top. Lightly dust the filling with sifted powdered sugar.

Serves 6.

Blackberry Sauce

2 cups blackberries, fresh or
   frozen (thawed)
½ cup sugar

¼ cup blackberry jam (seedless)
1 tablespoon lime juice

Place blackberries in a food processor or blender. Purée; strain into a medium-sized saucepan and discard seeds. Add sugar, jam, and lime juice; cook over medium heat until sugar dissolves. Continue to cook for an additional 3 minutes, stirring continuously. Remove from heat and allow to cool. Cover and refrigerate.

CHEESECAKE
Topped with Cherry Sauce

The Crust:

1½ cups unbleached flour

½ cup sugar

2 teaspoons lemon zest

¾ cup butter, cold

2 egg yolks, slightly beaten

½ teaspoon vanilla

Combine flour, sugar, and zest in a food processor. Gradually add butter, a little at a time, until fine and crumbly. Add egg yolks; pulse to blend. Pat in bottom of springform pan, using one-third of the mixture. Bake at 400° for 8 minutes. Cool completely. Pat remaining mixture around edges. Set aside.

The Filling:

5 (8 ounce) packages cream cheese

½ teaspoon vanilla

1½ teaspoons lemon juice

½ teaspon almond extract

1 tablespoon lemon zest

1¾ cups sugar

3 tablespoons unbleached flour

¼ teaspoon salt

5 eggs

2 egg yolks

¼ cup heavy cream

Bring all ingredients to room temperature. Place cream cheese in work bowl of electric mixer. Beat on medium-high speed until creamy. Add remaining ingredients in order given, mixing well, and gently adding the heavy cream last. Scrape sides of bowl as necessary. Pour into prepared crust. Bake at 450° for 12 minutes; reduce temperature to 300°, and bake an additional 55–65 minutes until set. Remove from oven and allow to cool. After 30 minutes, gently loosen the sides of pan (may need to run a knife around outer crust and pan to help loosen). Continue to cool. Cover and refrigerate at least eight hours.

Serves 10.

Cherry Sauce

1 (20 ounce) package frozen
   tart cherries

½ cup sugar

2 tablespoons cornstarch

¼ cup water

Thaw cherries; place in a medium-sized saucepan along with the sugar. Dissolve cornstarch in water; add to cherries. Cook over medium-high heat until thickened and bubbly; reduce heat and simmer for 10 minutes. Chill thoroughly before topping cheesecake.

BLUEBERRY CHEESECAKE

The Crust:

2 cups graham cracker crumbs

¾ cup sugar

¼ cup unsalted butter, melted

1 teaspoon ground cinnamon

Combine above ingredients in a large bowl; mix until well blended. Press into bottom and up the sides of an 8-inch springform pan. Bake at 350° for 8 minutes. Remove from oven; cool.

The Filling:

3 (8 ounce) packages cream cheese

1¾ cup sugar

3 tablespoons unbleached flour

¼ cup heavy cream

5 eggs, plus 1 egg yolk

8 ounces mascarpone cheese

8 ounces ricotta cheese

4 tablespoons toasted almonds, broken fine

1 tablespoon lemon zest

½ teaspoon vanilla extract

½ teaspoon almond extract

2 cups fresh blueberries, divided

Bring all ingredients to room temperature. Place cream cheese, sugar, flour, and cream in work bowl of electric mixer. Mix well to blend, scraping sides of bowl as necessary. Add eggs and yolk, one by one, beating well after each addition. Beat in mascarpone and ricotta. Stir in nuts, zest, and extracts; blend thoroughly.

Pour half of cheese filling into graham cracker crust. Top with one cup blueberries. Pour in remaining cheese filling and place the remaining blueberries on top. Bake at 400° for 5 minutes, then reduce temperature to 325° and bake for one hour. Turn oven off and leave in oven for one more hour. Remove from oven; allow to cool. Cover; place in refrigerator overnight before serving.

Serves 10.

If fresh blueberries are not available, then use frozen ones, but don't thaw them. Also, cream cheese may be substituted for the mascarpone and ricotta cheeses.

TRI-CHOCOLATE CHEESECAKE

½ cup sugar
3 tablespoons butter
1 egg white
2½ cups chocolate graham
  cracker crumbs
¼ cup rum
2 ounces semisweet
  chocolate
½ cup chocolate syrup

32 ounces cream cheese, softened
2 cups sugar
4 tablespoons cocoa
2 teaspoons vanilla
½ teaspoon salt
4 eggs
1 cup sour cream
2 tablespoons sugar
1 tablespoon cocoa

Place first three ingredients in work bowl of electric mixer. Beat at medium speed until blended; add graham cracker crumbs and mix well. Press into bottom, and four inches up the sides of an 8-inch springform pan coated with cooking spray. Bake at 350° for 12 minutes; cool.

Combine rum and chocolate squares in top of double boiler. Melt over medium-high heat, stirring frequently. Remove from heat; add chocolate syrup and mix until smooth. Set aside.

Place cream cheese in work bowl of electric mixer. Beat at medium speed until smooth. Add 2 cups sugar, 4 tablespoons cocoa, vanilla, and salt; beat until smooth. Add eggs; beat well, scraping sides of bowl as necessary. Gently stir in the rum and chocolate mixture, creating a swirled effect, but not mixing. Pour into prepared springform pan. Bake at 300° for 45 minutes, or until almost set. Combine sour cream, 2 tablespoons sugar, and one tablespoon cocoa in a small bowl; stir well. Turn off oven, and spread mixture over cheesecake. Allow cheesecake to stand for 45 minutes in oven with door closed. Remove; allow to cool to room temperature. Cover and chill for eight hours.

Serves 10.

TIRAMISU

⅔ cup powdered sugar
8 ounces cream cheese
2 cups Sweet Whipped Cream, divided (see index)
½ cup sugar
¼ cup water
3 egg whites

1 cup hot water
1 tablespoon sugar
1 tablespoon instant espresso coffee
2 tablespoons Kahlua
20 ladyfingers
½ teaspoon unsweetened cocoa

Place powdered sugar and cream cheese in work bowl of electric mixer. Beat on high speed until creamy. Using a rubber spatula, gently fold in 1 cup of the whipped cream. Set aside.

Combine ½ cup sugar, water, and egg whites in top of double boiler; place over simmering water. Using a handheld mixer, beat until stiff peaks form. Gently stir this mixture into the previous cream cheese mixture. Set aside.

Combine hot water, and following three ingredients in a small bowl; stir well. Split ladyfingers in half lengthwise. Arrange 20 of the halves, cut side up, in the bottom of an 8-inch square baking dish. Drizzle half of the espresso mixture over ladyfinger halves. Spread half of cream cheese mixture over ladyfinger halves; repeat procedure. Spread remaining one cup whipped cream evenly over cream cheese mixture; sprinkle with sifted cocoa. Cover and chill for at least two hours.

Serves 8.

Suggestion: *Freeze for two hours before cutting.*

STRAWBERRY TIRAMISU

12 ounces cream cheese
¾ cup powdered sugar
7 tablespoons Marsala wine, divided
½ cup sour cream
2 cups Sweet Whipped Cream, divided
½ cup sugar
¼ cup water

3 egg whites
¾ cup boiling water
2 tablespoons sugar
1 tablespoon instant espresso coffee
20 ladyfingers
2 cups strawberries, sliced
Grated chocolate, for garnish

Place cream cheese, powdered sugar and 5 tablespoons of the Marsala in work bowl of electric mixer. Beat on high speed until creamy. Using a rubber spatula, gently mix in sour cream and one cup of the whipped cream; set aside.

Combine ½ cup sugar, ¼ cup water, and egg whites in top of double boiler; place over simmering water. Using a handheld mixer, beat until stiff peaks form. Gently stir this mixture into the previous cream cheese mixture; set aside.

Combine ¾ cup boiling water, sugar, espresso powder, and remaining 2 tablespoons Marsala in a small bowl; mix well.

Split ladyfingers in half lengthwise. Arrange 20 of the halves cut side up, in the bottom of an 8-inch square baking dish. Drizzle up to half of the espresso mixture over ladyfinger halves, being careful to avoid making them soggy. Spread half of cream cheese mixture over ladyfinger halves. Spread 1 cup of strawberries on top of cream cheese mixture. Repeat procedure. Spread remaining 1 cup whipped cream evenly over cream cheese mixture; sprinkle grated chocolate on top. Cover and chill for at least two hours.

Serves 8.

Suggestion: *Freeze for two two hours before cutting.*

BANANA PUDDING

⅓ cup unbleached flour	2 teaspoons vanilla
¼ cup sugar	2 tablespoons butter
Dash of salt	3 bananas, sliced
2½ cups milk	45 vanilla wafers
2 egg yolks	4 egg whites
1 (14 ounce) can sweetened condensed milk	¼ cup sugar

Combine flour, sugar, and salt in medium-sized saucepan. Add just enough milk to make a smooth paste, gradually pouring in all but ½ cup. Pour the remaining ½ cup into a one-cup glass measuring cup; add egg yolks and whisk well. Strain into saucepan. Add condensed milk. Cook over medium heat, stirring constantly, until thickened and bubbly. Add vanilla and butter; mix to blend.

Arrange 1 cup of banana slices in bottom of a two-quart baking dish. Spoon one-third of the pudding mixture over bananas. Arrange 15 wafers on top of pudding. Repeat layers two times. Arrange the last 15 wafers around edge of dish; pushing cookies halfway into the pudding.

Place egg whites in work bowl of electric mixer. Beat at medium-high speed until foamy. Gradually add ¼ cup sugar, a little at a time. Beat until stiff peaks form. Spread meringue evenly over pudding, sealing to edge of cookies. Bake at 325° for 22 minutes, or until meringue is light golden.

Serves 8.

PUMPKIN ROLL

3 eggs	1 teaspoon ground ginger
1 cup sugar	½ teaspoon salt
1 cup canned pumpkin	1 cup nuts, chopped fine
1 teaspoon lemon juice	*Cream together following ingredients:*
¾ cup unbleached flour	1 (8 ounce) package cream cheese
2 teaspoons ground cinnamon	4 tablespoons butter
½ teaspoon nutmeg, freshly grated	½ teaspoon vanilla
1 teaspoon baking powder	1 cup powdered sugar

Place eggs in work bowl of electric mixer. Mix on medium speed; gradually add sugar. Add the next eight ingredients. Mix well, stopping twice to scrape sides of bowl. Pour into a greased and floured jellyroll pan; spread nuts on top. Bake at 375° for 20–25 minutes, or until wooden pick inserted in center comes out clean. Remove from oven. Invert onto dishtowel that has been dusted with powdered sugar. Gently roll up towel and pumpkin together, lengthwise. Set aside until cooled. Once cooled, unroll. Spread with cream cheese mixture; re-roll (without dishtowel). Wrap in plastic wrap and chill.

MOCHA-MARBLED MOUSSE

1 cup whole milk	2 cups heavy cream
4 teaspoons powdered instant coffee	1 teaspoon vanilla
4 cups miniature marshmallows	7 ounces semisweet chocolate

Combine milk and coffee powder in a heavy medium saucepan. Stir over medium heat until coffee is dissolved. Add marshmallows and stir until melted and mixture is smooth, about 3 minutes. Pour into a large bowl. Allow to stand at room temperature until cool, but not set, whisking occasionally.

Place heavy cream and vanilla in work bowl of electric mixer. Beat at medium speed until stiff peaks form. Fold half of the whipped cream into coffee mixture; mix to blend. Fold the remaining cream into coffee mixture in two separate additions, stirring gently to blend each time. Set aside.

Melt chocolate in top of double boiler over simmering water. Remove from heat, and pour chocolate into large bowl, reserving 1 tablespoon in double boiler for garnish. Cool chocolate to lukewarm. Whisk 1 cup coffee mousse into chocolate in bowl. Gently fold one more cup coffee mousse into chocolate in bowl. Pour remaining coffee mousse over. Using large spatula, gently swirl to create marbled effect. Spoon mousse into six goblets. Drizzle reserved one tablespoon chocolate over each dessert, reheating if necessary. Cover and chill overnight.

Serves 6.

CHOCOLATE ANGEL FOOD CAKE
with Irish Coffee Sauce

¾ cup sifted cake flour

4 heaping tablespoons cocoa

1¼ cups egg whites, room temperature

¼ teaspoon salt

1 teaspoon cream of tartar

1¼ cups sugar

1 teaspoon vanilla

Irish Coffee Sauce (recipe follows)

1 cup Sweet Whipped Cream

Instant espresso coffee powder

Sift flour and cocoa four times, until well mixed. Set aside.

Place egg whites and salt in work bowl of electric mixer. Beat on medium-high speed until foamy; add cream of tartar. Continue to beat, adding sugar a little at a time; add vanilla. Beat until stiff peaks form. Gently fold in flour-cocoa mixture, a little at a time, but working quickly. Pour the batter into an ungreased 10-inch tube pan and bake at 375° for 30 minutes, or until toothpick inserted in center of cake comes out clean. Cool completely before removing from pan.

To serve, pour some Irish Coffee Sauce onto individual serving plates; place a slice of cake on top. Garnish with Sweet Whipped Cream (see index) with espresso coffee powder dusted on top.

Irish Coffee Sauce

1 cup sugar

⅓ cup water

1 cup freshly made coffee

2 tablespoons Irish whiskey
(or bourbon)

Place the sugar and water in a large saucepan; bring to a boil over medium-high heat. Reduce heat; simmer for about 10 minutes, until the mixture begins to turn a caramel color. As mixture continues to cook, it will turn a medium caramel color (at this point, turn off heat but continue to stir—it will continue to darken). Add coffee carefully, for it will spatter; mix well. Allow to cool, and stir in whiskey. Refrigerate in a glass container until ready to use.

CARROT CAKE
with Cream Cheese Frosting

The Cake:

3 eggs
2 cups sugar
¾ cup vegetable oil
¾ cup buttermilk
2 cups unbleached flour
2 teaspoons baking soda
½ teaspoon salt
2 teaspoons ground cinnamon

2 teaspoons vanilla
2 cups grated carrots
1 cup crushed pineapple, drained
1 (3½ ounce) can flaked coconut
1 cup chopped pecans or walnuts
Buttermilk Glaze (recipe follows)
Cream Cheese Frosting
  (recipe follows)

Lightly grease and flour three 8-inch round cake pans; set aside. Using work bowl of electric mixer, add eggs, sugar, oil, and buttermilk; mix well at medium speed. Slowly add flour, soda, salt, cinnamon, and vanilla. Mix well, stopping to scrape bowl as necessary; add vanilla. Add carrots, pineapple, coconut, and nuts; gently mix to blend thoroughly. Pour batter equally into prepared cake pans. Bake at 350° for 25–30 minutes, or until a wooden pick inserted in center comes out clean. Remove from oven. Using a pastry brush, gently brush Buttermilk Glaze evenly over layers; cool in pans on wire racks 10 minutes. Invert pans to remove cakes onto wire racks. Allow to cool. Place in layers on cake plate, spreading Cream Cheese Frosting between layers, on sides, and on top of cake. Enjoy!

Option: *You can bake this in a 13 x 9 x 2-inch baking pan; increase cooking time to 50–60 minutes.*

Buttermilk Glaze:

1 cup sugar
1½ teaspoons baking soda
½ cup buttermilk

½ cup butter
1 tablespoon light corn syrup
1 teaspoon vanilla

Place first five ingredients in a large saucepan; bring to boil over medium heat. Continue to boil for about 4 minutes. Remove from heat; stir in vanilla.

Cream Cheese Frosting:

¾ cup butter, softened
11 ounces cream cheese, softened

3½ cups powdered sugar
1½ teaspoons vanilla

Combine butter and cream cheese in work bowl of electric mixer; mix on medium speed until creamy. Add vanilla and powdered sugar; mix until smooth.

ITALIAN CREAM CAKE
Plain or Chocolate

5 eggs, separated
2 cups sugar, divided
1 cup butter
1 teaspoon salt
1 teaspoon vanilla

1 teaspoon baking soda
1 cup buttermilk
2 rounded cups unbleached flour
1 cup flaked coconut
Cream Cheese Frosting
   (recipe follows)

Lightly grease and flour three 9-inch round cake pans; set aside.

Place egg whites in work bowl of electric mixer; beat on medium-high speed until frothy. Slowly add about ½ cup of the sugar; continue to beat until stiff peaks form. Using a rubber spatula, scrape into another bowl; set aside.

Place butter, egg yolks, and remaining sugar in work bowl of electric mixer; beat on medium speed until creamy. Add salt, vanilla, soda, buttermilk, and flour. Continue to mix until well blended. Using a rubber spatula, gently fold in egg white mixture; mix well. Fold in coconut; mix well. Pour equally into prepared cake pans. Bake at 325° for 25–30 minutes, or until wooden pick inserted in center comes out clean. Remove from oven; allow to cool 10 minutes on wire rack. Invert pans to remove cakes onto wire rack. Allow to cool completely. Place in layers on cake plate, spreading Cream Cheese Frosting between layers, on sides, and on top of cake.

Variation: Add ¼ cup cocoa, along with the flour, for a Chocolate Italian Cream Cake!

Cream Cheese Frosting

¾ cup butter, room temperature
12 ounces cream cheese, room
   temperature

1 teaspoon vanilla
1 pound (16 ounces) powdered sugar
1 cup chopped walnuts

Combine butter, cream cheese, and vanilla in work bowl of electric mixer; mix on medium speed until creamy. Add powdered sugar; continue to mix until smooth. Add chopped walnuts; mix to blend.

Variation: Mix ¼ cup cocoa with first three ingredients for Chocolate Cream Cheese Frosting!

CARAMEL FLAN

1¾ cups sugar, divided	3 eggs, room temperature
¼ cup water	5 egg yolks, room temperature
3 cups whole milk	2 teaspoons vanilla
2 (13 ounce) cans evaporated milk	¼ cup Grand Marnier

Bring 1 cup of the sugar and water to a boil in a heavy saucepan; continue to cook until it begins to turn golden (don't stir). Continue to boil the syrup, swirling pan instead of stirring, until it is a deep caramel color. Pour immediately into six ramekins.

Combine the remaining ¾ cup sugar, whole milk, evaporated milk, eggs, egg yolks, and vanilla into work bowl of electric mixer. Mix until well-blended, but not bubbly. Strain equally into six individual ramekins. Place ramekins in a 13 x 9 x 2-inch baking pan; add two inches boiling water to the pan. Place, covered, in 325° oven for one hour, or until set. Remove from oven; cool. Once cooled, cover; place in refrigerator to chill. When ready to serve, run a thin knife around edges and invert onto individual plates. Heat Grand Marnier in small pan until hot; ignite. Spoon over top.

Serves 6.

PUMPKIN BUNDT CAKE

4 tablespoons butter, softened	2½ teaspoons ground cinnamon
1½ cups sugar, divided	1 teaspoon ground nutmeg
2 teaspoons vanilla	¼ teaspoon salt
3 egg whites	3¼ cups unbleached flour
1½ cup canned pumpkin	1 teaspoon milk
½ cup applesauce	3 tablespoons rum
1 tablespoon baking powder	3 tablespoons brown sugar
1 teaspoon baking soda	3 tablespoons powdered sugar

Combine butter and ½ cup of the sugar in work bowl of electric mixer; mix on medium speed. Add vanilla and egg whites; mix well and slowly add the remaining one cup sugar. Add the pumpkin, applesauce, baking powder, baking soda, cinnamon, nutmeg, and salt; mix well. Add the flour; mix well, stopping to scrape sides of bowl as necessary. Pour into a greased and floured bundt pan. Bake at 350° for 50 minutes, or until wooden pick inserted in center comes out clean. Remove from oven and allow to cool 10 minutes in pan. Invert pan (to remove cake) onto a wire rack to continue cooling; turn cake back over to an upright position. Place milk, rum, and brown sugar in a small saucepan. Cook over medium heat until sugar dissolves. Remove from heat. Add powdered sugar, stirring with a whisk to blend. Spoon over top of cake.

CHOCOLATE BUNDT CAKE
with Dark and White Chocolate Frosting

1 cup butter, softened
1½ cups sugar
4 eggs
½ teaspoon baking soda
1 cup buttermilk
2½ cups unbleached flour
2 (4 ounce) squares semisweet
   baking chocolate

2 tablespoons vegetable shortening,
   divided
⅓ cup chocolate syrup
1½ cups chocolate chips
2 teaspoons vanilla
4 ounces white chocolate chips

Place first six ingredients in work bowl of electric mixer. Mix on medium speed until just blended, scraping sides of bowl one time. Melt chocolate squares and one tablespoon of shortening in top of double boiler. Using a rubber spatula, stir half of the melted chocolate into the batter along with the chocolate syrup, chocolate chips, and vanilla; mix well. Pour into a lightly oiled and floured bundt pan. Bake at 300° for 30–35 minutes, or until wooden pick inserted in center comes out clean. Remove from oven; invert onto wire rack to cool, then invert onto serving plate. Melt the white chocolate, along with the remaining tablespoon shortening, in top of double boiler. Drizzle, using a spoon, onto cool cake, from center to outside edges. Once cooled, drizzle remaining chocolate over white chocolate.

CHOCOLATE CHIP CAKE

1 box yellow cake mix
3 eggs
1 (6 ounce) box chocolate
   instant pudding

¾ cup water
½ cup vegetable oil
1 cup sour cream
1 cup chocolate chips

Place ingredients in work bowl of electric mixer. Mix on medium-high speed until thoroughly combined, scraping sides of bowl as needed. Pour into a lightly greased and floured bundt pan. Bake at 350° for 50–55 minutes, or until wooden pick inserted in center comes out clean. Remove from oven; cool 10 minutes. Invert pan to remove cake onto plate.

I used to mix this and put it in the oven during a commercial as I watched our favorite soap opera, "Dallas"!

CRANBERRY CAKE
with Hot Butter Sauce

2 tablespoons butter, room temperature	3 teaspoons baking powder
1 cup sugar	½ teaspoon salt
1 teaspoon vanilla	1 cup milk
2 cups unbleached flour	2 cups whole, raw cranberries

In work bowl of electric mixer, combine butter and sugar. Mix well on medium speed. Add remaining ingredients, except cranberries. Mix until thoroughly blended, stopping to scrape sides as needed. Using a rubber spatula, stir in cranberries; mix well. Pour into a lightly greased and floured 8-inch square baking pan. Bake at 400° for 30–35 minutes, or until wooden pick inserted in middle comes out clean. Remove from oven. Allow to cool approximately 10 minutes. Serve warm on individual dessert plates. Spoon Hot Butter Sauce (recipe follows) over top of each serving (about 4–5 tablespoons).

Hot Butter Sauce

½ cup butter	½ cup light cream
1 cup sugar	

Place the above ingredients in a small saucepan. Heat over medium heat until butter is melted and sugar is dissolved. Serve over individual pieces of warm Cranberry Cake.

This is our our traditional Christmas Eve dessert, and it takes less than an hour to make from start to finish!

CHOCOLATE PUDDING CAKE
Because we all need this recipe!

The Crust:

½ cup butter, room temperature   1 cup pecans, chopped fine
1 cup unbleached flour

Mix above ingredients in a medium-sized bowl. Press into a 13 x 9 x 2-inch baking dish. Bake at 350° for 20 minutes. Remove from oven; cool.

First Layer:

8 ounces cream cheese, room   1 cup powdered sugar
  temperature   1 cup sweet whipped cream

Place cream cheese and powdered sugar together in work bowl of electric mixer. Mix on medium speed until creamy. Fold in whipped cream. Spread over baked crust.

Second Layer:

1 (3.4 ounce) box instant   2½ cups milk
  chocolate pudding
1 (3.4 ounce) box instant
  vanilla pudding

Using the work bowl of electric mixer, pour the dry pudding slowly into the milk while mixing on medium speed. Continue to mix until well incorporated. Pour over cream cheese mixture.

Final Layer:

2 cups sweet whipped cream   Grated chocolate bar, for garnish

Top chocolate mixture with whipped cream. Garnish top with grated chocolate bar. Cover with plastic wrap and refrigerate until well chilled.

I think this is every child's favorite dessert!

CHOCOLATE SHEET CAKE
For Dr. Robert

2 cups sugar	2 eggs
2 cups unbleached flour	½ cup buttermilk
4 tablespoons cocoa	1 teaspoon baking soda
½ cup butter	1 teaspoon vanilla
½ cup vegetable shortening	1 teaspoon ground cinnamon
1 cup water	

Place sugar and flour in work bowl of electric mixer. Place cocoa, butter, and shortening in a small saucepan. Heat over medium heat until melted and cocoa is blended; add water. Remove from heat; pour over flour mixture and mix at medium speed. Add remaining ingredients, scraping sides of bowl as needed. Mix until well blended. Pour into 13 x 9 x 2-inch lightly greased and floured baking pan. Bake at 400° for 30 minutes, or until wooden pick inserted in center comes out clean.

Chocolate Fudge Frosting

½ cup butter	4 cups powdered sugar
4 tablespoons cocoa	1 teaspoon vanilla
6 tablespoons milk	¾ cup pecans, chopped

Melt butter in small saucepan over medium heat. Add cocoa; mix well to blend. Add milk and mix until slightly thickened. Remove from heat.

Place powdered sugar in work bowl of electric mixer. Pour chocolate mixture over top; mix well on medium speed. Add pecans; mix. Spread over warm cake, and allow to cool. Garnish top with extra chopped pecans. Bake this cake for a special friend from time to time!

PINEAPPLE UPSIDE-DOWN CAKE
For My Dad

3 eggs, separated
1 cup sugar, divided
5 tablespoons pineapple juice
⅛ teaspoon salt
1 teaspoon baking powder

1 cup unbleached flour
½ cup butter
1 cup brown sugar
1 (8 ounce) can sliced pineapple
Large pecan halves (about 8)

Place egg whites in work bowl of electric mixer. Beat on medium-high speed, gradually adding ½ cup of the sugar, until stiff peaks form. Using a rubber spatula, scrape into another bowl; set aside.

Place the egg yolks in work bowl of electric mixer. Beat on medium-high speed, gradually adding the remaining ½ cup of sugar. Add pineapple juice, salt, baking powder, and flour. Mix until well blended, scraping sides of bowl as needed. Using a rubber spatula, gently fold egg whites into mixture; mix well.

Preparing the skillet:
Melt butter in a large cast-iron skillet over medium-high heat. Add brown sugar; stir to moisten, but not necessarily to dissolve it. Turn off heat. Place pineapple rings in circular pattern and in center of mixture. Place pecan halves (top-side down) into circles of pineapple rings, and scattered about, if you choose. Pour prepared batter on top. Place in 375° oven; bake for 30–35 minutes, or until wooden pick inserted in center comes out clean. Remove from oven; allow to cool in pan for 10 minutes. Invert skillet over plate to release cake from pan. Serve warm with vanilla ice cream.

Serves 8.

CHOCOLATE DATE NUT CAKE

1 (8 ounce) package chopped dates
1 cup hot water
⅔ cup vegetable shortening
2 eggs
1 cup sugar
⅓ cup buttermilk
2 tablespoons cocoa

½ teaspoon salt
1 teaspoon baking soda
1 teaspoon vanilla
1¾ cup unbleached flour
½ cup chopped pecans, optional
¾ cup chocolate chips

Place dates and hot water in small bowl; set aside to soften and cool. Using work bowl of electric mixer, cream shortening, eggs, and sugar on medium speed. Add buttermilk and date mixture; mix slowly to blend. Add cocoa, salt, soda, vanilla, and flour; mix well, scraping sides of bowl as needed. Add nuts, if you choose; mix well. Pour into a well-greased and floured 13 x 9 x 2-inch baking pan; sprinkle chocolate chips on top. Bake at 350° for 40 minutes, or until wooden pick inserted in center comes out clean. Remove from oven; cool.

BLUEBERRY POUND CAKE

1½ cups sugar
½ cup butter, softened
½ cup cream cheese, softened
3 eggs
2¾ cup unbleached flour
1 teaspoon baking powder
½ teaspoon baking soda

½ teaspoon salt
1 cup plain yogurt (or sour cream)
1½ teaspoons vanilla
2 cups fresh or frozen blueberries
½ cup powdered sugar
4 teaspoons lemon juice

Place sugar, butter, cream cheese, and eggs in work bowl of electric mixer. Mix on medium speed until creamy. Slowly add flour, baking powder, baking soda, salt, yogurt, and vanilla. Mix until well-blended, scraping sides of bowl as necessary. Using a rubber spatula, fold in (thawed) blueberries. Lightly oil and flour bundt pan; pour batter into pan. Bake at 350° for approximately one hour, or until wooden pick inserted in center comes out clean. Remove from oven; allow to cool 10 minutes. Invert pan to remove cake onto a wire rack; cool. Transfer onto plate. Drizzle mixture of powdered sugar and lemon juice on top of warm cake.

SOUR CREAM POUND CAKE
For Elise

6 eggs, separated
1 cup butter, softened
3 cups sugar
1 cup sour cream, room temperature
3 cups unbleached flour

⅛ teaspoon salt
¼ teaspoon baking soda
1 teaspoon vanilla
1 teaspoon almond extract

Place egg whites in work bowl of electric mixer; beat until stiff peaks form. Transfer to another bowl; set aside.

Using the same work bowl, add egg yolks, butter, sugar, and sour cream; beat until creamy. Add remaining ingredients. Mix well, scraping sides of bowl as necessary. Using a rubber spatula, gently fold in beaten egg whites and mix to blend thoroughly. Pour into a lightly greased and floured tube pan. Bake at 300° for 90 minutes, or until a wooden pick inserted in center comes out clean. Remove from oven. Allow to cool for 5 minutes; invert onto a wire rack to cool.

FRUIT COCKTAIL CAKE

The Cake:
2 eggs
1½ cups sugar
2 cups unbleached flour
2 teaspoons baking soda

¼ teaspoon salt
1 teaspoon vanilla
1 (30 ounce) can fruit cocktail
    and juice

Place above ingredients, except fruit cocktail, into work bowl of electric mixer. Mix on medium-high speed until well blended, scraping sides as necessary. Pour in fruit cocktail; mix on low speed until well incorporated. Pour into a greased and floured bundt pan. Bake at 350° for 35–40 minutes, or until a wooden pick inserted in center comes out clean. Remove from oven. Allow to cool 5 minutes. Invert onto a wire rack to continue cooling. Invert, again, onto a serving plate. Frost with Coconut Frosting.

Coconut Frosting:
1 cup evaporated milk
1 cup sugar
¾ cup butter

1½ cups flaked coconut
½ cup pecans, chopped
1 teaspoon vanilla

Place the first three ingredients in a large saucepan. Cook over medium heat until thick and a light-medium caramel in color, stirring constantly. Remove from heat; stir in remaining ingredients.

GLAZED APPLE CAKE

1 cup butter
2 cups sugar
3 eggs
3 cups unbleached flour
½ teaspoon salt
1½ baking soda

1 teaspoon ground cinnamon
⅛ teaspoon ground nutmeg
2 teaspoons vanilla
3 cups apples, peeled and chopped
2 cups pecans or walnuts, chopped
Cooking spray

Combine butter, sugar, and eggs in work bowl of electric mixer; mix on medium speed until creamy. Add flour, salt, soda, cinnamon, nutmeg, and vanilla. Continue mixing until thoroughly combined, scraping sides of bowl as necessary. Using a rubber spatula, stir in apples and pecans; mix well. Pour into bundt pan that has been prepared with cooking spray. Bake at 325° for about 1½ hours, or until wooden pick inserted in middle comes out clean. Remove from oven. Allow to cool for 10 minutes. Invert pan onto a wire rack to remove cake. Invert again to place on plate. Pour glaze on top of cake.

Glaze:

1½ cups sugar

½ cup sherry or bourbon

Combine sugar and sherry in small saucepan. Bring to a boil over medium-high heat. Reduce heat to low, and simmer until a syrup consistency.

MOCHA PUDDING CAKE

1 cup unbleached flour
1 cup sugar, divided
⅓ cup cocoa, divided
2 tablespoons instant coffee powder
2 teaspoons baking powder
¼ teaspoon salt

½ cup milk
3 tablespoons butter
1 teaspoon vanilla
1 cup boiling water
Vanilla ice cream

Combine flour, ⅔ cup sugar, ¼ cup cocoa, instant coffee, baking powder, and salt in work bowl of electric mixer. Add milk, butter, and vanilla; mix well to blend. Grease and flour an 8-inch square baking pan; fill with batter. Combine the remaining sugar and cocoa; sprinkle over top of batter. Pour the boiling water over top. Bake at 350° for 30 minutes. Serve warm with vanilla ice cream.

STRAWBERRY SOUFFLÉ
with Sweet Strawberry Sauce

3 teaspoons unsalted butter, softened
4 tablespoons sugar
7 egg whites, room temperature
⅛ teaspoon salt
½ cup powdered sugar

2 pints fresh strawberries, puréed
   and strained
4 tablespoons beer foam
½ cup Strawberry Sauce
   (recipe follows)

Butter a 1½-quart soufflé dish; dust with sugar. Butter and sugar a collar made of foil; place it around the soufflé dish, two inches above the rim of dish.

Place the egg whites in work bowl of electric mixer. Beat the whites until foamy; add salt. Gradually begin adding the powdered sugar; continue beating until stiff peaks form.

Pour one cup of the strained strawberries into a large bowl. Thoroughly blend one heaping spoonful of the egg whites into the strawberry sauce. Gently fold the remaining egg whites, along with the beer foam, into the strawberry mixture, being careful to not overmix. Pour into prepared soufflé dish, and place in a preheated 350° oven. Bake for 20–25 minutes, or until lightly browned. Remove from oven, and serve immediately on warm plates, accompanied with sauce.

Serves 4.

For an even more impressive dessert, prepare four individual soufflé dishes. Once the soufflé is placed before your guest, serve the sauce by making a small well in the top of the soufflé in which to ladle the sauce.

Sweet Strawberry Sauce

½ cup strained strawberry purée

¼ cup sugar

Combine the above ingredients; mix well. Allow to stand until sugar is completely dissolved.

CHOCOLATE SOUFFLÉ
with Mocha Cream

The Soufflé:

¼ cup butter

3 (1 ounce) squares semisweet chocolate

¼ cup unbleached flour

1½ cups milk

⅛ teaspoon salt

6 eggs, separated

½ cup sugar

Hot Chocolate Mix (see index)

1 teaspoon vanilla

Melt butter and chocolate in medium-sized saucepan over medium heat. Stir in flour, mixing well to smooth. Gradually add milk, stirring constantly to smooth. Add salt; cook until bubbly and thick.

Place egg whites in work bowl of electric mixer. Beat on medium speed until stiff peaks form (but not dry peaks). Place egg whites in a clean bowl; set aside. Add egg yolks to same work bowl. Beat on medium speed; gradually add sugar, a little at a time. Beat until creamy. Gradually add hot chocolate mixture, mixing constantly until well incorporated; add vanilla and mix well.

Using a rubber spatula, gently fold one-fourth of the beaten egg whites into chocolate mixture; mix well. Add remaining egg whites, gently mixing until well incorporated.

Equally divide mixture into six lightly oiled, individual ramekins (custard cups), or into a single soufflé dish. Bake at 325° for approximately 30–35 minutes, or until puffy and set. Serve immediately with Mocha Cream (just before serving, poke hole in center of soufflé; spoon Mocha Cream inside).

Serves 6.

The Mocha Cream:

1½ cups heavy cream

¼ cup sugar

1 tablespoon powdered cocoa

2 teaspoons instant espresso granules

Combine the above ingredients in work bowl of electric mixer. Beat on medium-high speed until stiff peaks form. Chill until ready to use.

This cream is good to offer guests for flavoring their coffee, too! However, I don't suggest offering it when you serve this dish—keep it special for the soufflé.

GRANDMOTHER'S FUDGE BROWNIE PIE

2 eggs, room temperature
½ cup butter, room temperature
1 cup sugar
½ cup unbleached flour

4 tablespoons cocoa
Dash of salt
1 teaspoon vanilla
1 cup chopped pecans

Combine all ingredients, except pecans, in a medium-sized bowl. Mix well, using a fork, until well incorporated. Add pecans; mix to blend. Pour into a lightly greased and floured pie plate. Bake at 300° for 30–35 minutes. Eat by itself (one piece at a time), or serve warm with ice cream!

BROWNIES

2 cups sugar
2 cups unbleached flour
½ teaspoon salt
½ teaspoon baking powder
2 teaspoons vanilla

4 (heaping) tablespoons cocoa
4 eggs
1 cup butter, melted
1 cup pecans, chopped

Place the above ingredients together in a large bowl and mix well by hand. Pour batter into a lightly oiled and floured 13 x 9 x 2-inch baking pan. Bake at 350° for 35 minutes.

CARAMEL NUT BROWNIES

1 (14 ounce) package caramels, unwrapped
⅔ cup evaporated milk, divided
1 (1½ pound) box of German chocolate cake mix

¾ cup butter, melted
1 cup chocolate chips
1 cup pecans, chopped

Melt caramels and ⅓ cup of the milk in top of double boiler over medium heat. Combine cake mix, butter, and remaining milk in large bowl; mix well by hand. Pour ½ of mixture into a lightly oiled and floured 13 x 9 x 2-inch baking pan. Bake at 350° for 10 minutes. Remove from oven; sprinkle top with chocolate chips and pecans. Drizzle melted caramels over chips and nuts; pour remaining batter on top of all. Return to oven and continue baking for 20 minutes, or until firm. Cool before slicing.

BREAD PUDDING
with Bourbon Sauce

1 loaf French bread	2 tablespoons vanilla
4 cups milk, divided	4 tablespoons butter, melted
3 eggs	1 cup raisins
1½ cups sugar	

Tear bread into bite-sized pieces into a large bowl. Pour 3 cups of the milk over bread; set aside. Break eggs into work bowl of electric mixer. Mix on medium speed, adding the remaining cup of milk, sugar, vanilla, butter, and raisins; mix well to blend. Using a rubber spatula, gently mix with the bread mixture. Pour into 13 x 9 x 2-inch baking dish. Bake, uncovered, in Bain Marie (water bath) at 300° for 50–60 minutes, or until firm. Serve warm; top with Bourbon Sauce.

Bourbon Sauce:

½ cup butter	1 egg, well beaten
¾ cup sugar	¼ cup bourbon

Place butter and sugar in top of double boiler. Cook over medium heat until butter melts. Pour in beaten egg, whisking constantly, being careful to adjust heat to prevent curdling. Continue cooking until sugar is dissolved. Remove from heat; stir in bourbon. Serve warm over Bread Pudding.

PIE PASTRY

3 cups unbleached flour	1 egg
Dash of salt	2 tablespoons vinegar
1½ cups vegetable shortening	6 tablespoons water

Place flour, salt, and shortening in a large bowl. Using a pastry cutter or food processor, cut shortening into flour. In a small bowl, mix together the egg, vinegar, and water; whisk to blend. Pour this mixture into the flour mixture. Using your hands, knead to blend. If dough seems too sticky after kneading, add more flour, a little at a time. Divide dough into fourths; roll each into a circle 1½ inches larger than a 9-inch pie plate. Gently lift onto pie plate; fold outer edge of pastry under, then flute edge. (These may be covered and frozen at this stage. Allow to reach room temperature before baking, and resume with following instructions.) With fork, prick bottom and side of pie shell at 1-inch intervals to prevent puffing and shrinking during baking. Bake at 425° for 4 minutes. Reduce heat to 400° and bake 8 minutes, or until lightly golden.

My mother always sprinkled sugar and cinnamon on her leftover pastry and baked it as a special treat!

MOM'S PEACH COBBLER

2 pie crusts, rolled flat
1½ cups sugar
4 tablespoons unbleached flour

1½ quarts fresh peaches, sliced
½ cup butter, softened
Dash of salt

Place one pie crust on baking sheet. Bake at 400° for 10 minutes. Set aside.

Combine sugar and flour in medium-sized saucepan; mix to blend. Stir in peaches, butter, and salt; cook over medium heat, stirring, until hot and slightly thickened. Pour one-half of the mixture into a round casserole dish (about the size of pie crust). Place the precooked pie crust on top. Pour in the remaining peach mixture, and top with the unbaked pie crust. Make several tiny slits in crust to allow steam to vent. If you choose, top the crust with small dots of butter and sprinkle with sugar. Bake at 425° for 8 minutes; reduce heat to 350° and continue baking until a light golden brown. Serve hot with vanilla ice cream.

BRANDIED PUMPKIN ICE CREAM PIE
with Malted Pecans

1½ cups graham cracker crumbs
½ teaspoon cinnamon
2 egg whites, lightly beaten
Cooking spray
1 cup canned pumpkin
⅓ cup packed light brown sugar
1 teaspoon ground cinnamon

¼ teaspoon allspice
¼ teaspoon ground nutmeg
⅛ teaspoon ginger
2 tablespoons brandy
4 cups vanilla ice cream, softened
4 tablespoons pecans, roasted
2 tablespoons malted milk powder

Combine the first three ingredients in a large bowl; toss with a fork to moisten. Press into bottom and sides of a 9-inch pie plate that has been coated with cooking spray. Bake at 350° for 10 minutes. Cool.

Combine pumpkin and following six ingredients in a large bowl; mix well. Using a rubber spatula, fold in ice cream to create a marbled effect. Pour into prepared crust; cover loosely and freeze for 8 hours. Twenty minutes before serving, place in refrigerator. Place pecans and malted milk powder in food processor, and process until ground. Sprinkle around the edge of pie.

Serves 8.

TEXAS CREAM PIE
with Sweet Whipped Cream

1 package gelatin

¼ cup cold water

2 tablespoons cornstarch

2 cups milk, divided

2 eggs

1 cup sugar

¼ teaspoon salt

1 tablespoon butter

1 teaspoon vanilla

1 pie crust, baked

Grated chocolate, for garnish

Roasted slivered almonds, for garnish

Place gelatin and water in a small bowl. Allow to soften; set aside.

Combine cornstarch with ¼ cup of the milk in a medium saucepan; stir well to smooth. Add remaining milk and eggs in a small bowl; whisk well to blend. Strain through a wire strainer into the saucepan. Add sugar, salt, and gelatin mixture. Cook, stirring continuously, over medium-high heat until thickened. Remove from heat; stir in butter and vanilla. Cool slightly and pour into baked pie crust. Cover with plastic wrap and refrigerate until cold (about 4 hours). Serve in individual pieces. Top each piece with Sweet Whipped Cream. Garnish with grated chocolate and toasted slivered almonds.

Serves 8.

Sweet Whipped Cream

1 cup heavy cream

⅓ cup sugar

Place cream in work bowl of electric mixer. Mix on medium speed until it begins to thicken. Gradually begin to add sugar, a little at a time. Continue to mix until very thick, being careful to not overbeat.

This pie is so delicious, and it takes only a very short time to put together. The first time I made it, though, I was in the kitchen for hours. I thought that a pie this good must take all afternoon to make!

CHOCOLATE MERINGUE PIE

2½ cups milk, divided
2 heaping tablespoons cocoa
⅓ cup unbleached flour
1 cup sugar
¼ teaspoon salt

3 egg yolks (reserve whites for
   meringue)
2 tablespoons butter
1 teaspoon vanilla
1 prebaked pie crust
1 recipe Meringue (recipe follows)

Pour ½ cup milk into a two-cup glass measuring cup; set aside.

Place cocoa, flour, sugar, and salt in large saucepan. Add just enough of the remaining milk to make a very thick but smooth paste (this is to prevent the flour and cocoa from forming small lumps). Continue to add the remaining milk slowly, stirring constantly to dissolve the dry ingredients.

Add egg yolks to the reserved ½ cup milk. Using a fork, whisk well to blend. Pour through a wire mesh strainer into the saucepan containing the cocoa mixture. Cook over medium-high heat, stirring continuously, until very thick (with large, thick, open bubbles). Remove from heat; stir in butter and vanilla. Pour into a prebaked pie crust. Smooth meringue over top, making sure to connect the meringue well to the pie crust (this prevents shrinking away from the crust). Bake at 350° for about 10 minutes, or until light golden brown. Remove from oven; allow to cool.

Serves 8–10.

Meringue

3 egg whites, room temperature
¼ teaspoon cream of tartar

¼ cup sugar
½ teaspoon vanilla

Place egg whites in work bowl of electric mixer (always make sure that your equipment is oil-free and that your egg whites contain no little pieces of yolk, or the whites won't foam!). Beat on medium-high speed until the foamy appearance begins to lightly froth. Sprinkle in the cream of tartar. Continue mixing; begin adding sugar, one tablespoon at a time, until all used. Add vanilla, and continue to mix until stiff peaks form (but not dry peaks).

Cream of tartar aids the proteins in the egg whites in becoming stronger and more stiff. Sugar also strengthens egg white proteins, keeping the bubbles small and the foam more pliable. It's really best to use a copper mixing bowl, for the copper transfers the heat from the whites, and copper ions are released during beating, serving a similar purpose as the cream of tartar! A metal or glass bowl retains the heat, therefore producing larger bubbles. I tell you this because everyone I know has a little problem now and then with their meringue . . . including me!

COCONUT PIE
For Curt

3 eggs, separated
¼ cup sugar
1½ cups milk, divided
¼ cup unbleached flour
¼ teaspoon salt

½ cup sugar
2 tablespoons butter
½ teaspoon vanilla
½ cup flaked coconut
1 prebaked pie crust

Place egg whites in work bowl of electric mixer. Beat on medium-high speed until frothy. Gradually begin adding ¼ cup sugar, a little at a time. Continue to beat until stiff peaks form (but not dry peaks). Using a rubber spatula, transfer to another bowl. Set aside.

Place egg yolks and ½ cup of the milk in a two-cup glass measuring cup; using a fork, whisk well to blend. Set aside.

Place flour, salt, and sugar in a large saucepan. Add just enough of the remaining milk to make a very thick but smooth paste (this is to prevent the flour from forming small lumps). Continue to add the remaining milk slowly, stirring constantly to dissolve the dry ingredients. Strain the egg yolk mixture through a wire mesh strainer into the saucepan. Cook over medium-high heat, stirring constantly, until very thick (with large, thick, open bubbles). Remove from heat. Stir in butter, vanilla, and coconut; mix well.

Using a rubber spatula, fold in ⅓ of the egg white mixture (meringue); mix well. Pour into a prebaked pie crust. Smooth the remaining meringue over top, making sure to connect it well to the pie crust (this prevents shrinkage). Bake at 350° for about 10 minutes, or until light golden brown. Remove from oven; allow to cool.

Serves 8–10.

I'd like to emphasize that the filling must be cooked until very thick, with large, thick, open bubbles. In other words, when you think that it's thick, don't take it up—it's not ready until it's, really, extremely thick! The first time my son Curt made this pie, I didn't stress this point. His pie was runny. I jokingly asked him if I should get straws instead of forks; he failed to see the humor in my comment—and, of course, the runny pie was my fault due to my lack of instructions!

PECAN PIE
For Kelly

¼ cup butter, room temperature
½ cup sugar
1 cup light corn syrup
3 eggs

1 teaspoon vanilla
1 cup pecans, pieces or halves
1 pie crust, unbaked
Vanilla ice cream

Place butter and sugar in work bowl of electric mixer. Beat on medium speed until creamy. Add corn syrup, eggs, and vanilla; mix well to blend. Stir in pecan pieces. Pour into unbaked pie crust. Bake at 350° for 45 minutes, or until set. (If edge of crust seems to brown too much, make a foil "sleeve" to place over it.) Remove from oven; cool. Serve warm with vanilla ice cream!

Serves 8–10.

CHOCOLATE CHIP PECAN PIE

1 cup chocolate chips
1 pie crust, unbaked
¼ cup butter, room temperature
1 cup light corn syrup

½ cup sugar
3 eggs
1 teaspoon vanilla
1 cups pecans, pieces or halves

Sprinkle chocolate chips into pie crust; set aside. Place butter, corn syrup, sugar, eggs, and vanilla in work bowl of electric mixer. Beat on medium speed until well blended. Stir in pecans; pour over chocolate chips in pie crust. Bake at 350° for 45 minutes, or until set. Remove from oven; cool. Serve with vanilla ice cream!

Serves 8.

CHESS PIE

4 eggs
2 cups sugar
1 tablespoon unbleached flour
1 tablespoon yellow cornmeal

1 teaspoon vanilla
1 cup flaked coconut
1 cup crushed pineapple
1 pie crust, unbaked

Place eggs, sugar, flour, cornmeal, and vanilla in work bowl of electric mixer. Mix on medium-high speed until smooth, scraping sides of bowl as necessary. Using a rubber spatula, fold in coconut and pineapple; mix well to blend. Pour into unbaked pie crust. Bake at 425° for 5 minutes. Reduce heat to 350°; bake for one hour or until set. Remove from oven; allow to cool.

Serves 8.

LEMON MERINGUE PIE
For Martha

1 cup sugar	½ cup lemon juice
⅓ cup cornstarch	2 tablespoons butter
⅛ teaspoon salt	½ teaspoon vanilla
1 cup milk, divided	½ cup sour cream
½ cup heavy cream	1 prepared pie crust, baked
3 egg yolks, slightly beaten	1 recipe meringue (see index)

Place sugar, cornstarch, salt, and ½ cup milk in large saucepan. Whisk well to dissolve cornstarch; add remaining ½ cup milk. Combine cream and egg yolks in a small bowl; whisk well to combine. Pour through a strainer into the saucepan. Cook over medium-high heat, whisking constantly until hot and very thick. Remove from heat; whisk in lemon juice. Continue to cook, about 2 minutes, until very thick. Remove from heat; whisk in butter and vanilla. Pour a small amount into a separate bowl containing the sour cream; whisk well to blend. Combine with remaining mixture; mix well. Pour into prepared crust and top with meringue. Bake at 350° for 10 minutes, or until light golden brown. Remove from oven; cool. Cover and chill for six hours, or until set.

Serves 8.

CHOCOLATE MOUSSE PIE
in Meringue Shell

2 egg whites	Sweet chocolate baking squares
⅛ teaspoon cream of tarter	(8 ounces)
⅛ teaspoon salt	3 tablespoons water
½ cup sugar	1 teaspoon vanilla
½ cup pecans, chopped fine	1 cup heavy cream, whipped
½ teaspoon vanilla	

Combine egg whites, cream of tartar and salt in work bowl of electric mixer. Beat on medium speed until foamy. Gradually add sugar, a little at a time. Beat until stiff peaks form (but not dry peaks). Using a rubber spatula, fold in nuts and ½ teaspoon vanilla. Spoon into a lightly oiled 9-inch pie plate, making a shell by building up the sides about ½-inch above the pie plate rim. Bake at 300° for 50–55 minutes. Remove from oven; cool.

Place chocolate and water in top of double boiler. Melt over simmering water. Remove from heat; stir in teaspoon vanilla. Allow to cool completely. Fold in whipped cream; pile into meringue shell. Cover and refrigerate. Chill for at least three hours.

Serves 8.

APPLE PIE
with Hot Butter Sauce

Pie pastry, for two pies (see index)
6 apples, peeled and sliced thin
2 tablespoons lemon juice
¼ teaspoon ground cinnamon
¼ teaspoon ground nutmeg
½ cup sugar

¼ cup raisins
1 cup light brown sugar
2 tablespoons unbleached flour
½ cup pecans, chopped
2 tablespoons butter
¼ cup water

Prepare one pastry to fit a 9-inch pie plate, reserving the remaining pastry to place on top.

Mix apples, lemon juice, cinnamon, and nutmeg in a large bowl. Place in pie shell. Spread sugar and raisins over the apples. Combine the brown sugar with flour; spread on top. Place nuts on top; dot with butter. Sprinkle water over all.

Roll out remaining pastry; place on top of apple mixture. Seal edges, and flute. Make a few slits in top crust. Bake at 400° for 10 minutes. Reduce heat to 350° and continue to bake for 30 minutes. Serve warm with Hot Butter Sauce.

Serves 8.

Hot Butter Sauce

½ cup butter
1 tablespoon water

1 teaspoon brandy
1½ cups powdered sugar

Using a large saucepan, melt butter in water over medium heat. Remove from heat; add brandy. Beat in powdered sugar with a whisk. If too thick, add a little more hot water.

STRAWBERRY PIE

1 cup sugar
¼ cup cornstarch
⅛ teaspoon salt
1 cup water

6 cups fresh strawberries, quartered
1 pie crust, baked (see index)
Sweet whipped cream (see index)

Combine sugar, cornstarch, and salt in a medium saucepan. Slowly add water to dissolve cornstarch. Cook over medium heat until thick and translucent; cool. Place strawberries in pie shell; pour mixture over top. Cover and refrigerate. Serve with whipped cream.

Serves 8.

PUMPKIN PIE
with Pecan-Carmel Sauce

3 eggs
½ cup light brown sugar
2 cups canned pumpkin
¾ cup heavy cream
½ cup milk
½ teaspoon salt

1½ teaspoon ground cinnamon
¼ teaspoon ground nutmeg
¼ teaspoon ground ginger
¼ teaspoon ground cloves
1 pie crust (baked halfway)
Pecan-Carmel Sauce (recipe follows)

Place eggs in work bowl of electric mixer. Beat on medium speed until smooth; add brown sugar and mix until creamy. Add pumpkin, cream, milk, and salt, followed by the four spices listed. Mix on medium speed until well incorporated, scraping sides as necessary. Pour into prepared pie crust. Bake at 350° for 50–60 minutes, or until knife inserted in center comes out clean. Remove from oven and allow to cool for about an hour. Pour hot Pecan-Carmel Sauce over top; cool. Cover top with plastic wrap and allow to cool at least four hours.

Serves 8.

Variation: Instead of pouring sauce on top of pie, a different choice of topping could be offered. I personally enjoy sweet whipped cream (see index) on my pumpkin pie!

Pecan-Carmel Sauce

1 cup light brown sugar
¼ cup heavy cream
2 tablespoons light corn syrup
2 tablespoons butter

1 tablespoon distilled white vinegar
1 cup roasted pecans, broken
1 teaspoon vanilla

In a large saucepan, heat brown sugar, cream, corn syrup, butter, and vinegar to a boil; stir frequently. Reduce heat to low; simmer 5 minutes. Remove from heat; stir in pecans and vanilla. (The topping will be runny when hot, but will thicken somewhat as it cools.)

MOCHA ICE CREAM PIE

The Crust:

1½ cups chocolate wafers, crushed

⅓ cup butter, softened

3 tablespoons sugar

2 tablespoons Kahlua liqueur, optional

Mix ingredients together in a medium-sized bowl. Press into a 9-inch pie plate that has been coated with cooking spray. Bake at 350° for 8 minutes. Remove from oven; cool completely.

The Filling & Topping:

1 quart coffee ice cream, slightly softened

1 tablespoon Irish whiskey, or bourbon

Fudge Sauce (see index)

2 cups Sweet Whipped Cream (see index)

½ cup toasted slivered almonds

Place ice cream in a large bowl and stir in whiskey with a large spoon or rubber spatula. Pour into prepared pie crust. Cover with plastic wrap and place in freezer for at least 4 hours. When ready to serve, allow to set out for about 10 minutes. Cut into eight pieces. Drizzle chocolate sauce on top, followed with a dollop of sweet whipped cream; sprinkle toasted almonds on top.

Serves 8.

CHARLENE'S SWEET POTATO PIE

3 large sweet potatoes, peeled and sliced

6 tablespoons butter

1 (14 ounce) can sweetened condensed milk

2 eggs

2 teaspoons ground cinnamon

2 teaspoons ground nutmeg

2 teaspoons ground allspice

2 heaping tablespoons flour

2 teaspoons vanilla

Sugar, to preferred taste

2 pie crusts (baked halfway)

Sweet Whipped Cream, for topping

Barely cover potatoes with water in large saucepan. Bring to a boil over medium-high heat. Reduce heat and simmer until soft and tender; drain. Add butter; allow to melt. Mash potatoes and butter with potato masher or electric mixer until smooth. Add condensed milk with the following seven ingredients. Stir well to incorporate thoroughly. Taste to adjust seasonings. Pour into two prepared pie crusts. Bake at 350° for 45 minutes, or until knife inserted in center comes out clean (may need to make a foil sleeve to place around crust if it seems to brown too much). Remove from oven; cool. Top individual servings with sweet whipped cream.

Serves 8.

KEY LIME PIE

1 cup chocolate wafers, crushed
5 tablespoons butter, melted
¼ cup sugar
½ cup macadamia nuts, chopped fine
1 cup sugar
⅓ cup cornstarch
⅛ teaspoon salt
1 cup milk, divided
½ cup heavy cream

3 egg yolks, slightly beaten
½ cup Key lime juice
2 tablespoons butter
½ teaspoon vanilla
½ cup cream cheese
Sweet whipped cream, for topping
Macadamia nuts, chopped fine,
 for garnish

Combine wafers, butter, ¼ cup sugar, and ½ cup macadamia nuts in a large bowl; press into a 9-inch pie plate. Bake at 350° for 10 minutes. Set aside to cool.

Combine the cup of sugar, cornstarch, salt, and ½ cup of the milk in large saucepan. Whisk well to dissolve cornstarch; add remaining ½ cup milk. Combine cream and egg yolks in a small bowl; whisk well to combine. Pour through a strainer into the saucepan. Cook over medium-high heat, whisking constantly until hot and very thick. Remove from heat; whisk in lime juice. Continue to cook, about 2 minutes, until very thick. Remove from heat; whisk in butter and vanilla. Pour a small amount into a separate bowl containing the cream cheese; whisk well to blend. Combine the two mixtures; mix well. (At this point, you may want to add just a bit of green food coloring.) Pour into prepared crust. Cover and refrigerate for at least six hours, or until set. Serve on individual serving plates and top with whipped cream. Garnish with chopped macadamia nuts.

Serves 8–10.

APRICOT FRIED PIES
Squaw Mountain Style

The Pastry:

2½ cups unbleached flour
¾ teaspoon baking powder
½ teaspoon salt
½ teaspoon sugar

½ cup vegetable shortening
1 egg (beaten with evaporated milk)
¾ cup evaporated milk

Place flour, baking powder, salt, sugar and shortening in medium-sized bowl. Cut shortening into flour mixture until crumbly. Add egg and milk mixture; mix until dough forms a smooth ball. Pinch pieces of dough into small balls (about golf ball–sized). Using a rolling pin, roll a ball onto a lightly floured surface, making a 6-inch circle. Repeat with remaining dough, placing a piece of waxed paper in between each. Cover and set aside until ready to fill.

The Apricot Filling:

2½ pounds dried apricots
1½ cups sugar

4 tablespoons butter
1 tablespoon unbleached flour

Barely cover dried apricots with water in medium-sized saucepan. Cook over medium heat until soft (about 30 minutes). Add sugar; cook until sugar is dissolved and mixture has thickened slightly. Stir in butter and flour; mix well and continue to cook until thickened. Cool to room temperature.

Assembly: Place approximately 1½ tablespoons of apricot filling onto one side of a pastry circle. Fold the other half side of pastry over filling. Crimp edges together, using fork tines, to seal. Repeat procedure for remaining pies. Deep fry at 275°–300° until lightly browned. Drain on paper towels.

BAKLAWA
Cathy's Recipe

1 pound walnuts, chopped fine

¾ cup sugar

1 teaspoon ground cloves

1 teaspoon ground cinnamon

1 pound package filo pastry sheets

1 cup butter, melted

3 cups sugar

2 cups water

Juice of 1 lemon

1 teaspoon rosewater, optional

Combine walnuts, sugar, cloves, and cinnamon in a medium-sized mixing bowl. Set aside.

Carefully spread one pastry sheet, and brush with melted butter. Continue to layer pastry sheets, brushing each with butter, until the stack has six or seven layers.

Spread a thin layer of the walnut and spice mixture on top, and roll each short edge to the center. Cut down the center to make two long rolls. Place the rolls on a shallow baking sheet (it must have sides!). Continue to layer, fill, and roll the remaining sheets until they are all used (should have six to eight rolls on the baking sheet). Cut each roll halfway through, diagonally, about every 1½ inches, creating a diamond-shaped pattern. Bake in 350° oven for approximately 25 minutes, or until light golden brown on top and bottom.

Combine sugar and water in a large saucepan. Bring to a boil over medium-high heat; cook until the sugar is dissolved. Remove from heat; add lemon juice and optional rosewater. Pour mixture over slightly cooled baklawa and allow to stand until the syrup is absorbed (at least overnight). Cut completely through your diagonal cuts to separate pieces.

ICEBOX FRUIT PIE

1 (16 ounce) can red cherries, drained

1 (16 ounce) can crushed pineapple, drained

1¾ cups sugar

4 tablespoons unbleached flour

1 (3 ounce) package orange gelatin

3 bananas, sliced

1 cup pecans, chopped

2 (purchased) graham cracker pie shells

12 ounces frozen whipped cream, thawed

Place cherries, pineapple, sugar, and flour in a large saucepan; mix well. Cook over medium heat until hot and thickened. Remove from heat; add gelatin and mix well. Chill. Divide bananas and pecans; place in bottoms of pie shells. Pour equal amounts of cherry mixture over tops. Cover and refrigerate. Top with sweet whipped cream!

MOM'S MILLIONAIRE PIE

1 (14 ounce) can sweetened
　　condensed milk
½ cup lemon juice
1 (15½ ounce) can crushed
　　pineapple, drained

1 cup pecans, chopped
½ cup flaked coconut, optional
9 ounces frozen whipped cream, thawed
2 prepared graham cracker pie crusts

Combine the milk, lemon juice, pineapple, pecans, and optional coconut in a large bowl; mix well. Using a rubber spatula, gently fold in whipped cream. Equally divide into prepared pie crusts. Cover and refrigerate for at least 4 hours.

PINK LEMONADE PIE

½ cup butter
2 tablespoons sugar
1 cup unbleached flour
1 (6 ounce) can pink lemonade,
　　thawed

1 (14 ounce) can sweet
　　condensed milk
12 ounces frozen whipped cream,
　　thawed

Cream butter and sugar in work bowl of electric mixer; add flour and mix until combined. Place ⅓ cup of the mixture in the bottom of 9-inch pie plate. Press remaining dough around edges and flute. Bake at 375° for 12–15 minutes, or until lightly browned; cool.

Place lemonade and condensed milk in a large bowl; mix well to blend. Gently fold in a generous half-portion of the whipped cream. Spoon into prepared pie crust; freeze. When ready to serve, top with remaining whipped cream.

SNOW ICE CREAM

2 eggs
¾ cup sugar

¾ cup milk, plus 1 teaspoon vanilla
Freshly fallen snow

Place eggs in work bowl of electric mixer. Beat on medium speed, slowly adding sugar. Mix until creamy. Add milk and vanilla; mix well. Spoon clean snow into mixture. Using a rubber spatula, mix in as much snow as mixture will allow. Hop into bed under an electric blanket, and watch a good movie while you enjoy your ice cream! (This makes a fine impression on your grandchildren!)

My mom made this for us when it snowed, about once every five years! From when I was very young, I recall the haunting warning, "Don't eat the snow, because it's contaminated with nuclear fallout." I guess that's why I glow in the dark!

PECAN ICE CREAM
with Bourbon and Fudge Sauce

3 cups light cream
½ cup light brown sugar (packed)
¼ cup sugar

1¼ cups broken pecan pieces
2 tablespoons bourbon
Fudge Sauce (recipe follows)

Combine cream, brown sugar, sugar, pecans, and bourbon into ice cream freezer bowl. Blend with a rubber spatula; allow to sit a few minutes to help dissolve sugars. Once the sugars are dissolved, place the churn in the work bowl, and freeze according to the manufacturer's instructions. Serve with Fudge Sauce drizzled on top.

Yield: 2½ quarts.

Fudge Sauce

1 cup semisweet chocolate, chopped
1 cup butter
⅔ cup evaporated skim milk
⅓ cup light corn syrup

¼ cup light brown sugar (packed)
1 teaspoon vanilla
4 tablespoons bourbon

Place ingredients, except bourbon, in top of double boiler. Simmer over medium-low heat until hot and sugars are melted. Stir in bourbon. Serve warm.

Yield: 3½ cups.

HOMEMADE VANILLA ICE CREAM

2 cups sugar
8 cups milk, divided
⅛ teaspoon salt
3 egg yolks

14 ounces sweetened condensed milk
2 cups light cream
1 cup heavy cream
1 tablespoon vanilla

Combine sugar, 2 cups of the milk, and salt in large saucepan. Whisk egg yolks with a small amount of milk; strain into the saucepan. Cook over medium heat, stirring constantly, until hot. Do not boil. Remove from heat; cool. Add remaining milk, condensed milk, creams, and vanilla; stir well. Place in ice cream freezer and follow manufacturer's instructions for freezing.

Yield: 1½ gallons.

MAPLE-NUT ICE CREAM

1½ cups maple syrup
2 egg yolks, lightly beaten
1½ cups milk, divided

2 cups heavy cream
2 teaspoons vanilla
1 cup walnuts, chopped fine

Place syrup and egg yolks in top of double boiler. Cook over medium heat, whisking continuously. Add 1 cup of the milk; continue to cook until slightly thickened. Remove from heat; whisk in remaining milk, cream, and vanilla. Stir in nuts. Place in ice cream freezer and follow manufacturer's instructions.

Yield: 1 quart.

BANANA-NUT ICE CREAM

2 egg yolks, lightly beaten
1 cup sugar
2 tablespoons lemon juice
1½ cups mashed banana

2 cups heavy cream
1 cup milk
2 tablespoons rum
1 cup roasted pecans, chopped fine

Combine eggs, sugar, and lemon juice in medium-sized bowl. Allow to rest 5 minutes. Add remaining ingredients; stir well. Place in ice cream freezer and follow manufacturer's instructions.

Yield: 1 quart.

BANANA SPLIT ICE CREAM

6 eggs, well beaten
2 cups sugar
1 quart heavy cream
1½ quarts chocolate milk
1 (15½ ounce) can crushed
  pineapple

1½ cups frozen strawberries,
  thawed
4 bananas, roughly mashed
1 tablespoon vanilla
1 cup chocolate syrup
1 cup roasted pecans, chopped

Place eggs, sugar, and heavy cream in large saucepan. Cook over medium heat, stirring constantly, until slightly thickened. Cool. Pour into freezing container. Add remaining ingredients; mix well to blend. Freeze in ice cream freezer, following manufacturer's instructions.

Yield: 1 gallon.

PINK CHAMPAGNE SORBET

5 cups fresh pink grapefruit
  juice, divided
1¼ cups sugar
½ cup light corn syrup
1 tablespoon grated pink
  grapefruit peel

¾ cup champagne
  (or other sparking wine)
Fresh mint, for garnish

Place 3 cups of the grapefruit juice and sugar into a large saucepan. Heat over medium heat until sugar is dissolved. Turn off heat. Pour in corn syrup; stir to blend. Add the remaining 2 cups grapefruit juice, grapefruit peel, and champagne (this should be cooled by now). Place in ice cream freezer and freeze according to manufacturer's instructions. Transfer sorbet to a plastic container; cover and place in freezer until ready to serve.

Yield: about 8 cups.

Serving suggestion: Sorbets are delicious for a dessert, or as a palate cleanser. This particular sorbet was served as dessert at a luncheon. The sorbet was "fluffed" into beautifully fluted fresh grapefruit bowls and garnished with fresh mint sprigs!

SIMPLE SYRUP

4 cups sugar   **4 cups water**

Place the sugar and water in a large saucepan. Simmer over medium heat until sugar is dissolved. Allow to cool. Store in a covered jar in refrigerator for use in sorbets.

Yield: 4 cups.

LEMON SORBET
For my Family

1 cup fresh lemon juice   **2½ cups simple syrup**
1 tablespoon lemon zest   **(previous recipe)**

Combine the above ingredients in ice cream freezer; follow manufacturer's instructions for freezing.

Yield: 4 cups.

If you like lemons, there'll be no leftovers!

FRESH STRAWBERRY SORBET

1½ pints strawberries, puréed   **2 tablespoons lemon juice**
¾ cup simple syrup (see index)

Combine the above ingredients in ice cream freezer; follow manufacturer's instructions for freezing.

Yield: 3 cups.

CANTALOUPE SORBET

1 cantaloupe, peeled, seeded,   **1 cup Simple Syrup (see index)**
**   and puréed**   **2 teaspoons lemon juice**

Combine the above ingredients in ice cream freezer; follow manufacturer's instructions for freezing.

Yield: 4 cups.

KIWI SORBET

6 kiwi fruits, peeled and puréed   **3 teaspoons lemon juice**
1 cup Simple Syrup (see index)

Combine the above ingredients in ice cream freezer; follow manufacturer's instructions for freezing.

Yield: 4 cups.

CRANBERRY SORBET

2¼ cups cranberry juice   **½ cup Simple Syrup (see index)**

Combine the above ingredients in ice cream freezer; follow manufacturer's instructions for freezing.

Yield: 3 cups.

Cookies, Candies, Beverages

From Chocolate Truffles to Popcorn Balls

CHOCOLATE BISCOTTI

1¾ cups unbleached flour
1 teaspoon baking soda
¼ teaspoon salt
⅓ cup cocoa
1 cup sugar
2 tablespoons instant coffee powder
4 (1 ounce) bittersweet chocolate
    squares, chopped

3 eggs
1 teaspoon vanilla
½ teaspoon almond extract
1 cup toasted almonds, chopped
Cooking spray
4 (1 ounce) squares semisweet
    chocolate
1 teaspoon vegetable shortening

Place first seven ingredients in food processor; process until chocolate is finely chopped (about 20 seconds), stopping once to scrape sides of bowl.

Place eggs, vanilla, and almond extract in work bowl of electric mixer. Beat on medium speed until creamy. Gradually add flour mixture, decreasing speed as it thickens (make sure you have the proper mixing blade on). Stir in almond pieces; mix well to blend.

Place dough on a lightly floured surface; divide in half. Lightly flour hands, and shape each half into a 12-inch log. Place on insulated baking sheet that has been prepared with cooking spray. Bake at 300° for 50 minutes. Remove from oven; cool.

Using a serrated knife, cut each log crosswise into ½-inch slices. Place slices on baking sheet and bake at 300° for 40 minutes, turning once after the first 15 minutes. Remove from oven; cool.

Melt semisweet chocolate squares in top of double boiler over medium heat. Add shortening, and mix until smooth. Spread on top sides of biscotti. Cool until chocolate has hardened.

Yield: 3 dozen.

CHOCOLATE-OATMEAL DROP COOKIES

½ cup butter
¼ cup cocoa
2 cups sugar

½ cup milk
1 teaspoon vanilla
2 cups (quick-cook) oatmeal

Place the first four ingredients in a large saucepan. Bring to a boil, stirring continuously, over medium-high heat. Boil for 5 minutes; remove from heat. Add vanilla and oatmeal; mix well. Carefully drop by small spoonfuls onto parchment or waxed paper. Allow to cool.

Yield: about 4 dozen.

CHOCOLATE COOKIES

1 cup butter, softened	1 teaspoon ground cinnamon
1 cup sugar	3 cups unbleached flour
1 cup light brown sugar (packed)	1 teaspoon baking soda
2 eggs	1 teaspoon salt
1 teaspoon kahlua	1 cup chocolate chips
1 tablespoon vanilla	1 cup chocolate candy bar, chopped
1 cup cocoa	1 cup roasted walnuts, chopped

Place butter, sugar, and brown sugar in work bowl of electric mixer. Beat on medium speed until creamy, scraping sides of bowl as necessary. Add eggs, kahlua, and vanilla; beat until well blended. Add cocoa, cinnamon, flour, soda, and salt; beat well, scraping sides of bowl as necessary. Add chocolate chips, chopped candy bar, and walnuts. Mix only to blend thoroughly. Drop by very small spoonfuls, one inch apart, onto insulated baking sheet that has been prepared with cooking spray. Bake at 350° about 8 minutes. Remove from oven; allow to cool.

Yield: 8 dozen.

CHOCOLATE CHIP PEANUT BUTTER COOKIES

½ cup crunchy peanut butter	½ teaspoon vanilla
¾ cup vegetable shortening	1¼ cups unbleached flour
½ cup light brown sugar (packed)	½ teaspoon baking soda
½ cup sugar	¼ teaspoon salt
1 egg	1 cup chocolate chips

Place peanut butter, shortening, brown sugar, and sugar in work bowl of electric mixer. Beat on medium speed until creamy. Add egg, vanilla, flour, soda, and salt; mix well, scraping bowl as needed. Add chocolate chips. Mix only to blend thoroughly. Drop by small spoonfuls, one inch apart, onto insulated baking sheet that has been prepared with cooking spray. Bake at 375° for 10–15 minutes. Remove from oven; allow to cool.

Yield: 3 dozen.

CRUNCHY COCONUT COOKIES

1 cup butter, softened
1 cup sugar
1 cup light brown sugar (packed)
2 eggs
2 cups unbleached flour
1 teaspoon salt

1 teaspoon baking soda
1 teaspoon baking powder
1 teaspoon vanilla
1 cup coconut
1 cup puffed rice cereal
1½ cups pecan pieces

Place butter, sugar, brown sugar, and eggs in work bowl of electric mixer. Beat on medium speed until creamy. Add flour, salt, baking soda, baking powder, and vanilla. Mix well, scraping sides of bowl as necessary. Add coconut, cereal, and pecan pieces; mix only to incorporate. Make small balls, then flatten—or drop by spoonfuls onto lightly oiled baking sheets, two inches apart. Bake at 350° for 8–10 minutes. Remove from oven; allow to cool.

Yield: 4 dozen.

FRUITCAKE COOKIES

½ cup butter, softened
1 cup brown sugar (packed)
4 eggs
3 tablespoons milk
3 cups unbleached flour
1 teaspoon baking soda
¼ teaspoon salt
1 teaspoon vanilla

2 cups pecan halves
1 cup dried cherries
1 cup dried pineapple
1 cup raisins
1 teaspoon ground cloves
1 teaspoon ground nutmeg
1 teaspoon ground cinnamon
½ cup bourbon

Place butter, brown sugar, and eggs in work bowl of electric mixer. Mix on medium speed until creamy. Add milk, flour, baking soda, salt, and vanilla; mix well, scraping sides of bowl as necessary. Add remaining ingredients; mix well to blend. Drop onto lightly oiled baking sheets by very small spoonfuls (cookies will be about the same size as dough you spoon out). Bake at 250° for about 30 minutes. Remove from oven; allow to cool. (Oven temperatures vary; sample to see if these are cooked as well as you like them.) The bourbon gives these cookies a nice sheen!

Yield: 8 dozen.

I've never really enjoyed fruitcakes, but I have always appreciated these fruitcake cookies. I think it's their look—nice and festive!

OATMEAL COOKIES
For Don

1 cup vegetable shortening
1 cup light brown sugar (packed)
1 cup sugar
2 eggs
1½ teaspoons vanilla

1½ cups unbleached flour
1 teaspoon baking soda
1 teaspoon salt
3 cups (quick-cook) oatmeal
1 cup chopped pecans

Place shortening, brown sugar, sugar, eggs, and vanilla in work bowl of electric mixer. Mix on medium speed until creamy. Add flour, soda, and salt. Mix well, scraping sides as needed. Add oatmeal and pecans; mix well to incorporate. Drop by spoonfuls onto lightly oiled baking sheet. Bake at 350° for 10–12 minutes. Remove from oven; cool.

Yield: 4 dozen.

PARTY COOKIES

1 cup butter, softened
1 cup light brown sugar (packed)
½ cup sugar
2 eggs
1½ teaspoons vanilla
2½ cups unbleached flour

1 teaspoon baking soda
1 teaspoon salt
2 cups candy-coated chocolates,
OR chocolate chips and
1 cup chopped nuts

Place shortening, brown sugar, sugar, eggs, and vanilla in work bowl of electric mixer. Mix on medium speed until creamy. Add flour, baking soda, and salt; mix well, scraping sides of bowl as necessary. Add candy-coated chocolates; mix well to incorporate. Drop by spoonfuls onto lightly oiled insulated baking sheet. Bake at 375° for 10–12 minutes.

Yield 4 dozen.

FORGOTTEN COOKIES

2 egg whites
Pinch of salt
⅔ cup sugar

1 cup chopped pecans
1 cup chocolate chips

Place egg whites and salt in medium bowl; beat until foamy. Gradually add sugar. Beat until stiff peaks form. Stir in pecans and chocolate chips. Drop by spoonfuls onto baking sheets lined with parchment paper. Place in 350° oven. Immediately turn off oven, leave until oven is completely cool.

Yield: 4 dozen.

SUGAR COOKIES
(Rolled)

½ cup vegetable shortening
½ cup butter
2 cups sugar
4 eggs

1 teaspoon vanilla
⅛ teaspoon salt
4 teaspoons baking powder
4⅓ cups unbleached flour

Place shortening, butter, sugar, eggs, and vanilla in work bowl of electric mixer. Beat on medium speed until creamy. Add salt, baking powder, and flour. Mix well to incorporate, scraping sides as needed. Cover with plastic wrap and refrigerate for about 30 minutes. Working with one-third of the dough at a time, roll about ¼-inch thick on a lightly floured work surface. Cut in shape you prefer, using a cookie cutter. Place on a lightly oiled insulated baking sheet. Bake at 400° for 8–12 minutes, or until lightly browned. Remove from oven; cool. Frost cookies and decorate as you choose!

Yield: 4 dozen.

WHITE FROSTING
for Cookie and Cake Decorating

¾ cup vegetable shortening
2 tablespoons butter, softened
½ teaspoon salt
⅔ cup milk

1 teaspoon vanilla
1 teaspoon almond extract (only if
   frosting a cake)
2 pounds powdered sugar

Combine shortening, butter, salt, milk, and vanilla; mix well on low speed to blend. Add powdered sugar; mix on slow speed to blend. (Mix just enough to blend thoroughly. Beating the frosting will incorporate air into the frosting, which is not what you want!) If frosting seems too moist, add more powdered sugar, a little at a time. If it seems too dry, add more milk, a little at a time. Keep covered, to prevent drying out, until ready to use.

Yield: 4½ cups.

My mother has used this recipe all of my life, which is almost all of hers, too! Some of my memories of her baking our birthday cakes and baking these cookies for special holidays are from as long ago as I am old, and as recent as this past Easter! She enjoys the happiness it brings to others—Thanks, Mom!

KISS COOKIES

1 cup butter, softened
⅔ cup sugar
1 teaspoon vanilla
¼ cup cocoa

1⅔ cup unbleached flour
1 cup pecans, chopped fine
42 chocolate candy kisses
Powdered sugar, optional

Combine butter, sugar, vanilla, and cocoa in work bowl of electric mixer. Mix on medium speed until creamy. Add flour; mix well to blend. Add pecans; mix well. Cover with plastic wrap and place in refrigerator. (Allow to chill as you unwrap the candy kisses.) Roll approximately one tablespoon dough around each candy. Place on lightly oiled insulated baking sheet. Bake at 375° for 10–12 minutes. Remove from oven; cool thoroughly. Roll in powdered sugar, if you choose!

Yield: 3½ dozen.

PEANUT BUTTER KRISPIES

¾ cup sugar
¾ cup light corn syrup
4 tablespoons butter

¾ cup (creamy) peanut butter
½ teaspoon vanilla
2½ cups puffed rice cereal

Place sugar, corn syrup, and butter in large saucepan. Bring to a boil over medium heat. Continue to boil for two minutes. Add peanut butter and vanilla; stir quickly to blend. Turn off heat; add puffed rice cereal; mix well. Drop by small spoonfuls onto parchment or waxed paper; cool.

Yield: 4 dozen.

PIZELLE COOKIES

6 eggs
1½ cups sugar
3½ cups unbleached four

1 cup butter, melted and cooled
4 teaspoons baking powder
2 tablespoons vanilla

Place eggs in work bowl of electric mixer; beat on medium speed, slowly adding sugar, until well blended. Add remaining ingredients; mix well. Drop by spoonfuls onto preheated Pizelle iron and cook according to manufacturer's instructions. While hot, you may form into cones or various other shapes. I like to leave mine flat and dust with powdered sugar!

Variation: *May substitute by adding ½ cup ground nuts to the dough for ½ cup of the flour.*

POPCORN BALLS

2 cups sugar
1½ cups water
½ cup light corn syrup
¼ teaspoon salt

1 teaspoon vanilla
1 teaspoon vinegar
5 quarts freshly made popcorn

Place sugar, water, corn syrup, and salt in large saucepan. Cook over medium-high heat until it reaches very hard ball stage; add vanilla and vinegar. Continue cooking to light crack stage. Remove from heat. Very carefully, pour over popcorn that is placed in a very large mixing bowl. Stir well with a wooden spoon to coat every kernel. Place some vegetable shortening on your hands to keep mixture from sticking. Very quickly (and cautiously), using your hands, press into balls.

Yield: 20.

FROZEN TREATSICLES
For Michelle

1 small package flavored gelatin
1 small package flavored drink mix

1 cup sugar
1 cup water

Combine all ingredients in a pitcher; stir to dissolve. Pour into individual molds and freeze.

PEANUT BRITTLE

1 teaspoon baking soda
1 teaspoon water
1 teaspoon vanilla
1½ cups sugar

2 cups water
1 cup light corn syrup
2 cups raw peanuts, shelled
3 tablespoons butter

Spread a thin layer of butter onto two insulated baking sheets. Dust tops with sugar; set aside. Mix soda, teaspoon water, and vanilla in small bowl; set aside.

Place sugar, 2 cups water, and corn syrup in heavy, medium-sized saucepan. Bring to a boil over medium-high heat; cook until temperature reaches 240° (soft ball stage) on candy thermometer. Add peanuts and butter. Continue cooking, stirring continuously, until temperature reaches 300° (hard crack stage). Remove immediately; quickly stir in baking soda mixture until light and foamy. Pour one-half of the mixture onto each baking sheet. Using a metal spatula (working quickly and carefully, as the mixture is very hot), slide lightly oiled spatula under brittle and pull to stretch as thin as possible, turning pans as needed. Allow to cool; break into pieces.

SHERRIL'S CREAMY PRALINES

1 cup sugar	1 cup heavy cream
1 cup light corn syrup	4 cups pecan halves
1 cup butter	1 teaspoon vanilla

Combine sugar and corn syrup in large saucepan. Cook over medium-low heat until thermometer reaches 250°. Remove from heat; add butter and cream, stirring to blend well. Return to heat and cook until thermometer reaches 242°, stirring constantly. (You will know it's ready when it's golden with brown streaks—watch carefully!) Remove from heat; add pecans and vanilla. Stir well. Drop by teaspoonfuls onto parchment paper or buttered foil. When cool, wrap each piece in plastic wrap.

BUTTERMILK PECAN PRALINES

2 cups light brown sugar	2 cups pecan halves
1/8 teaspoon salt	2½ tablespoons butter
1 cup buttermilk	

Combine sugar, salt, and buttermilk in a large saucepan. Stirring constantly, cook over medium-high heat until it reaches 236° (soft ball stage). Remove from heat. Add pecans and butter. Stir just until butter melts; cool slightly. With wooden spoon, beat until mixture is creamy but looks lighter in color. Drop by teaspoonfuls onto parchment paper or buttered foil.

Yield: 3 dozen.

PAULA'S BUTTERSCOTCH NOODLES

12 ounces butterscotch chips	1½ cups Spanish peanuts
4 cups Chinese noodles	

Place butterscotch chips in top of double boiler and melt over low heat. Stir in noodles and peanuts; mix well. Drop by spoonfuls onto parchment paper.

Yield: 4 dozen.

MILLIONAIRES

2 tablespoons water

2 tablespoons butter

1 (14 ounce) package caramels, unwrapped

3 cups pecan halves, cut into halves

⅓ of a ¼-pound bar of paraffin wax

1 (10 ounce) package chocolate chips

Place water, butter, and caramels in top of double boiler. Melt over low heat; stir in pecans. Drop by small spoonfuls onto buttered foil. Place in refrigerator until cold and firm.

Place paraffin and chocolate chips in top of double boiler; melt over low heat. Using a wooden pick or ice pick, quickly dip each caramel cluster (one at a time) into chocolate. Place on parchment or waxed paper to cool and set.

MILLION DOLLAR FUDGE
For Gay

3 (4½ ounce) plain chocolate candy bars

1 (12 ounce) package chocolate chips

2 cups marshmallow cream

1 tablespoon butter

1 teaspoon vanilla

4½ cups sugar

1¾ cup evaporated milk

1 pound walnuts or pecans, chopped

Melt candy bars, chocolate chips, marshmallow cream, butter, and vanilla in large, heavy saucepan over low heat.

As chocolate is melting, place sugar and milk in a medium, heavy saucepan. Bring to a boil over medium-high heat, stirring occasionally. Continue to boil for 6 minutes. Pour over chocolate mixture; stir well to blend. Add nuts; mix well.

Drop by small spoonfuls onto parchment or waxed paper. Allow to stand until completely cooled.

TRISHA'S TIGER BUTTER

1 pound almond bark
1½ cups crunchy peanut butter

1½ cups chocolate chips

Place almond bark and peanut butter in large bowl. Microwave at 50% power; stir to mix.

Place chocolate chips in medium-sized bowl. Microwave at 50% power; stir to mix.

Spread almond mixture on parchment-lined baking sheet. Drizzle chocolate over it, and swirl. Place in refrigerator to cool. Once cool, break into pieces. Store in refrigerator or other cool place.

CHOCOLATE-COATED COCONUT BALLS

½ cup butter
1 (14 ounce) can sweetened
  condensed milk
2 pounds powdered sugar
⅛ teaspoon salt

2 cups flaked coconut
2½ cups pecans, chopped fine
4 cups semisweet chocolate chips
¼ pound paraffin

Place butter in large bowl; microwave until just melted. Add milk, sugar, salt, coconut, and pecans; mix well. Place in refrigerator until well-chilled. Roll into one-inch balls. Return to refrigerator or place in freezer; chill until very firm.

Place chocolate chips and paraffin in top of double boiler. Melt over medium-low heat; stir until smooth.

Using a wooden pick or ice pick, quickly dip each coconut ball (one at a time) into melted chocolate. (Keep coconut balls cold, or they will become too soft to hold while dipping. Also, the cold temperature will aid in quick setting of chocolate!) Place on parchment or waxed paper to set.

And I must tell you, if there is a hole in your candy where you were holding it with a pick, just add a little chocolate over it to cover it up! (Mom made me say that!)

CHOCOLATE TRUFFLES

6 ounces semisweet chocolate
1 ounce unsweetened chocolate
½ cup heavy cream
2 tablespoons butter

¾ cup powdered sugar, sifted
1 egg yolk, lightly beaten, optional
3 teaspoons brandy
1 cup sifted cocoa, or crushed nuts

Place chocolates, cream, and butter in top of double boiler. Stir over hot water until chocolate melts. Add sugar and egg yolk, whisking to a smooth consistency; heat thoroughly. Add brandy; mix well to blend. Remove from heat; cool. Cover pan and place in refrigerator until malleable. Lightly dust hands with cocoa to prevent sticking, and shape into bite-sized balls. Roll in sifted cocoa or crushed nuts, and place in paper candy cups. Refrigerate.

Yield: 3 dozen.

ROCHELLE'S PEANUT PATTIES

2½ cups sugar
¾ cup white corn syrup
1 cup light cream
3 cups raw peanuts

1 teaspoon vanilla
2 tablespoons butter
¾ cup powdered sugar, sifted
Red food coloring

Combine first four ingredients in a heavy saucepan. Cook over medium-high heat until candy thermometer reads 242°. Remove from heat. Add remaining ingredients, adding a few drops of food coloring at a time, until mixture is the color you desire. Beat until creamy. Drop by spoonfuls onto parchment paper.

Have a little Irish blood in ya'? Add green food color, versus the red, and have yourself a "Saint Patty"!

HOT CHOCOLATE

½ cup sugar
1 heaping tablespoon cocoa
Dash of salt

4 cups milk
1 teaspoon vanilla
Sweet Whipped Cream, optional
    (see index)

Combine sugar, cocoa, and salt in large saucepan. Add just enough milk to make a smooth paste. Continue to add milk slowly, stirring continuously and adjusting strength to your liking. Add vanilla. Place over medium heat until hot. Serve with Sweet Whipped Cream on top.

BEVERLY'S EGG NOG

6 eggs, separated
¾ cup sugar
2 cups Sweet Whipped Cream
   (see index)

2 cups milk
1 cup Canadien Whisky
2 cups vanilla ice cream, softened
Nutmeg, for garnish

Place egg whites in work bowl of electric mixer. Beat on medium speed, adding a little bit of sugar, until stiff peaks form. Place in a large bowl; set aside.

Place egg yolks in same work bowl. Beat on medium speed, adding remaining sugar, until smooth and creamy. Fold in egg whites, whipped cream, milk, whiskey and ice cream. Sprinkle top with nutmeg. Serve very cold.

For over twenty years, our friends Jim and Beverly have made this wonderful egg nog to share with their family and friends on Christmas morning. We have always looked forward to our doorbell ringing, and seeing Jim standing there, grinning. I've never known if he thinks that Santa has been better to him than to us, and we don't know about it, or if he enjoys seeing us look so wired! Maybe he is just happy—probably so (know so!). Anyway, we have enjoyed the egg nog, and we are ever so thankful that they have been a special influence on our children through our years of friendship.

SISSY'S ICED TEA
For Tim

¾ cup fresh squeezed lemon juice
2 cups sugar

14 sprigs fresh mint
3 tablespoons instant tea

Place lemon juice and sugar in large glass measuring cup; bring to a boil in microwave. Add mint; return to a quick boil. Allow to cool; strain mint. Cover and store in refrigerator overnight. Make 1 gallon of tea, or use 3 tablespoons instant tea per 1 gallon of water. Add sugar solution; mix well. Serve over ice.

SPICED TEA MIX

2 cups instant orange drink mix
1 cup instant tea
1 package lemonade mix

2 cups sugar
1½ teaspoons ground cinnamon
¾ teaspoon ground cloves

Mix above ingredients together in a large bowl. Store in airtight container. Use 2 teaspoons mix per 6 ounces hot water.

HOT CHOCOLATE MIX

Powdered milk (to make 8 quarts)
11 ounces powdered coffee cream

1 pound box of powdered sugar
2 pound box of hot chocolate mix

Mix above ingredients together in a large bowl. Store in airtight container. Use ⅓ cup mixture per 6 ounces hot water.

FRUIT SMOOTHIE
Another Habitual

1 cup frozen blueberries or
    strawberries
1 orange, orange rind peeled, white
    left intact
1 apple, cored removed

1 banana, peeled
1 (8 ounce) can crushed pineapple
1 cup orange juice
½ cup skim milk
6 ice cubes

Place above ingredients in blender; blend on high speed until smooth!

Serves 2–4.

Variations: There are so many different options to choose from when making a smoothie. It just so happens that I do this one all the time, because I always have these particular ingredients on hand. So, use your imagination! Try adding some sherbets—or apple juice, yogurt, peaches, kiwi, dates, prunes, mango . . . Just have fun nutritiously—it'll make you feel better about some of the other "sinful" things you've eaten that day!

PINEAPPLE PUNCH

2 cups hot water
2 (3 ounce) packages pineapple
    gelatin
1½ cups sugar

2 cups water
1 quart pineapple juice
1 (2 liter) bottle ginger ale,
    chilled

Place hot water in large container. Add gelatin and sugar; stir to dissolve. Add the remaining ingredients, except ginger ale; chill. Just before serving, add the ginger ale. (If you would like a floating ring in your punch bowl, use the solution of hot water, gelatin, and sugar; place in a mold and freeze.)

Serves about 25.

ALMOND TEA PUNCH
A Favorite

1 cup (strong) brewed tea
1¾ cups sugar
½ cup lemon juice
1 tablespoon vanilla

1 (1 ounce) bottle almond extract
1 quart water
1 (1 gallon) zip-closure plastic bag
1 (2 liter) bottle of ginger ale, chilled

Mix hot tea and sugar in large pitcher until sugar is dissolved. Add lemon juice, vanilla, almond extract, and water; mix to blend. Pour into zip-closure plastic bag and freeze. When ready to use, remove from freezer and place in refrigerator about 3 hours before ready to serve (keep a watch on it and put the bag in a bowl!) When ready to serve, mash up to make slushy; add to punch bowl with ginger ale. Serve immediately.

Serves about 12.

Of course, you will probably need more than one recipe for your function. The nice thing is, the frozen bags will keep—so, better to have too much than too little! I make an ice ring using the concentrate. If you do this, add just a bit more ginger ale to compensate as it melts.

HOT CHRISTMAS PUNCH

3 quarts apple juice
1 quart cranberry juice
1 (46 ounce) can pineapple juice

1 (5 ounce) package red hot candies
Red food coloring, optional

Place the above ingredients in a large Dutch oven. Heat over medium heat until hot and candy is melted. Reduce heat to low to keep warm.

Serves about 25.

FROZEN MARGARITAS

¾ cup triple sec (Cointreau)
½–1 cup tequilla
1 (12 ounce) can frozen limeade, thawed

1 (12 ounce) can frozen lemonade, thawed

Combine the above ingredients into a one gallon ice cream freezer. Add enough water to reach the fill line on the freezing container. Follow manufacturer's instructions on freezing.

SAUCES

FROM MORNAY SAUCE
TO SOP SAUCE

ORANGE-CRANBERRY SAUCE
For Janet

1 cup sugar	**⅛ teaspoon Worcestershire sauce**
½ cup water	**½ teaspoon salt**
¾ cup white raisins	**¼ teaspoon ground cloves**
½ cup dried cranberries	**⅛ teaspoon ground mace**
1 cup orange, chopped with rind	**1 cup currant jelly**
1 tablespoon butter	**¼ cup ham drippings (optional)**
2 tablespoons red wine vinegar	**2 teaspoons cornstarch**

Place above ingredients, excluding cornstarch, in a medium-sized saucepan. Cook over medium heat until cranberries and raisins become plump. Using a small bowl, mix cornstarch with just enough water to stir into a smooth, slightly thin, paste. Slowly pour into sauce mixture, stirring constantly. Cook until sauce's cloudy appearance turns to a more clear appearance. This sauce should be light-bodied and of a thin consistency. Serve on the side with ham, turkey, chicken, pork chops, pork tenderloins, or beef tenderloins!

Yield: 2½ cups.

PEARS IN MAPLE SAUCE

3 pears	**2 tablespoons butter**
1 cup apple juice	**½ cup maple syrup**
2 tablespoons lemon juice	**Nutmeg, cinnamon, salt (to taste)**

Halve pears; core and peel. Cut each half into fourths or fifths, depending on size of pears. Place ingredients in a large skillet and bring to a boil over medium-high heat. Reduce heat to simmer, and continue to cook until pears are just tender, turning once. Remove pears. Increase heat to medium-high and continue to cook liquid until it reduces to syrup (about 4 minutes). Pour syrup over pears. Serve warm. This is good alongside gingerbread (see index), over ice cream, or as an accompaniment with pork.

Yield: 2½ cups.

APRICOT GLAZE

½ cup sugar
¼ teaspoon ground cloves
2 tablespoons cornstarch

2 cups apricot nectar
1 tablespoon lemon juice

Combine ingredients in small saucepan. Cook over medium heat until slightly thickened.

SPICY PEANUT SAUCE

1 tablespoon onion, chopped
1 garlic clove, pressed
1 jalapeño chile, seeded, chopped fine
1 tablespoon peanut oil
2½ tablespoons soy sauce

1 tablespoon lime juice
2 tablespoons light brown sugar
1 teaspoon molasses
½ cup creamy peanut butter
¼ teaspoon red pepper

Place onion, garlic, chile, peanut oil, soy sauce, and lime juice in food processor. Process until smooth; transfer to bowl. Whisk in remaining ingredients.

Yield: 1 cup.

LAMB SAUCE

½ cup brown sugar
½ cup currant jelly
1 tablespoon dry mustard

2 egg yolks
½ cup vinegar

Combine the above ingredients, except vinegar, in top of double boiler. Cook over medium heat until thickened. Slowly add vinegar, stirring constantly.

Yield: 1 cup.

CARAMELIZED ONION SAUCE

2 teaspoons butter
1 cup onion, chopped fine
½ cup red wine

1½ cups chicken broth
Salt and pepper, to taste

Melt butter in large skillet. Add onion; sauté over medium-high heat until golden brown. Add wine to deglaze pan; cook until liquid almost evaporates. Add chicken broth, salt, and pepper; bring to a boil. Cook until mixture is reduced to about ¾ cup. Serve warm with pork or chicken.

Yield: ¾ cup.

HAM GLAZE

½ cup brown sugar

1 teaspoon vinegar

¼ teaspoon ground cloves

1 teaspoon dry mustard

Combine the above ingredients in a small bowl; mix. Pat over top of ham before baking.

Yield: ½ cup.

ANCHO CHILE SAUCE

2½ cups water

3 ounces dried Ancho chiles

½ teaspoon salt

¼ teaspoon pepper

Bring water to a boil in medium-sized saucepan; add chiles and remove from heat. Allow to stand until cool, 30–40 minutes. Remove chiles, reserving water; discard seeds and stems. Place in food processor or blender and process until a thick paste forms; add salt and pepper. Gradually add approximately ¼ cup of the reserved water to thin the paste to desired consistency. This makes a good marinade and basting sauce. It is also used as one of the ingredients in Adobo Sauce (recipe follows).

ADOBO SAUCE

1 recipe Ancho Chile Sauce
    (previous recipe)

1–2 Serrano chiles, stems removed

1½ cups chicken broth

¾ cup chopped onion

4 garlic cloves, cut into halves

2 teaspoons sugar

¼ cup red wine vinegar

½ cup orange juice

1 tablespoon lemon juice (or lime)

½ teaspoon ground cumin

½ teaspoon dried oregano

¼ teaspoon dried thyme

½ teaspoon salt

⅛ teaspoon ground white pepper

Place ingredients in food processor or blender; process until smooth. Strain into a medium-sized saucepan; bring to a boil. Remove from heat; cool. Place in a pastry bag and pipe a small amount onto food for garnish, or use sparingly as a sauce.

BEEF MARINADE
with Garlic

⅓ cup red wine	1 tablespoon brown sugar
¼ cup beef broth	¼ teaspoon fresh ground pepper
2 tablespoons balsamic vinegar	3 garlic cloves, pressed

Combine ingredients in a large zip-closure bag. Marinate beef, such as tenderloin, in refrigerator for at least 2 hours.

Yield: 1 cup.

JIMMY'S BEEF MARINADE
with Jalapeños

1 cup water	1 teaspoon fresh ground pepper
¼ cup red wine vinegar	1 teaspoon garlic salt
2 tablespoons tomato paste	1 bay leaf
1 garlic clove, pressed	2 tablespoons butter (for grilled
½ cup jalapeños, seeded and diced	meat only)
½ teaspoon salt	

Combine ingredients in a large zip-closure bag. Marinate meat in refrigerator overnight.

Yield: 1¾ cups.

This is a good marinade for chicken or beef fajitas.

JOE'S SOP SAUCE

1 onion, chopped	¼ cup vinegar
½ cup butter	2 quarts water
Juice of 4 lemons	

Place onion and butter in Dutch oven; sauté over medium-high heat until onions are translucent. Remove from heat; add remaining ingredients, and cool to room temperature.

Yield: 1 cup.

My friend Joe says that this is the sauce to use for basting meat while grilling. If you use a sweet sauce, the sugar will cause meat to char, and we don't want that, do we?

BARBECUE SAUCE # 1

¾ cup prepared barbecue concentrate
   sauce
3 cups prepared ketchup
1 tablespoon Worcestershire sauce

3 tablespoons Liquid Smoke
3 tablespoons lemon juice
3 tablespoons brown sugar

Place the above ingredients in a medium-sized saucepan. Bring to a boil over high heat; reduce heat to low and simmer for 5 minutes.

Yield: 3¾ cups.

BARBECUE SAUCE # 2

1½ cups ketchup
½ cup prepared chili sauce
¼ cup steak sauce
3 tablespoons dry mustard
2 tablespoons prepared horseradish

1 tablespoon molasses
1 tablespoon red wine vinegar
1 tablespoon jalapeño, minced
1 tablespoon garlic, pressed
1 tablespoon hot pepper sauce

Whisk together the above ingredients in a medium-sized bowl. Cover and chill.

Yield: 2½ cups.

BARBECUE SAUCE # 3

1 small onion, chopped and sautéed
1 garlic clove, minced and sautéed
1 cup ketchup
3 tablespoons brown sugar
2 tablespoons vinegar

¼ teaspoon Liquid Smoke
3 tablespoons lemon juice
1 teaspoon prepared mustard
3 tablespoons Worcestershire sauce
¼ teaspoon hot sauce

Combine the above ingredients in a large saucepan. Cook over medium heat until hot. If sauce seems too thick, thin it just a bit with water. This sauce is good to use with miniature sausage franks, as an appetizer!

Yield: 1½ cups.

CRANBERRY BARBECUE SAUCE

1½ cups teriyaki sauce
1½ cups brown sugar
1 garlic clove, pressed
4 tablespoons molasses
½ teaspoon ground cumin

2 teaspoons ground red pepper
¼ cup hot pepper sauce
1 teaspoon fresh ground pepper
1 (16 ounce) can cranberry sauce

Combine the above ingredients in a medium-sized bowl; mix well. Use as a marinade for meat, or for basting. If basting, do so during the last 30 minutes of grilling to prevent charring.

Yield: 4 cups.

RICK'S MUSTARD SAUCE

1 cup butter
1 onion, chopped fine
½ cup brown sugar
2 tablespoons vinegar

¾ cup prepared mustard
1 tablespoon salt
1 teaspoon pepper
1 teaspoon garlic salt

Combine butter and onion in medium-sized saucepan. Sauté over medium-high heat until onion is tender. Add remaining ingredients. Reduce heat and cook for an additional 5 minutes.

Yield: 1½ cups.

This is a nice sauce to accompany brisket, along with barbecue sauce! Rick, a sculpter of Western art, really enjoys outdoor grilling. When using this sauce for basting brisket, he thins it just a bit with some water.

MUSTARD SAUCE

3½ teaspoons brown mustard
1 cup mayonnaise
2 teaspoons Worcestershire sauce

1 teaspoon steak sauce
⅛ cup light cream
⅛ teaspoon salt

Combine mustard and mayonnaise in small bowl; whisk to blend well. Add remaining ingredients; whisk until mixture is creamy. Chill.

Yield: 1 cup.

TERIYAKI SAUCE

1 teaspoon sesame (or vegetable) oil
1 tablespoon onion, minced
2 garlic cloves, minced
1 tablespoon ginger root, grated

1 cup light soy sauce
⅓ cup Japanese sake (or dry sherry)
¼ cup brown sugar
Salt, to taste

In a small saucepan, combine the oil, onion, garlic, and ginger root. Sauté over medium heat until just tender, being careful to not brown. Add remaining ingredients; salt to taste. Cook until sugar has dissolved. Use as a marinade for chicken or shrimp; reserve some of the sauce to serve on the side.

Yield: 1½ cups.

PIZZA SAUCE
Green or Red

Pesto (green):
3 cups cilantro or basil leaves
3 garlic cloves, chopped
1 tablespoon pine nuts

1 teaspoon each, salt and pepper
¾ cup olive oil
½ cup Parmesan cheese, grated

Combine ingredients, except cheese, in food processor or blender. Process on high until smooth (may need to add a bit more oil). Stir in cheese; mix well.

Yield: 1½ cups.

Tomato (red):
2 tablespoons olive oil
½ teaspoon fennel
1 cup onions, chopped fine
3 garlic cloves, minced
4 cups tomatoes, chopped fine
1 (6 ounce) can tomato paste
1 teaspoon sugar

1 bay leaf
½ teaspoon dried oregano
1 teaspoon dried basil
¼ teaspoon cinnamon
1½ teaspoon salt
1 teaspoon fresh ground pepper
1 tablespoon brandy

Sauté oil and fennel in Dutch oven over medium heat for 30 seconds; add onions and cook until onions are just tender. Add garlic; continue to cook until just turning brown. Add remaining ingredients, except brandy. Reduce heat, cover, and simmer for one hour (mixture will thicken as it cooks—which is what you need for a pizza sauce!). Add brandy during the last 10 minutes of cooking.

Yield: 3 cups.

HOLLANDAISE SAUCE

3 egg yolks, room temperature
2 teaspoons lemon juice
1 tablespoon water

¾ cup butter, cut in small pieces
⅛ teaspoon salt
¼ teaspoon ground white pepper

Whisk together egg yolks, lemon juice, and water in top of double boiler. Cook over medium heat, whisking constantly, until hot and fluffy (never allow to boil, for it will curdle). Reduce heat to low. Begin adding butter slowly, piece by piece, whisking to blend, but not to melt. (If at any time the butter seems to melt, rather than blend, remove from heat and allow mixture to cool just a bit. Continue to whisk more butter into the sauce, and it will recover its proper consistency.) Serve warm with steamed fresh veggies, such as broccoli and asparagus—or with poached salmon!

Yield: 1 cup.

WHITE SAUCE

½ cup butter
3 tablespoons onion, minced
½ cup unbleached flour
3½ cups milk

3 sprigs parsley
8 whole peppercorns
⅛ teaspoon fresh nutmeg, grated
Salt, to taste

Place butter and onion in medium saucepan. Sauté over medium heat until onion is tender. Remove from heat and stir in flour; mix well. Slowly stir in milk, a little at a time, until well blended. Add remaining ingredients and return to heat. Cook, stirring constantly, until thickened. (If the mixture seems to become too thick, thin it with just a little more milk.) Remove from heat; strain.

Yield: 3 cups.

MORNAY SAUCE

3 egg yolks
⅓ cup heavy cream
2 cups White Sauce (previous recipe)

¼ cup Parmesan cheese, grated
¼ cup butter, cut into small pieces

Whisk yolks and cream in top of double boiler. Add white sauce; cook over medium heat until thoroughly heated, but not boiling. Remove from heat; whisk in cheese and butter; mix well. Serve hot with steamed veggies, chicken, or fish.

Yield: 2½ cups.

CHEESE SAUCE

2 tablespoons butter
2 tablespoons unbleached flour
1 cup milk
½ teaspoon prepared mustard

1 teaspoon chicken stock granules
1 teaspoon hot pepper sauce
2 tablespoon dry sherry
¾ cup Cheddar cheese

In heavy medium-sized saucepan, heat the butter over medium heat. Stir in flour; mix well. Gradually add milk, a little at a time, until well blended. Add remaining ingredients, except for the cheese. Continue to cook, stirring continuously, until thickened and bubbly. Remove from heat; add cheese and stir until thoroughly blended. Serve immediately.

Yield: 1½ cups.

This is good with veggies, chicken, or fish!

TARTAR SAUCE

½ cup onions, chopped fine
½ cup dill pickles, chopped fine
2 cups mayonnaise

1–2 tablespoons lemon juice
Salt and Pepper, to taste

Place ingredients in a small bowl; mix well. Adjust seasonings to preferred taste. Cover and refrigerate.

Yield: 3 cups.

LEMON & BUTTER SAUCE

½ cup butter
2 tablespoons lemon juice

2 tablespoons fresh parsley, chopped

In a small saucepan, heat the butter over medium heat until lightly browned. Remove from heat. Stir in lemon juice and parsley. Serve hot, spooned over broiled fish.

Yield: ½ cup.

Variation: *Sauté two thin-sliced green onions with the butter; add 2 teaspoons Worcestershire sauce. Salt and pepper to taste.*

CREOLE SAUCE

¼ cup butter

⅓ cup mushrooms, sliced thin

1 onion, chopped fine

¼ green bell pepper, chopped fine

½ red bell pepper, chopped fine

2 tablespoons parsley, chopped fine

2 cups Sauce Espagnole (recipe follows)

½ teaspoon salt

¼ teaspoon fresh ground pepper

Dash of red pepper

Place butter and next five ingredients in medium-sized saucepan. Sauté over medium heat until onions are translucent. Slowly add Sauce Espagnole, stirring constantly. Add seasonings and adjust to preferred taste. Simmer over low heat for about 45 minutes. Serve with grilled steaks.

Yield: 2 cups.

SAUCE ESPAGNOLE

½ cup onion, chopped fine

1 stalk celery, sliced thin

1 carrot, sliced thin

¼ cup butter

¼ cup unbleached flour

5 cups brown stock (see index)

Bouquet garni*

Salt and pepper, to taste

Using a large skillet, sauté onion, celery, and carrot in butter over medium heat until onion is barely translucent. Remove from heat and stir in flour, making a smooth paste. Return to heat, and continue to cook until roux is well-browned. Remove from heat and allow to cool just a bit. Slowly whisk in brown stock, stirring constantly to prevent lumping. Add bouquet garni,* salt, and pepper. Continue to cook, uncovered, over low heat for 1½ hours. Remove bouquet garni; strain. This sauce is wonderful with roast and is a good base sauce.

Yield: 4 cups.

*Bouquet garni: *5 sprigs parsley, 1 sprig thyme, and 1 bay leaf, tied together with cooking string.*

SAUCE DIABLE

2 green onions, chopped fine
½ cup dry white wine
½ cup red wine vinegar
1 tablespoon Worcestershire sauce
¼ cup butter

¼ cup unbleached flour
1 cup brown stock (recipe follows)
¼ teaspoon fresh ground pepper
⅛ teaspoon red pepper
2 teaspoons parsley, chopped fine

Combine onions, white wine, vinegar, and Worcestershire sauce in medium-sized saucepan. Cook over medium heat until liquid is reduced to ¼ cup. Set aside. Melt butter in large skillet over medium heat. Slowly add flour to make a smooth roux; cook until browned. Slowly add brown stock, whisking constantly to prevent lumping. Add onion mixture; mix well and continue to cook for an additional 5 minutes. Strain into a gravy boat. Stir in fresh ground pepper, red pepper, and parsley. Serve hot as an accompaniment with broiled red meat or sautéed chicken breasts.

Yield: 2 cups.

BROWN STOCK
And Demiglace

7 pounds beef bones
1 onion, quartered
6 garlic cloves
1 cup turnips, chopped
1 cup carrots, sliced
1 cup celery, sliced
1½ teaspoons dried thyme

4 bay leaves
1 cup parsley, stems removed
1 teaspoon assorted peppercorns
8 medium tomatoes, chopped
1 (6 ounce) can tomato paste
7 cups dry red wine
12 (14½ ounce) cans chicken broth

Place bones in large roasting pan and bake, uncovered, at 450° until well browned, approximately 1½–2 hours. During the last 30 minutes, add the onion, garlic, turnips, carrots, and celery.

Remove pan from oven. Transfer ingredients to a twelve-quart stockpot; add remaining ingredients. Bring to a boil over medium-high heat; reduce heat and simmer gently 8–10 hours, covered.

Remove from heat; cool. Strain the stock into a clean pan, discarding solids. Place in refrigerator, and allow to cool completely, bringing fat to a solid state. Using a large spoon, remove fat and discard. Return pan to medium heat; continue cooking to reduce stock to one-half (this will enhance and intensify the flavor). Allow to cool. Divide into desired portions, and freeze in airtight containers until ready for use (up to three months). Makes approximately two quarts stock, or one quart demiglace. (To make a demiglace, reduce the stock further by one-half.)

CHICKEN STOCK

1 small onion, quartered	1 cup celery, sliced
3 garlic cloves	1 teaspoon dried thyme
1 tablespoon butter	3 bay leaves
5 pounds chicken wings	1 teaspoon peppercorns
1 cup carrots, sliced	4 quarts water

Place onion, garlic, and butter in large skillet. Cook over medium-high heat until well browned. (This gives the stock additional color and flavor.) Remove from heat; place in a large stockpot, along with the remaining ingredients. Bring to a boil over medium-high heat. Reduce heat to low. Simmer for 4 hours, adding water as necessary, and cooking an additional 30 minutes after the last addition.

Remove from heat; cool to room temperature. Strain into a clean pan. Place in the refrigerator or freezer long enough for fat to solidify on top of broth, then remove the fat. At this point, you may use the broth or return it to the stove top for further cooking! To reduce the broth by one-half will greatly intensify the flavor.

Yield: 3 quarts.

To make a Brown Chicken Stock, *place chicken wings in large roasting pan. Cook at 450° for one hour. During the last 30 minutes of cooking, add the onion, garlic, carrots, and celery. Remove from oven, and transfer the baked ingredients to a large stockpot, along with the remaining ingredients. Bring to a boil over medium-high heat. Reduce heat to low. Simmer for 4 hours, adding water as necessary and cooking an additional 30 minutes after the last addition of water. At this point, resume with the above instructions for completion of cooking (paragraph two).*

CREAMY WHITE SAUCE

1 onion, chopped fine	1 cup sour cream (or crème fraîche)
2 tablespoons butter	3 tablespoons lemon juice
⅓ cup dry white wine	⅛ teaspoon salt
1 teaspoon unbleached flour	⅛ teaspoon ground white pepper

Using a small saucepan, sauté onion in butter over medium heat. Cook until just tender; add wine. Continue cooking until reduced by one-half. Remove from heat. Add flour; mix until smooth. Add sour cream; return to heat. Continue to cook, stirring constantly, until thoroughly heated. Add remaining ingredients; mix well. Serve hot with poultry or red meat . . . or with chicken enchiladas!

Yield: 1 cup.

FRESH PEACH SALSA

3 cups peaches, chopped
1 cup red onion, chopped fine
¼ cup lemon juice
4 tablespoons cilantro

½ jalapeño pepper, seeded
  and minced
2 teaspoons honey
⅛ teaspoon salt

Place the above ingredients in a medium bowl; toss well to mix.

Yield: 3 cups.

Variation: *Substitute papaya, mango, or combination of the two for the peaches. Add a small amount of fresh corn kernels; adjust seasonings.*

GARDEN-FRESH SALSA

2 cups fresh corn kernels
1 cup fresh tomato, chopped
½ cup jicama, chopped
¼ cup red onion, chopped

2 tablespoons cilantro, chopped
¼ teaspoon each, salt and pepper
¼ teaspoon paprika
1 jalapeño pepper, seeded and
  minced

Combine the above ingredients in a medium bowl; toss well to mix.

Yield: 3¾ cups.

This is good with chicken or fish!

PINEAPPLE SALSA

2 cups pineapple, chopped fine
½ cup red onion, chopped fine
½ jalapeño chile, seeded and minced
1 garlic clove, minced

1 cup chopped tomato
¼ cup cilantro, chopped
1 tablespoon brown sugar
1 tablespoon cider vinegar

Combine the above ingredients in small bowl; mix well. Cover and refrigerate. This is a nice accompaniment for grilled pork chops!

Yield: 3½ cups.

PAPAYA SALSA

½ cup tomato, chopped
½ cup purple onion, chopped
½ cup papaya, chopped
¼ cup green bell pepper, chopped
¼ cup yellow bell pepper, chopped
¼ cup cilantro, chopped fine

2 jalapeño peppers, seeded and
  minced
3 tablespoons lime juice
½ teaspoon chili powder
1 tablespoon honey

Combine the above ingredients in a medium-sized bowl; mix well to coat. Cover and refrigerate.

Yield: 2 cups.

MANGO SALSA

4 mangos, peeled and chopped
¼ cup celery, chopped fine
¼ cup red bell pepper, chopped fine
1 jalapeño pepper, seeded and minced
¼ cup cilantro, chopped fine

¼ cup honey
3 tablespoons olive oil
2 tablespoons lime juice
Salt, to taste

Combine the above ingredients in a small bowl; mix well to blend. Cover and chill.

Yield: 2 cups.

FRESH RED PEPPER RELISH

1 tablespoon butter
¼ cup green onions, chopped
½ cup cilantro, chopped
3 tomatoes, peeled and chopped
1 red bell pepper, seeded and chopped

3 tomatillos, husked and minced
1 jalapeño, roasted, peeled, seeded
  and minced
2 tablespoons lime juice
Salt and Pepper, to taste

Combine butter and onions in small skillet. Sauté over medium heat until onion is just tender. Remove from heat; add remaining ingredients. Mix well. Serve at room temperature. This is a really delicious garnish for grilled tuna steaks!

Yield: 1 cup.

CUSTARD SAUCE

4 egg yolks   2 cups milk
4 tablespoons sugar   ½ teaspoon vanilla

Whisk egg yolks and sugar in top of double boiler, over medium heat. Gradually whisk in milk. Continue cooking, whisking continuously, until thick enough to coat the back of a spoon. (Overcooking the sauce will cause it to separate.) Remove from heat; whisk in vanilla. Serve warm with desserts, such as bananas, blackberries, etc.!

Yield: 1¾ cups.

Variation: *Should you like a flavored custard, whisk in 2–3 teaspoons of your favorite liqueur before serving, such as: amaretto, brandy, crème de banana, or praline. Or whisk in some fruit purée or nectar—be creative! Serve with fresh fruit, ice cream, or gelatin molds, waffles . . .*

CARAMEL SAUCE

1 cup sugar   ½ cup water

Combine the sugar and water in a small, heavy saucepan. Cook over medium-high heat, stirring only until sugar is dissolved. Cook until solution turns light golden brown. Remove from heat. Stir with a wooden spoon to help cool. (Have a cool water bath ready, just in case it begins browning too much; set the pan in the water, and stir with wooden spoon to cool.)

Yield: 1¼ cups.

LEMON SAUCE

1 tablespoon cornstarch   ¼ cup sugar
¼ cup lemon juice   Zest of 1 lemon
¾ cup water

Dissolve cornstarch in lemon juice in a small saucepan. Add water, sugar, and lemon zest; mix well. Cook over medium heat until mixture is thickened, stirring constantly. Serve hot with cakes, pastries, and ice cream!

Yield: 1 cup.

BUTTERSCOTCH SAUCE

½ cup butter
2 cups light brown sugar

½ cup heavy cream
1 teaspoon lemon juice

Place ingredients, except lemon juice, in top of double boiler. Cook over medium-high heat until sugar is dissolved, stirring frequently. Reduce heat to low; simmer 30 minutes, continuing to stir frequently. Serve with ice cream or bananas.

Yield: 1¾ cups.

FRESH BERRY SAUCE

2 pounds berries (blackberries,
    blueberries, etc.)
1 tablespoon cornstarch

2 teaspoons lemon juice
4 tablespoons sugar

Place berries in food processor or blender; process until smooth. Pour through a wire sieve, pressing to make three cups purée. Discard seeds. Place berries in a medium-sized saucepan. Dissolve cornstarch in lemon juice in a small bowl; add to the berries, along with the sugar. Cook over medium-low heat, stirring constantly, until sugar is dissolved and mixture has thickened. Serve with fresh berries and cream, cake, pastries, or ice cream!

Yield: 2 cups.

HOT FUDGE SAUCE

1 cup water
2 teaspoons butter
1 cup sugar

2½ tablespoons cornstarch
3 tablespoons cocoa
1½ teaspoons vanilla

Combine water and butter in a four-cup glass measuring cup; bring to a boil in microwave oven.

Combine sugar, cornstarch and cocoa in small bowl; mix well to blend. Add to water mixture; stir well. Return to microwave; cook until thickened, stopping frequently to stir. Remove from microwave; add vanilla. Serve hot with ice cream and brownies!

Yield: 1½ cups.

HOLIDAY WAFFLE SYRUP

⅔ cup maple syrup
⅓ cup honey
½ teaspoon cinnamon

¼ teaspoon allspice
⅛ teaspoon caraway seeds
¼ teaspoon lemon juice

Place syrup and honey in small saucepan. Cook over medium heat until hot. Remove from heat; stir in remaining ingredients. Serve over hot waffles.

Yield: 1 cup.

ORANGE BUTTER

¼ cup orange juice concentrate
¾ cup butter, room temperature

1 pound powdered sugar

Combine above ingredients in small bowl; whisk until smooth. Serve with popovers, muffins, or hot breads. Cover and refrigerate until ready to use.

Yield: 1½ cups.

Variation: For other butter flavors, substitute orange juice concentrate with various preserves!

CRÈME FRAÎCHE

½ cup heavy cream

½ cup sour cream OR
2 tablespoons buttermilk

Combine heavy cream and sour cream (or buttermilk) in a small glass bowl; whisk well. Cover and leave sitting out on counter for 48 hours, then refrigerate. Will keep up to a week in the refrigerator.

Yield: 1 cup.

Crème Fraîche is similar to sour cream. The heavy cream is allowed to thicken and ferment to create a pleasant but sour taste. The main advantage in preparing crème fraîche is that when used in cooking sauces, it won't curdle like sour cream does. For that reason, it is well worth making!

MISCELLANEOUS

PRESERVES TO PLAY DOUGH

PEACH PICKLES

2 quarts water
½ cup vinegar
4 pounds sugar

4 sticks cinnamon
1 tablespoon whole cloves
16 pounds semi-cling peaches, peeled

Place water, vinegar, and sugar in large Dutch oven. Wrap cinnamon and cloves in cheesecloth; tie, and add to water mixture. Bring to a boil over medium-high heat. Add peaches and return to boil. Cook for approximately 10 minutes, depending on size of peaches. Place in prepared canning jars; seal.

Yield: 4–5 quarts.

FREEZING FRESH PEACHES

Peel and slice peaches into appropriate-sized bowl. Using a rubber spatula, gradually add sugar until you've reached sweetness desired. Add sorbic acid, following package instructions (this is to prevent peaches from turning brown). Allow sugar to dissolve. Place in zip-closure freezer bags; freeze.

PEACH PRESERVES

Using one pound fruit to 2 cups sugar; peel and slice peaches into a Dutch oven. Bring to a boil over medium-high heat. Cook until thickened and syrupy. Pour into prepared canning jars; seal.

FREEZING BLACK-EYED PEAS

Place unwashed, shelled peas into plastic zip-closure bags. Freeze. (How simple can it get?) When ready to cook, empty peas into a colander and wash. Place in a medium saucepan and cover 2 inches above peas with water. Bring to a boil over medium-high heat; reduce heat and simmer until done (about 1½ hours). Season with bacon or ham, salt, and pepper.

GRANDMOTHER'S SWEET PICKLES

7½ pounds cucumbers, sliced
4 cups lime (for pickling)
2 gallons water
9 cups sugar

8 cups vinegar
3 tablespoons pickling spice
1 tablespoon salt
1 tablespoon celery seed

Soak cucumbers in pickling lime and water for 24 hours, using appropriate-sized container. After 24 hours, wash thoroughly several times and soak in clear water for 3–5 hours. Drain on cloth.

Combine remaining ingredients in Dutch oven; cook over medium heat long enough to dissolve sugar. Allow to cool completely. Place the cucumbers in solution and let soak overnight. The following day, bring to a boil over medium heat and boil gently for one hour. Place in prepared canning jars; seal.

POLLY'S DILL PICKLES

Use a wide-mouthed pint jar—how many? Just depends on amount of cucumbers you have . . . let's plan for 10! Place 2 garlic cloves and 1 grape leaf in bottom of each jar. Add 1 tablespoon dill seed, or 2 bunches of fresh dill. Place sliced cucumbers into jars.

Make a solution containing the following ingredients:
1 quart cider vinegar, 2 quarts water, ½ cup pickling salt. (Calculate for amount you need per pint!)

Cook above solution over medium-high heat until hot. Pour over cucumbers. Add a pinch of alum and a grape leaf on top; seal.

JUST FOR FUN

Play Dough:

1 cup flour	1 cup water
½ cup salt	1 tablespoon oil (scented, but edible)
2 teaspoons cream of tartar	Food coloring

Combine ingredients in medium-sized saucepan. Stirring constantly, cook over medium-low heat for approximately 3 minutes (a soft dough will form). Cool.

Christmas Tree Ornaments:

2 cups flour, plus ½ cup salt	¾ cup water

Mix ingredients in a medium-sized bowl, adding a little more water if needed to form a soft, pliable dough. Using a rolling pin, roll dough out and cut designs using a cookie cutter. Bake at 300° on ungreased baking sheet for about 45 minutes. Remove just before they begin to brown. Allow to cool. Decorate by painting with acrylic paints; allow to dry. Cover with a clear coat of acrylic to finish.

Suggestion: *Create other crafts, such as tiny woven wreaths! To make decorations adhere to the ornament, use a little water.*

Taffy:

1 cup sugar	2 tablespoons butter, unsalted
¾ cup light corn syrup	1 teaspoon salt
⅔ cup water	Food color, optional
1 tablespoon cornstarch	2 teaspoons vanilla, or other flavoring

Butter an 8-inch square pan; set aside. Combine all ingredients, except vanilla, in a medium-sized saucepan; mix to combine. Bring to a boil over medium heat. Continue to boil (but don't stir) until temperature reaches 260° on candy thermometer, or until a small amount of mixture dropped into cold water forms a hard ball that holds its shape, but is still pliable. Remove from heat; stir in vanilla. Pour into prepared pan. Once cool enough to handle, pull taffy until it's satiny, lighter in color, and stiff. If at any time the taffy becomes too sticky, just put a little butter on your hands. Pull into long strips about one inch wide; cut with kitchen shears. Wrap with parchment paper to help hold its shape.

Definitely a hands-on project—children love this!

GLOSSARY

Adobo sauce: A rich, spicy marinade, or basting and cooking sauce, for various poultry and meat dishes. It's often used for pickling chipotle chiles, for it contains vinegar.

Allspice: A nutmeg-like spice with cinnamon, clove, and juniper flavors. Good for pumpkin, sweet potatoes, and mincemeat pies.

Ancho chiles: Dried poblano chiles, deep reddish-brown in color and about four inches long. The sweetest of all dried chiles.

Asiago cheese: Similar to Monterey Jack cheese. It has a slightly tart flavor and melts easily.

Basil: An herb with hints of mint, cloves, and anise. Good in soups, Italian dishes, and various sauces.

Bay leaf: Woody herb, with a bit of a cinnamon flavor and a sweet smell. Good in stews, red beans, and various meat dishes.

Brown sauce: A basic sauce used in French cooking, it forms the foundation for many sauces. It takes time to make but is well worth the effort. I divide mine into two-cup portions and freeze to have on hand and share with friends from time to time!

Butavan: Butter/vanilla flavoring, found in specialty food stores.

Capers: Small green buds from the caper bush. It is used primarily to add a piquant flavor to various dishes. They're generally bottled and found in the pickle section at the food market.

Caramelized onions: Sliced onions sautéed over medium heat in a small amount of olive oil and sugar. They will turn soft and caramel brown in color. Stir, and watch closely to prevent them from burning! These are delicious served on burgers, fajitas, and various grilled meats.

Cardamom: A spice with hints of cinnamon, eucalyptus, and lemon. Good in coffee cakes.

Celery seed: Used as a spice, and tastes a little bitter! Good for potato salad, pimiento cheese, and soup.

Cheddar cheese: Mild or sharp flavor. It's a semi-soft cheese that is easily grated.

Chili powder: A spice that is a combination of ground chile peppers, cumin, salt, and oregano. Good in Mexican dishes and for flavoring red beans.

Chipotle chile: Dried, smoked jalapeños, with dark, reddish skin. They have a smoky, sweet flavor . . . and they're hot! They're generally bottled and packed in adobo sauce at the food market.

Cilantro: Fresh, somewhat lemony in fragrance, this herb is also known as coriander and Chinese parsley. Good in Mexican and Oriental dishes, as well as in various salads and salsas.

Cinnamon: A spice with a sweet, nutty flavor—a little warm to taste. Good for cinnamon toast, various cakes and pies, sweet potatoes, and hot chocolate.

Clarified butter: Melted butter that has had the milk solids removed. It's often used to sauté, because it doesn't burn easily, like whole butter does. To make clarified butter, melt butter over low heat until foam disappears from top. The milk solids will collect in bottom of pan. Pour off the clear butter and discard the milk solids.

Cloves: An aromatic dried flower bud from an evergreen tree, which may be used whole or ground. Good cooked with ham, chutneys, and gingerbread.

Confit: This term is generally seen when using a recipe for roasted duck or goose. It's cooked meat that lies under layers of fat.

Coriander: Lemony fragrant, the herb coriander is the same as cilantro. Good in various Oriental and Mexican dishes, as well as in Mideastern cuisine.

Coulis: Fruits or vegetables that are puréed.

Cream of tartar: A white, crystalline salt.

Crème fraîche: Similar to sour cream, but with a richer taste. Chances are you won't find it in your grocery market, so you'll have to make it yourself!

Cumin: Hot, bitter spice with a faint taste of caraway. Also known as *comino*. Good in various Mexican dishes, black bean soup, dips and curried vegetables.

Curry powder: A combination of cumin, turmeric, coriander, ginger, fenugreek, and cayenne. Good in various sauces and Mexican and Oriental dishes.

Deglaze: Adding a liquid called for in recipe to a warm pan that has had fat removed after sautéing. Its purpose is to loosen cooked-on brown bits to add back into the recipe.

Demi-glace: Reducing brown stock by one-half further to make an even richer brown sauce.

Dill: A mild herb with a faint anise taste. Good for various fish dishes and potatoes.

Egg wash: A mixture of one egg and one tablespoon water. Brush on pastry or breads before baking. It gives a nice shiny finish.

Fennel seed: Very intense spice with a sweet, licorice-like taste. Good in potatoes, cakes, and various seafood dishes.

Feta cheese: A soft, white Greek cheese made from sheep's milk or goat's milk. Served on salads, appetizers, and various entrées.

Flambé: To enflame a dish by adding liquor or liqueurs. Use only amount called for in recipe, and light with a tapered match. Exercise extreme caution.

Fontina cheese: A creamy, semi-soft, Italian cheese with a nutty flavor. Melts easily.

Frenched: Vegetables cut into thin, lengthwise strips before cooking; or, a rib chop with the meat trimmed from the end of the rib.

Ginger: A sweet spice with a bite! Good in various cakes, cookies, fish, and soups.

Goat cheese: Fresh goat cheese is soft and crumbly and has a somewhat earthy flavor. Delicious served on salads and in various Mexican dishes.

Heavy cream: Generally labeled "whipping cream." It contains a lot of butterfat, which doubles its volume when whipped.

Herb measurements: Use one teaspoon dried herbs for every three teaspoons fresh called for in recipe. Dried herbs lose flavor over time. Crush a small amount in your hand, and if there's no fragrance, discard.

Hungarian wax chiles: Sweet bell peppers.

Jalapeño chiles: These chiles are generally purchased when dark green. They turn red when fully ripe and are very hot. They are about two inches long, with rounded tips. I wear surgical gloves when I'm cutting these chiles!

Julienne: To cut into long, small strips, approximately one-fourth inch in diameter.

Light Cream: Generally labeled "coffee" or "table" cream. It contains about half the fat as heavy cream.

Mascarpone cheese: Similar to cream cheese, but much richer. It has a very short shelf life.

Mint: A cool and refreshing herb—there are many varieties! Good in iced tea as a garnish, or in mint jelly for your rack of lamb!

Monterey Jack cheese: A semi-soft cheese that is mild in flavor. Melts easily.

Nutmeg: A milder spice than cinnamon, yet warm and spicy. Good in Italian sauces, eggnog, and poundcakes.

Olive oil: Extra-virgin olive oil is the finest quality olive oil and has a pleasing flavor. It is used mainly in salad dressings and non-cooked recipes, for it has a low smoking point. Store in a cool, dark place.

Oregano: A peppery, strong-tasting herb. Good in Italian dishes, on garlic bread, and in stews.

Paprika: As spice that is earthy and rich, hot or mild. Sweet paprika (which is what I prefer) is made from sweet peppers and is good for Hungarian dishes, stew, and chicken.

Parmesan cheese: A hard cheese with a bit of a salty, sharp taste. Good on salads and Italian food.

Poblano chiles: Usually mild, dark green in color, and about two inches wide by four inches long. Their flavor is pleasing for many dishes. I roast mine and peel off the outer skin. (See index.)

Pizelle iron: Similar to a waffle iron, but not as deep. It cooks a thin cookie batter, creating a thin, crisp cookie. Great for making waffle cones for ice cream, as well as creating various presentations (such as small bowls) for desserts. May be found in most small kitchen-appliance sections in stores.

Ricotta cheese: A soft cheese that blends well with herbs for various dishes. It is also a good cheese to use for dessert dishes.

Roasted garlic: Garlic that has been oven roasted to make a soft inner pulp. (See index.)

Roasted chiles and peppers: Peppers that have had the outer skin blistered and removed, generally by placing under the broiler in the oven. (See index.)

Rosemary: Bittersweet, tea-like flavored herb with a hint of pine. Good in soups, potatoes, and poultry.

Roux: A combination of flour and fat, cooked to thicken gravy, sauces, or soups.

Sage: A woodsy-flavored herb. Good for stuffing, poultry, and pork dishes.

Sauté: To fry quickly, using very little fat.

Scald: To heat just until bubbly (usually refers to milk).

Scallions: Also known as green onions. Related to onions, garlic, and leeks. They have a subtle, peppery flavor.

Serrano chiles: Generally bright green when purchased and turn bright red, then yellow as they ripen. Small, pointed chiles, about one-and-a-half inches long. They are very hot.

Shallots: A member of the onion family. Their flavor lies somewhere between the flavors of onion and garlic.

Spaetzle maker: A traditional German noodle maker. It is similar to a flat, metal cheese grater but designed to strain a soft dough for making firm-textured mini-dumplings. Commonly stocked in stores alongside various cooking utensils, and inexpensive.

Spices: Ground spices are good for up to a year. Whole spices will keep for two to three years.

Stock: Homemade broth. When using canned broth, buy one of a good quality that is low-sodium and fat-free.

Tarragon: An herb with a hint of licorice and vanilla. Good cooked with roast, chicken, seafood, and omelets.

Thyme: A peppery herb with hints of mint and lemon. Cook in clam chowder and Italian dishes.

Truss: To bind together the wings or legs of fowl in preparation for cooking.

Zest: Small shavings of the outer, colored part of a peel, such as that of a lemon.

INDEX

Notes

NOTES

Notes

NOTES